DADDY,
WE HARDLY
KNEW YOU

DADDY, WE HARDLY KNEW YOU

BY

GERMAINE GREER

ALFRED A. KNOPF

NEW YORK

1990

THIS IS A BORZOI BOOK
PUBLISHED BY ALFRED A. KNOPF, INC.

Copyright © 1989 by Germaine Greer
All rights reserved under International and Pan-American
Copyright Conventions. Published in the United States by
Alfred A. Knopf, Inc., New York. Distributed by Random
House, Inc., New York. Originally published in
Great Britain by Hamish Hamilton, Ltd., London, in 1989.

Library of Congress Cataloging-in-Publication Data
Greer, Germaine.
Daddy we hardly knew you/Germaine Greer.
p. cm.
ISBN 0-394-58313-2
1. Greer, Germaine—Family. 2. Greer, Reg (Eric
Reginald). 3. Feminists—Biography. 4. Veterans,
Disabled—Australia—Biography. 5. Fathers and
daughters—Australia. I. Title.
HQ1413.G74A3 1989
306.874′2′092—dc20   89-45867
CIP

Manufactured in the United States of America
First American Edition

To the memory of
my three grandmothers,
Alida Jensen Lafrank,
Emma Wise Greeney,
Rhoda Elizabeth King.

Author's Acknowledgments

The author wishes to thank all the members of the Greer clan who replied to her letters, all the genealogists amateur and professional who offered their assistance, and all the individuals named in the text who were so kind as to offer to share their impressions of Reg Greer with her and answer questions about the background to Reg Greer's career. Not named in the text, but equally deserving of her thanks, are George Randall, Sheila Helpmann, Bob Walker, Bob Piper, Tom Greer, Netta Ward, the Stoward family, Joyce Greer de Holesch, Sir Arthur Lee, Sir Murt and Lady Lee, Lloyd Brown, Helen Doxford Harris, Mary Polis, and Bruce Ruxton. As well, she is anxious to acknowledge the assistance that she received from the Archives Office of the State Library of Tasmania, the Northern Regional Library of Tasmania, the Library of the University of Tasmania, the Tasmanian Permanent Trustees Association, the Latrobe Library and the Newspaper Room of the State Library of Victoria, the Public Record Office of Victoria, the University of Melbourne Archives, the Mitchell Library and the N. S. W. Public Library, the Public Library of South Australia, the State Library of Queensland, the Archives of the State of Queensland, the Australian National Library, the compilers of the Australian Dictionary of National Biography, the National Library of Malta, the India Office Library and Records, the Newspaper Library of the British Library, the National Library of Ireland, the Cambridge University Library, the Office of Population Censuses and Surveys at St Catherine's House, London, the Public Record Office at Chancery Lane and Ruskin Avenue, Kew, the Royal Artillery Association at Woolwich, the Artillery Museum at Devlali, the Air Force Office of the Australian Department of Defence, the Victorian Department of Veterans' Affairs, the National War Museum Association of Malta, the War Museum, London, the Libraries of the Friends' Houses at London and Hobart, the General Register Office in Belfast, and the Probate Offices of Melbourne and Belfast, among others. And, not for the first time, special thanks are due to Leanne Winfield, who kept Mill Farm on an even keel, while the author was leaving no stone unturned.

Contents

The Quest

Your dangers are many. I
Cannot look much but your form suffers
Some strange injury

And seems to die: so vapours
Ravel to clearness on the dawn sea.
SYLVIA PLATH, 'FULL FATHOM FIVE'

IT IS silly of me, a middle-aged woman, to call my dead father
Daddy. It's not as if I were some giddy heiress anticipating the
next instalment of my allowance or Little Orphan Annie learning
to get what she wants out of Daddy Warbucks, or yet some
southern belle refusing to be her age. My brother and sister called
my father Reg, but they knew him better than I did and could
permit themselves such familiarity. I always called him Daddy,
and much mockery did I take from Mother for doing it. Daddy is
a baby's palatal word; the word *mother* on the other hand is
admirably adapted for saying through clenched teeth.

When it would have been appropriate for me to have called
my father Daddy, I didn't have the chance. Just when he should
have been dandling me on his knee while I searched through his
pockets for surprises he went away. He wasn't there to see me
turn from being a baby into Daddy's little girl. It was the war he
left me for – I knew that much. There was no war in Melbourne.
I saw no tanks, no planes, no marching, yet the war was more
real to me than many things I had seen. I knew it was there, just
out of sight, round a corner, behind the house fronts, ready to
burst deafeningly out. I was taken to the movies once but I
screamed in such terror at the cartoon that showed aeroplanes
with teeth like sharks tearing at each other in the sky that Mother
was forced to take me outside. Then I wept so unconsolably that
I was never taken to a cinema again. I felt the war had engulfed

the whole world, leaving us on a tiny promontory that would soon go under. Daddy was on the other side of the world somewhere trying to hold back the tide. I knew he could never come home on leave, and I wasn't angry or resentful, but I was worried as only children can be. I didn't dare to wish him home. Instead I wished with all my might for the war to end.

This is what I remember. Or rather, this is what I remembered until I found out the truth. Nobody told me any of this, you understand. I was told nothing. I made this all up myself when I was too young to remember that I had made it up. They call it confabulation, when people who are brain-damaged fill the vacancy in their minds with plausible matter, believable but unrelated to the truth. What is written above, dear reader, is such a confabulation. I do not remember the calamity that befell the little girl who made up this stuff; most victims of severe strokes do not remember the precise moment that they were struck down. I could be hypnotised into remembering every snapping strand in my four-year-old heart-break, but there is a limit. I am exhausted now. I can go no further. Some of the keloid must be left in place or my entire personality, gnarled and misshapen as it is, will collapse.

I should have listened when my good friend Jeffrey said, 'You mustn't face up to facts too much. Make little excuses for yourself, for your father.' Not I, I thought stoutly. Now that I see that life is too hard for most people, I regret my thoughtless cruelty. I have been a cow in a china shop, and the result is ruin.

In the last months of his life, when Daddy's anxiety threatened to overwhelm him, he would grow quiet if my little niece was set on his knee. He would sit quite still as she chirped and babbled and dribbled on him, as far as anyone could tell, happy. I like to think that he took her for the me he missed out on, his lost baby girl rescued from the maw of time, come to fill up the blank years that yawn between us.

Daddy did come home of course. But, during the years and years that we lived in the same small house, Daddy never once hugged me. If I put my arms around him he would grimace and pretend to shudder and put me from him. It was a joke, of course, a tiresome, hurtful, relentless, stupid joke. I told myself it was a ritual that Daddy needed to bridge some chasm of anxiety. I clung to the faith that he was not genuinely indifferent to me and did

2

not really find me repulsive, although I never quite succeeded in banishing the fear of such a thing. When I was twelve I read *Dombey and Son* and cried myself blind every night for a week, but I cried for Florence Dombey and not for myself. I *knew* Daddy's strangeness was different, to be expected of a man who was forced to abandon a cuddlesome toddler and allowed to come back only when she had become a sharp-faced skinny little girl who scrutinised him intently with his own longsighted eyes. If he had let me under his guard, I should have crept into his heart and found the wound there.

Women are always ready to believe that men love them, despite all appearances to the contrary. I had no grounds for supposing that I was anything but deluded about my father's affection for me, until the last months of Daddy's life. My sister Jane telephoned and told me that he wanted to see me. The call was unexpected and it took me a little time to get my affairs in order and myself to Australia. When I arrived I found that Mother had turned Daddy out of his own house and committed him to a hostel, a shabby weatherboard house where derelicts of one sort or another could be fed and housed two or three to a room in return for their pension cheques, out of which the management would take its profit. When Jane and I arrived the proprietor opened the door in singlet and shorts, with a cigarette hanging out of his mouth. We found Daddy along with all the other inmates of the hostel, in the 'lounge-room'.

Daddy was sitting in a chair backed up against the wall. A huge television set boomed from a corner, but no one was watching it. They were all too busy cackling, raving, mouthing obscenities, scratching themselves or cursing. Over all hung a miasma of frying fat and the scent of tinned baked beans.

'Daddy!' I croaked. Jane wheeled and fled. In the musty depths of the house I heard a screen door bang as she raced outside and flung herself full-length under a lemon tree to bawl aloud. She didn't see Daddy get courteously to his feet and take my arm as if he had been expecting me all along. We walked out of the cacophony and into the room he had been assigned, which he shared with the occupational therapy equipment. He had with him no possessions whatever except some shabby clothing which seemed to have come from an opportunity shop somewhere. His

3

chequebook lay on top of the nightstand. The last stub showed that he had paid $2,500 to my brother and the balance was nil. He had been stripped and dumped in that awful place for me to find. A smart move, and in every subtle and crazy detail the work of my mother.

Jane and I went into action immediately to see that Daddy was rescued from squalor and humiliation. The Returned Servicemen's League (of which Daddy was not a member) made a place available for him at once at RSL Park. I was given a form to fill in for him with details of his service 'overseas', a mere formality, but for me a challenge that made my heart knock. Ever since I could remember I had wondered what had happened to Daddy during those years he had been away but I had never dared to question him. He had never collected his medals, didn't go to reunions, didn't keep up with his old comrades, didn't spin yarns about his adventures. We children had always known that he was not to be badgered on the point. Now I was obliged to ask and he obliged to answer.

He answered quietly and simply, with a faintly abstracted air, until I came to the two years I thought he had spent in India. 'What about India?' I asked. He turned his eyes to me, those eyes which had been tired ever since I could remember; in them I could read something dreadful. His composure was completely gone. 'Not India,' he said in a voice that had risen to a wail, 'not active service, not India.' His mouth was working and the breath had come harsh into his throat. I threw down the papers and took him into my arms.

The RSL waived the formalities. Somewhere in the files there was an official diagnosis, 'Anxiety neurosis'. 'We've got more old soldiers suffer from anxiety than heart disease,' said Bruce Ruxton, Victorian president of the RSL. 'There's no need to distress the old man any more'.

I could have gone further. I could have kept on at him, taking advantage of his helplessness, to find out what I had always wanted to know. What did they do to him? Why was he in such anguish? What was the unnameable emotion I could see in his eyes? Panic? Shame? To grill him would have been to go against the habit of a lifetime. We children knew next to nothing at all about Daddy and we knew too that we had no right to find out.

He knew that he could function adequately only within strict limits and he imposed those limits on us, by what seems to me now an extraordinary exercise of will. If we had breached those limits out of idle curiosity, Pandora's box would have opened and confusion engulfed us all.

In the months of Daddy's rapid journey towards death, the anxiety rose up towering in the gathering darkness of his brain, and terrorised him, but, although he roamed endlessly around the hospital at night, he bore his anguish stoically. The more he suffered, the gentler and more courteous he became. Jeffrey went to see him for me, and told me that the nurses adored him. I was jealous of them, for they gave him all the hugging and kissing he had never been able to accept from me. The whole family except me was with him on the day he died, but he waited patiently until they had gone to get something to eat and then, typically, quietly snuffed it.

Now that Daddy's need to have us not know is at an end, my need to know can be satisfied. The leads I have are few. I know that he was stationed in Malta and then sent to Deolali, nowadays Devlali, in India. British army slang for 'mad' is 'Doolally tap'. I don't know when I first started noticing that Daddy was continually sedated or when I learned to interpret the names on bottles of Tropinal and Triptophen that I found on his bedside table. There is one appalling memory which I cannot date. I am sitting on the carpet in front of the full-length mirror in my parents' bedroom. In the mirror I can see my father who is abjectly pleading with my mother, 'Don't do that to me, Peg. Please. Don't do it.' And his face breaks up the way it did when I had to interrogate him in the hostel thirty-five years later. His mouth twists and opens and terrible gasping sobs are torn out of him. That's all I can remember, but I remember it with appalling vividness. It is about my first memory and it was the worst thing I had ever seen or ever saw. I probably began to scream and got myself flung out of the room.

Generally Daddy was droll. He was even droll about his anxiety state. When we met for the first time after I had been 'overseas' myself for seventeen years, he conducted himself with great suavity and aplomb, resplendent in a cream tussore suit. He told me later on the telephone that when lunch was over and the tension released, and he was walking back over Princes Bridge to where he had parked the car, he suffered a mass reflex and purged upwards and downwards all over his pale silk. I was aghast, but he chuckled ruefully and made light of my consternation. When I asked when I could come to see him again, though, he begged to be excused. There was no alternative. My presence was a source of stress and he had to avoid stress as rigorously as an alcoholic has to avoid drink.

To outsiders everything must have appeared quite normal. Daddy inhabited and functioned quite normally in a world of casual bonhomie. To silence the echoes he packed his brain with sports trivia and floated it in a sea of beers at the Commercial Travellers' Association. He dressed elegantly, even slightly foppishly, in a masculine sort of way: pigskin gloves for driving but not quite furled umbrella. And hats. At the dinner-table where we children were forbidden to speak, he occasionally held forth, but every opinion he expressed could have been traced to the leader pages of the two conservative newspapers he read every day. If I pounced on some statement that seemed to me to reflect however dimly upon the real world, he would stab his finger towards my plate, signifying that I should eat up and shut up. 'I've forgotten more than you're ever likely to know,' he would say. This fatuous hyperbole dismayed me even more than his shuddering routine, but perhaps after all it was literally true. Daddy's whole life was an exercise in forgetting. He never referred to any kin, neither father nor mother nor sisters nor brothers nor aunts nor uncles, not even in a chance anecdote. He was a man without a past.

What we knew about him could be summed up in a few words. We knew, or thought we knew, that he was born in Durban in 1905 or so. And came to Launceston where he went to school. He had mentioned being a boy soprano, perhaps even a choir scholar. We thought his parents had gone back to England and died, but the Australian composer Peter Sculthorpe told me once that his grandfather in Launceston used to play draughts with an 'old Mr Greer'. It gave me a funny feeling to think that I had a grandfather just across Bass Strait who had no idea I existed. If I did, why would Daddy give us the impression that his family was lost without trace?

Somehow I gained the conviction that my paternal grand-mother was named Rachel Weiss, but I'm afraid I probably made that up in my intense yearning to be Jewish. I wasn't deflected in my desire to make Daddy a Jew even by his own anti-Semitism, which I found only too easy to understand in a British Jew compelled to do business every day with central European Jews who could barely speak English and kept their working capital in paper bags under- their beds. Besides, anti-Semitism was imposed on anyone who wanted to be reasonably popular in a society as chauvinistic as the one we lived in. For Daddy it was an occupational disease, and its symptoms were aggravated by the difficulty he had in dealing with the central European *schmatte* merchants, whose trading *sechel* and capacity for hard work left their Australian-born competitors gasping. Lots of sensitive children who came to the age of reason in the last years of the war and the first of the peace grew up longing to be Jewish, as the only way of escaping the collective guilt for what was done to the Jews.

As if there was any escaping the stain that lies across our world, for any of us. Like Tsvetayeva in 'The Poem of the End' we ask,

> *Isn't it more worthy to*
> *become an eternal Jew?*
> *Anyone not a reptile*
> *suffers the same pogrom.*

We war-time children are a strange generation. Our lives spin out of control in the wake of a sin that makes our first parents look no more vicious than puppies chewing up a slipper. Tsvetay-eva killed herself; so did Sylvia Plath whose father was one of the 'men in black with a Meinkampf look and a love of the rack and the screw.' She too identified with the dead masks we saw piled in heaps in the open graves at Dachau and Belsen, and made of herself an honorary Jew.

> *A Jew to Dachau, Auschwitz, Belsen.*
> *I began to talk like a Jew.*
> *I think I may well be a Jew.*

Sylvia Plath did not speak like a Jew, but like a well-educated lady from New England; I learned Yiddish and joined the Habimah players. I did not know if I had any Jewish blood or not, but I felt Jewish and I went out with Jewish boys. My father said once, when Peter Sapir came to take me to a dance, 'Taking the princess out? You take good care of her.' 'He must be Jewish,' said Peter. Oy weh.

Another muddled notion that we children somehow got was that Daddy had gone jackerooing after he left school and wanted to go on the land, but his rich father refused him the nominal sum required to secure a lease, so Daddy severed relations with him and sold advertising space instead. Somehow he got himself to Adelaide, where he knew the young Robert Helpmann. And then to Melbourne where he met and married my mother. Then I was born, the war broke out and Daddy went away.

I was five when my mother and I went by train to Spencer Street Station to bring Daddy home. I was sure I would recognise him from the photograph on the maple sideboard. This ikon showed a collection of distinguished features, dark hair brushed back from a high forehead, a relaxed smile, and an ironic glint in the eyes. I knew the exact proportion of the ears to the head, the precise bend in the narrow nose, the set of the long head on its square shoulders. We trailed up and down the platform peering into every face. The heavy skirts of the men's greatcoats kept knocking me off my feet. The kissing, hugging knots of people began to gather up their belongings and disperse; the platform was emptying and still we hadn't found Daddy. The war had lasted all my life and I had difficulty imagining how it could end. I began to drag my feet and day-dream, convinced that Daddy wasn't there. Mother grabbed my arm, nearly wrenching it from its socket as she became more agitated, turning and hurrying hither and yon. Suddenly she stopped and dropped my arm. An old man was standing sightlessly by a pylon. His neck stuck scrawnily out of the collar of his grey-blue greatcoat. His eyes were sunken, his skin grey and loose. I ran up to look at Mother's face. Surely she wasn't going to take this old man instead of Daddy. She was standing with her head cocked, peering like a wary bird in the jaunty hat that she wore on her forehead like a crest. If she was shocked she made no sign. She bundled the old man up and took him home and a year later my sister was born.

8

By then I had learned to match the old man's features with the photograph and to admit that this distant, speechless wreck was indeed my father. I would rather have had one of the handsome big Americans who used to hang around my mother. So would she, I shouldn't wonder, but she stuck to her commitment, with an ill grace, but faithfully.

This is what I remember. It may be all wrong, but it cannot be irrelevant. I used to think that truth was single and error legion, but I know now that none of us grasps more than a little splinter of the truth. The blind men all observed the elephant correctly; their mistake was to infer an entire object consistent with the patch that came under their hands. I may make the same error – indeed I don't see how I could avoid it – but I have no choice but to try to build up a picture of who my father might have been, if only because I have a lurking fear that a great wrong was done to him.

And, however silly it sounds, I'm going to call him Daddy.

I never called him Father because priests are called that. If Daddy hated anything as much as he hated carrots and dried fruit, it was priests. During the months of the siege of Malta, the only way of getting enough Vitamin C to ward off scurvy was to eat quantities of carrots and dried fruit. When the war was over, Daddy eschewed carrots and dried fruit forever. Malta had something to do with his passionate anti-clericalism too. On the rare occasions when he spoke of 'overseas' Daddy would tell us how poor and wretched the Maltese people were, while their priests were rubicund and fat. The people lived ten or twelve to a room, but the churches were vast, encrusted with gilding, crowded with painted plaster statues and miraculous gew-gaws. The priests were well-educated and worldly; the people illiterate, trusting and deeply religious. When Daddy went to India he must have realised that on the world scale of poverty the Maltese were very far from the bottom, but perhaps he thought if they could just get the priests off their backs they would be as rich as Australians. To my mind, having the British on their backs was a rather more serious problem for the Maltese, as it was getting their island bombed flat, but Daddy was not receptive to this heretical notion.

Daddy's loathing of priests went back further than Malta.

9

When he was courting Mother, who was a Catholic, he had to take instruction in the faith. When the couple knocked on the door of the presbytery to ask the parish priest to do the honours, it was a suspiciously long time before the door opened to reveal the priest in his singlet and smelling strongly of liquor. Listening to Daddy tell it, and other stories of Maltese priests frequenting brothels, I despaired of Daddy's salvation. I thought there was some conspiracy in heaven to scandalise my father, so that he would never enter the true Church but die a heathen and go to hell. The priests I confessed myself to were chaste, unworldly and sober, but Daddy had never met any of them.

In fact Daddy's agnosticism was one of the few surviving indications of a native strength of mind. He used to tell a story of collapsing in the street with pleurisy and waking up in a Catholic hospital where they were busy administering to him the last rites. According to him, the fierce pleasure he took in throwing the priests and nuns with all their regalia and sacramental impedimenta out of his room saved his life. When everything else in his brain had dissolved, he clung fast to his disbelief, which wasn't easy seeing as everyone around him was a mick and praying hell-for-leather that he'd get the grace of final perseverance and be hauled to heaven.

Another reason for not calling Daddy Father was the existence of 'Father Gilhooley'. This imaginary personage was the principal of a reformatory, where the doors were perpetually open to receive us. Daddy invoked him whenever we showed some feeble sign of insubordination. He would demonstrate some of Father Gilhooley's disciplinary methods, including a nasty rabbit-killer chop to the nape of the neck, which caused electric tingles along your arms and legs that curdled in your fingers and toes. Daddy would imply darkly that he knew Father Gilhooley very well. The only religion he professed, which he called Calathumpianism, had been imparted to him by Father Gilhooley. Other children have bogeymen to frighten them and have the seeds of racism sown in them forever. We had an Irish Catholic priest lying in wait for us, which was odd for we were part Irish and wholly Catholic ourselves. Perhaps Father Gilhooley is a clue to who Daddy really was, a fossil trapped in some layer of his subconscious.

A clue to what? A clue to the man who courted my mother, to the half of my genetic inheritance, to a personality, a culture, a somebody I thought I could just glimpse from time to time. I never saw him read a book. His favourite music, indeed his only record, was Al Jolson's greatest hits. Sometimes he would intone a little verse:

> *Breathes there a man with soul so dead*
> *Who never to himself has said,*
> *This is my own, my native land . . .*

And he would sing in the shower,

> *Hi think that Hi shall never seeng*
> *Ha powem lervly as er treeng!*

Or

> *Ho Sole Mio,*
> *O gran divi dero*

and so on with nonsense words, or

> *Ho for the weengs, for the weengs hof a derv . . .*

two octaves below the key he would have sung it in as a boy soprano, and 'The Maori Farewell' with the word 'Tiddleypush' where 'goodbye' should be. Not too many clues there. There was an elaborate family word-play on the phrase 'Tosti partood' (the *tood* to rhyme with *wood*) which I realised many years later was an encoded memory of Tosti's 'Farewell'. And another silly set of phrases to do with 'bread dipped in bravery', an incantation of unknown significance to us, but perhaps it meant something to Daddy. He would never answer when you asked him what the time was, except to say, 'Must be, look how dark it is.' Every time.

A man I was in love with met my father once at the St Kilda Cricket Club. Daddy was showing around a cheque I had sent him in payment of a debt and telling everyone what a clever daughter he had, the more surprisingly to me, as he had never given me to understand that he thought of Ph.D.s as any but long-haired rat-bags. As he was describing the scene, my friend added an observation that surprised and hurt me, 'Your father's not very bright, is he?' I was mortified to think that the emptiness

11

of my father's head was obvious on first acquaintance. In that case it ought to have been obvious to my mother when she met him, unless he had been different then. The only man successfully to woo my mother, whose wit, if utterly undisciplined and often perverse, is certainly sharp, must have been clever, original, amusing, or interesting at least. Daddy was older than Mother to be sure, but how had he grown so rapidly senile? (You will be wondering why I did not simply ask my mother. Suffice it to say that for Mother language is a weapon rather than a means of communication.)

As if it was not bad enough that outsiders could see my father as an agreeable dimwit, at home I had undeniable proof that he was feeble. When Mother's frustration boiled over and she lit into me with anything she could lay her hands on, Daddy would 'keep out of it', even though he was sitting reading the paper in the next room where the thud of blows was clearly audible. His response to Mother's goading was always the same, silence and distance. 'It takes two to quarrel,' he would say, apparently unaware that I could not go off to my club until the mad dog in the kitchen had stopped foaming at the mouth. I suppose he thought I could take it, and he was right, but I thought him weak and craven. Nevertheless I could not forgive my mother for calling him 'a senile old goat', as she often did.

That my father never once struck or reviled me was reason enough for me to love him, but I could not respect him. Not until the terrible months of his decline, when his suburban character armour fell away and I could dimly see the grand ruin which was his mind. Mother kept away from him, but he never ceased to ask for her. She treated him abominably, but he never uttered a disloyal word about her. He died in love with her, an achievement which she doubtless credits to herself. Only when he was dead did we begin to have some idea of the devastation that he had suffered.

He died of advanced athero-sclerosis of the brain. He had no cancer, no heart disease, no blood-pressure disorder. Only his mind was aged, prematurely turned to porridge. What if he had been a strong, intelligent, brave and energetic man before he was needed to fight a war? And sent home when they had done with him, old and broken before his time? Would that not explain my mother's furious frustration? What if he was deliberately broken, broken say by electro-convulsive therapy during those two years in Deolali? What if he spoke so little of the war and of his life before it because he simply couldn't remember it?

There are men who were treated for anxiety neurosis by electro-convulsive therapy, or deep narcosis, the sleep cure, who completely forgot the cataclysm that sent their synapses gibbering out of control. The treatments made them stop weeping and stammering, made them manageable, silent, obedient. Who cared if they stopped laughing as long as they stopped crying? A zombie, provided he is neatly dressed, punctual and punctilious, is a useful individual in our society. He pays his taxes, commutes every day, does meaningless monotonous work and does not complain. And if he no longer dances with his little daughter held high on his shoulder, or makes up nonsense games for her to play, or puts her to sleep when she is tearful and overtired, if he does not hear her nervous vomiting in the night because he is too drugged to wake, who will give a damn? The child like him is 'highly-strung'; the inherent defect runs in their genes. *What runs in our genes, Daddy, is humanity, which will not survive except by extraordinary shifts in this inhuman world.*

In this most Christian world
poets are all Jews

Daddy told me a story once about the war in which there was a decoding machine. He said he was a Secret and Confidential Publications Officer in Malta. The programme the British called Ultra, by which they exploited information arising from their knowledge of the German Enigma machine, remained a military secret for years after the war ended. What if Daddy broke down while he was privy to this most important secret and had to be debriefed by shock therapy? Brainwashed, in other words. By the allies. It seems a mad suspicion, but once it has been entertained I have no choice but to investigate it. What if his brain turned to slush as a long-term consequence of his drug therapy or shock treatment? What if his relationship with me was jettisoned because it was part of a period in his life that he was *made* to forget? The mere suspicion of an injustice so terrible is unbearable.

All the Australians who served overseas had a difficult war.

They were assailed by culture shock, appalled by the poverty and inequality that they encountered for the first time, too far from home to touch base for years on end, a despised rabble among the fighting forces. Thousands of them came home to live out their lives as walking wounded, carrying out their masculine duties in a sort of dream, trying not to hear the children who asked, 'Mummy, why does that man have to sleep in your bed?' Australians don't whinge. There was no way these damaged men could explain their incapacity for normal emotional experience except by complaining and they would not complain. But their children must.

I don't know what I shall find on the other side of Daddy's curtain of silence. Perhaps he was after all a pompous ass, a dimwit or a coward. Perhaps he was a criminal, a traitor, a sexual deviant even. What I saw in his eyes that day in the hostel, the same spectre that looked at me out of the mirror in my parents' bedroom, struck me like a blow in the face. The most unbearable thought of all is that shame was planted in my father's heart and, all the time that he was heroically holding the fragments of his life together, he thought he was hiding from our censure.

It is a wise child that knows her own father. I knew as I held my father's old hand in my own, its exact replica, and watched my own skull emerging through his transparent skin, that I am my father's daughter. Now that he can be hurt no more, it is time to find out what that means.

Tuscany,
December 1986

Outside the window the poplars rustle:
'Your king is on this earth no more.'
AKHMATOVA, 'THE GREY-EYED KING'

MANY PEOPLE, probably most of the people on this planet, take special spiritual precautions before a journey. Old ladies in Italy never allow the train to pull out of the station before they have crossed themselves and uttered a swift prayer for a safe arrival. I embarked on the most important quest of my life without so much as crossing my fingers or touching wood. The only ritual I engaged in was the prodigal pouring out of money to acquire an airline ticket from London to Melbourne, with a stopover in Italy.

Nothing was amiss in my little Tuscan house. My housekeeper was less unwell than usual, and her husband had not had an accident for months. My old Tuscan cat sat in the amber sunlight and warmed his nephritic bones, and at night crept smelling of bracken and leaf-mould into my bed and lay against my side with his claws carefully tucked under my bare arm where they could flex with glee without piercing anything but sheets.

In my desk I found the old notebook in which I had begun to plot *The Female Eunuch*. I turned to a blank page and began to write:

Here we go, Daddy, in at the deep end. I discover, Papa, that I am like you in one thing at least. I hate remembering. There are days when I wander for hours in a spacious sewer of memory. And there are other days when memories stick up like dark spars in a sunlit river and I feel myself dragged under by them, struggling in darkness while the sparkling present slides over my head. These stubs of half-rotten lumber catch up junk, pieces of string too short to use, stoppers from vanished bottles, and choke my mind with them. I never remember you giving

15

me advice or encouragement, but I can remember you singing:

> *Pack up all my cares and woe,*
> *Here I go,*
> *Swinging low,*
> *Bye bye blackbird.*
>
> *Where my honey waits for me,*
> *Sugar's sweet,*
> *So is she,*
> *Bye bye blackbird.*
>
> *Not a soul to love or understand me,*
> *All those hard luck stories they all hand me,*
> *Make my bed, light the light,*
> *I'll be home, late tonight,*
> *Blackbird bye bye.*

Useless to ask what it all means. You can't treat such gibberish as oracular. Some children can remember their fathers reciting Urdu poetry or Marlowe, or teaching them to recognise birds and butterflies, to spot trains, to play chess or cricket. But you, Daddy dear? Not a curve-ball, not a cover-drive, not a card-trick. Not a maxim. Not a saw, adage or proverb. Except 'You're big enough and ugly enough to take care of yourself.' This is my *Enchiridion Militis*, my soldier's breastplate. This and 'Bye bye blackbird'.

> *Sometimes I love you,*
> *Sometimes I hate you,*
> *But when I hate you,*
> *It's 'cos I love you.*

This section of the notebook ends: 'How shall I keep sane during this pilgrimage, Daddy?' I can almost hear Daddy saying, 'It's news to me that you were sane when it started.' Daddy once stopped a friend in the street and said to her about my mother, 'She's mad of course.' He probably thought my genes were all my mother's, despite my Greer face. Probably thought we were all mad but he. But no, the sedatives in the bathroom cupboard were his, not ours. Except when the hospital put me on the same ones, Tropinal, for nervous exhaustion, Daddy's own disease. *Bone of your bone, Daddy. You shall not escape me.*

Should I be listening to the warnings? Tiresias said to Oedipus:

> *How terrible is wisdom when*
> *it brings no profit to the man that's wise!*

If my ignorance is bliss who am I wilfully to pick it to pieces? Like a teenager working on a pimple, I could end up with a pus-filled crater. A scar conspicuously worn, instead of the common suburban hypocrisy that was my birthright. My mother asked me on Christmas Day why I wanted so much to know my father's background and early life. Looking for an answer she would not ridicule I said, 'Hamish Hamilton have paid me a lot of money to write a book about him.'

'Gee,' said Mother, 'I'm glad I don't have to do that to earn a crust.'

At the next blank page the notebook continued:

I go without your blessing, without your knowledge, unless you are sitting on a cloud ledge somewhere above me, dressed in a sheet with a tin circlet floating over your head. There's more than one way of knowing; my bones know more than my brain can handle. The software is in the genes, Papa, and the mind is just the VDU. I need a way into the memory bank though, some filenames. The programme cannot be wiped, but it is not write-protected. Each time a memory comes up on the screen new material is incorporated. Until I begin to forget I cannot remember.

Perhaps, if each day I do a keeping-in-the-present exercise, I shall keep my bearings. Whatsay?

The telegraphic word forces a memory to pop up; when advertising men got married they could expect to read out at the reception the following telegram from Reg Greer, the Melbourne Representative of the *Adelaide Advertiser*: 'Six more insertions needed to complete contract.' Ho ho. Children never share their parents' sense of humour. Or vice versa.

The sun is on my hands. I could say the Italian sun, but the sun has no nationality. The sun is on my eyelids too, and on a strand of grey-blond hair which lifts across my face on the almost imperceptible movement of the breeze. My house sits on the side of a great basin of luminous air, surrounded by low hills that look like huge people sleeping under grey blankets, the same recycled wool blankets that soldiers were issued in the Middle

East when Reg Greer was there in 1942, and famine-stricken Ethiopians when I was there in 1985.

The holm oaks will keep their leaves till spring; now they are tarnished gold, made transparent by the heavy dew of the long night. The ash carries its heavy posies of brown seeds. The fig has dropped its leaves but its fruit clings to the bare branches. The honeysuckle over the door is still green and the wisteria is just turning faintly quince yellow. When the dew dries, I'll put on my overalls and walk up the hill through the brambles. There should be cyclamen, maybe a mushroom or two for an omelette.

Gardening is a good defence against memory, for it is all in the future. I can see branches to be lopped, fronds to be staked, briars to be tied in. There has been too much lax growth. The first frost will be punishing.

Jays and magpies are screaming in the wood. The air is so clear that when the woodsmen speak from the other side of the river, I can hear them as if they were at my elbow. They are nurses from the hospital in Cortona and keep quiet much of the time; if they were real *boscaioli* they would keep up a stream of human noise, whistling, singing, blaspheming, telling jokes, coughing, to warn huntsmen and foraging boar and sleepy vipers of their whereabouts. The real *boscaioli* are all old now; a sudden silence can mean accident, injury or seizure, a leg ripped by a chain saw, a tree trunk fallen the wrong way, an unwary step into the ravine, a snake bite, a heart attack. Our steep wooded hillsides are dangerous; a man who steps backwards without thinking can fall hundreds of feet into sharp shale and jagged rocks. The first rule is never to go alone, but many of the peasants are unmarried these days and all of them are old. Those who found wives and made sons see their sons only at holiday time. The olives must be picked and the firewood got in before the harsh winter, if the old peasants who are all the population we have left are to survive. Nobody wants to go to the *ospizio*.

Lisa's husband, Berto, is working on the hillside opposite. As long as the sun is on the slope we can see him loading the timber he has cut but, when the sun goes behind the hill and the blue shadow creeps up from the river, Lisa grows uneasy. Only a few months ago, Berto took one step too many in the long grass and brambles that masked a precipice, and split himself in half, one

18

leg down and one leg up and nothing to haul himself up by. They encased him in plaster of Paris from the waist down and a week later he cut it off. They had it on crooked anyway. Now, like me, he limps at the end of the day.

There's not a cloud in the sky. It's all in the valley below me, like a flat blue dish of white soup. My neighbour's Rottweiler bitch, spooked by the mist and the strange crackling noises that condensation makes when fat drops bounce on the dead leaves, won't stop barking.

When he died Daddy hadn't any money. Not a bean. And yet I've never felt poor. I always called myself middle of the middle class. All my life I have felt rich, but, now I come to think of it, Advertiser Newspapers paid my father badly for more than thirty years. 'His boss, Sir Lloyd Dumas, thought it was an honour to be allowed to work for the 'Tiser,' his old friends told me. For some reason (a reason I understand only too well now!) Daddy took this preposterous notion to heart. He stayed poor and penny-proud all his life. He never owed anyone anything; his only credit was the war-service loan that paid off our mortgage, his only perk a company car. We were poorer than many members of the Australian working class, but we did not share working-class aspirations, didn't dress up to feed money into the slot machines at the RSL club, didn't go to the dogs, or bet on the horses with the SP bookies, or play two-up down the lane. We were posh.

Re-reading the notebook, my old fears surface again. Why did we not identify with the working class and with popular Australian culture, beer and housie housie? Curiouser and curiouser. Was it because we belonged to the make-believe world of advertising and had to pretend that we were better off and better bred and better educated than we were? Were we phonies? Was my father's toff act a lie? A conscious fraud? My mother had no class pretensions, no snobbery, no toffery. She was too eccentric to merge with the mass of suburban housewives. She watched no soap-opera, played no bridge, belonged to no women's organ-isation, worked for no charity, drank coffee with no girlfriends. Come to think of it, I don't know what she did with herself before she began to study accountancy and Japanese – besides working on her tan, that is.

The house I grew up in had no music, no instrument, no record player, no paintings, no books, no flowers, no good cooking, no pretty furniture, no pudding, no cheese, no wine, no parties, none of the things I now deem essential to the good life. School was infinitely more interesting than my parents' house, where the only relief from tedium was trouble. Daddy used the house as a place to feed, sleep, wash and get his laundry done. To avoid conversation he watched television while waiting for his 'tea' and shared a bottle of beer with Mother. He went to bed immediately afterwards and got up next morning when we were leaving for school. I stayed at school later and later as I got older, inventing all kinds of extra-curricular activities to explain why I got home at seven o'clock when school finished at four.

There was something very unbourgeois and unworldly about this lifestyle, which I imagine emanated from my mother, who was perfectly happy to dress in hand-me-downs and cast-offs, supplemented by her own rather haphazard dress-making. Father used to give her money for furs and evening dresses, but somehow she never bought them. When my father's strength began to fail and he could no longer drive himself to his clubs and while away the day lunching with his friends and reading the newspapers, he fell more and more under Mother's aegis. All his swagger was resolutely pared away. By the time he died, all his beautiful tailored suits were gone; the alpaca cardigan my sister Jane knitted for him was gone too. Instead he was wearing a sagging threadbare number from St Vincent de Paul. His old watch had been replaced by a cheap digital one with a plastic strap. Even his shirts seemed to have been worn out by somebody else before he got them.

I sent him a Braun shaver and a silk dressing gown, in memory of his old glory, but within weeks they had gone the way of everything else. The money that I put into his bank account, which in the event of his not spending it was meant to pay for some small gift to the hospital in his memory, followed them. I was left not so much as a cuff-link or a fountain pen, or a book with his name in it. My name was not mentioned in his will. Everything he died possessed of was destined for my mother (who had already taken it) or for my brother and sister if she pre-deceased him.

As I sat in the golden winter light of Tuscany, scribbling in my old notebook, I did not know that my father being of sound mind had chosen not to mention me in his will. It never crossed my mind. I need never have seen the will, never have known that I was not even disowned, simply forgotten. Big enough and ugly enough to take care of herself. One look in the mirror is enough to prove to me that he can't disown me. Perhaps I have taken the hair off my face to expose his skull as a way of defying him; the cleft in the end of my nose, my receding hair-line, my lantern jaw, my large ears, my blunt fingers and my narrow chest are all he left me. They will have to do.

The white fog boiled over and crept up the ravines like smoke. A pheasant honked from the wood; all round me the world seemed made of love, although I was alone in it. The mason bees bumped sleepily around the window frames, putting finishing touches to the brood cells, topping up the food capsules, before sealing them off and going to die on a bed of pollen in the last of the Bourbon roses.

The next morning I went down from my golden mountain into the valley of the mist to change money. It was like making Dante's journey in reverse, from the peak of the *paradiso terrestre* to the Inferno. Below *in pianura* there was no horizon, no light or shade, only a damp, bleak cold in which objects loomed and vanished as my hired car rolled by. Rags of frost hung motionless on the trees and great drops slid down the bare branches like tears, to splat on my tiny windscreen. Pedestrians, wound up like bobbins in scarfs against the cold, floated towards me in the white murk, walking on the road to avoid the ice and slush. In sheltered spots I could see white rime lying thick on the ground. Above the cold steam the air was echoing and clear; below there was a muffled not-quite silence, like breathing under blankets.

The bank robbed me badly, taking nearly thirty points off yesterday's fixing. I complained and took the rate they offered. I hadn't the energy to shop around. The day before I had found the mushrooms for my omelette, the big white ones Lisa calls *brumani* which in my etymology means 'children of mist'. I ate them fried with chopped chives in olive oil, with three eggs. All night I dreamed in Technicolor while my gut roared and growled. At five in the morning the purging of the toxins began. Each time I slid out of bed and padded across the freezing tiles to the bathroom with my candle, the little cat hauled himself up on to the pillow and said loudly, 'Nao.' Usually he would follow me into the bathroom but this time he was intimidated by the uproar. Each time I crawled back into bed to warm my chilled bones before the next onslaught, he slipped under the covers and tried to purr my entrails back to quiet.

It is important to be sick sometimes, to bring home the extraordinary luckiness of being well. I am impressed by the way peristalsis speeds up as the body prepares to expel a wog, for I had picked up a wog, not in my moon-coloured mushroom, but in a sealed packet of *tortellini* that I found in the local food mart. I knew they were dodgy, but I was too tired to think of an alternative, so I trusted to the chemical preservatives in them and ate them. All day the bacteria had been proliferating; the plate of mushroomed eggs was simply the last straw. Whoosh. Boom. The fire hoses came into action and the riot was put down.

When at eight o'clock I set off for the bank, I was still feverish. I had to concentrate hard to get my errands done without messhap, but illness has its bonus too. In my fevered sight the trees on the hills stood out more clearly than if they had been beaten in gold and bronze and copper. Their hard edges burned against the web of long violet shadows cast by the low sun. I imagined that I was explaining what I could see to my father as if he was blind.

The colour of the sky is impossible to explain, Papa, because it is so many different colours. At the horizon, three o'clock, it's almost white, a sort of duck-egg colour, then at one-thirty o'clock it's forget-me-not and at the zenith, a warm cobalt. Quite unlike the enamelled Australian sky with its expanded polystyrene clouds bumping on the air currents. The richness of this blue shows best behind a persimmon tree at this time of year; after the frosts come the leaves take themselves off and the fruit hangs in the bare branches like lit lamps. I've never wanted to grow a persimmon; the fruit is mushy and insipid, a sort of half-rotten seedless tomato, but it looks, how? Out of this world? thrilling? stunning? heavenly? wondrous fair? tophole? amazing? takes your breath away? It reminds me of my favourite part of the Mass, when the celebrant used to say in the bad old days of Latin, which we all knew by heart:

Domine dilexi domus tuae, et locum habitationis gloriae tuae.

22

You would have known it, Daddy, and if you were were a chorister you must have known it, as 'Lord, I have loved the habitation of thy house, and the place where thine honour dwelleth'. Give me the Vulgate every time. Habitation of thy house indeed. I suppose it means house as in house of David. What is the house of Reg?

I could imagine Daddy brushing aside my gush about my landscape, 'Very nice, very nice, where's the beer?' only half serious, sending himself up, not wanting to appear 'sensitive' or artsy-fartsy, bored by having the obvious pointed out to him. The only landscape that excited Daddy was flat green grass striped by the mower and dotted with men in white flannels.

My notes break off at this point. Behind the myriad whispers of the dry leaves, and the clicking and fussing of the birds, there came a faint, solid sound. My concentration wavered. My gut had just been given a piece of dry bread and honey as encouragement to keep up the struggle against salmonella and was rather painfully deciding what to do with it. The solid sound grew to a faint drumming. Sophy, the Rottweiler, gave a single baritone bark of warning.

Into the sunlit field below me came three inhabitants of darkness. I could see their razor-backs and their long, night-black bristles clearly. They were small but, though their tusks could not be seen, the baby stripes along their flanks had faded. Adolescent boar, playing like puppies in the afternoon sun. Hungry boar will sometimes sneak up the gullies by day to feed on the oak-mast and huntsmen occasionally flush them out into the open, but this sighting was extraordinary. Round and round the field they trotted, playing chasey in and out of the clumps of Spanish broom, their half-cloven feet striking the dry earth like drumbeats. I saw no omen in their being so unusually exposed and fearless in the afternoon, but I did write in my notebook:

In two days I am to abandon the weak December sun of the northern hemisphere and cross the world to summer, short nights and blazing days, but I feel as if I am going into the dark. And I'm afraid.

I did not open my Bible and did not read Genesis IX:

And Ham, the father of Canaan, saw the nakedness of his father and told his two brethren without.
And Shem and Japhet took a garment and laid it upon both their

23

shoulders, and went backward, and covered the nakedness of their father; and their faces were backward, and they saw not their father's nakedness.

And Noah awoke from his wine, and knew what his younger son had done unto him.

And he said, Cursed be Canaan; a servant of servants shall he be unto his brethren.

All unaware of the primal elder's curse I gave my helpers their Christmas cheer and went on my way. The little cat followed me out to the gate and sat on the dry stone wall to watch me drive away. I did not know that I would never see him again. The Autostrada del Sole was strangely unterrifying; no juggernaut tried to crack my little car against the crash barrier like a flea on a fingernail; fewer Ferraris than usual wedged their snouts up my tail-pipe. In the crush by the passport control my journey suddenly took on a new, disaster-prone complexion.

There was as usual some sort of go-slow on. A clot of people had built up at the entrance to the passport-control booths, and stood pressing anxiously forward, festooned with cabin baggage, last-minute gifts, things too oddly shaped to go in their checked luggage, and restless children. The woman in front of me had both hands full and, hanging from her shoulder, a very large squashy overnight bag. As she moved off I bent to take my passport from the outside compartment of my cabin bag. At that precise milli-second she gave the overnight bag, which was embellished with ornamental straps and buckles, an almighty heave. One of the buckles caught in the hair at my temple. A pain clouted me on the side of the head like a hot poker and I shrieked. The woman tramped off towards the baggage examination bench, unaware that she was dragging me to the bench with her, sideways, bent in two and completely off-balance. All that stopped me falling was the hank of my hair clasped in the buckle. I kept on squealing, the crowd gasped and shouted in half-a-dozen languages and all she did was to pull harder against me. At last the clump of hair tore free. The woman staggered and looked over her shoulder.

I stood with tears streaming down my face, holding my head. 'Why didn't you stop when you heard us all shouting?'

'What? What's the matter with you? How was I to know?' she said in an offended tone and walked off. I was appalled but not surprised to discover that she was Australian.

When the immigration officer asked me if I needed medical attention I said no. The security officers waved me through and I groggily made my way to the bathroom. A trickle of mixed blood and lymph was creeping down my cheek. My fingers found a raw wound about an inch square; besides my hair, the unknown Australian was carrying a chunk of my flesh to Australia with her. I looked for her on the plane to tell her that raw meat is a prohibited import, but she had disappeared. I realise now that she was the first of the Eumenides.

I should have done as Oedipus did, visited the thicket of the ladies whose eyes are terrible, and brought bowls of spring water and honey, chaplets of fresh flowers, and the fleeces of new-born lambs. I should have poured the water into the earth and laid three times nine young shoots of olive on it, and then repeated my prayer as the Chorus told Oedipus, who was no blinder than I:

> *That as we call them Eumenides,*
> *Which means the gentle of heart,*
> *May they accept with gentleness*
> *The suppliant and his wish.*

Melbourne,
December 1986

But do not speak aloud or raise a cry;
Then come away, and do not turn again.
If you will do all this, I shall take heart
And stand up for you; otherwise, O stranger,
I should be seriously afraid for you.
SOPHOCLES, *OEDIPUS AT COLONUS*

TWENTY-TWO HOURS later by my watch and two days later by the calendar, my airliner crossed the rim of the island continent. Flying north-west to south-east, our day had been telescoped; as we crossed the coast of the biggest island in the world, not a pin-point of light pierced our second night. Unseen around us and above us were threatening pinnacles of cloud, spun off the monsoon winds. Inside our aluminium and plastic cocoon, the passengers lay like larvae, twitching slightly. Those young enough or drunk enough to find sleep lay with their mouths open, like victims of some poison gas. The kerosene fumes we were all obliged to breathe were being enriched with the effluvium created by a party of rich Italians who, unable to stop smoking, stop talking or stop running around, spread their stink as effectively as possible, to the toilets, the corridors and the galleys, in concerted defiance of the IATA regulations. In its curtained alcove, the Italian cabin crew was concentrating on growing its own cancers.

By holding my pillow up to the porthole I could see out into the Australian night, where some titanic electrical commotion was brewing. Far to the west, great bursts of sulphur-yellow, blood-red and a sort of fizzing purply-orange light would boil up out of the black velvet and spill on to the horizon, backlighting tiers of cloud hanging in great slabs. A trickle of magnesium white would slip down them and bounce to earth, then all would vanish and the blackout would be seamless once more.

The storm system was hundreds of miles across. The 747 scuttled down its eastern flank as the horizon turned gun-metal grey, then indigo, then RAF blue and suddenly the cabin crew laid down their cigarettes to serve us a breakfast just as terrible as the other five meals I had already looked at. My appetite was not improved by a certain nervousness to do with something in my luggage.

My intention had been to give all my family presents of a distinctly Italian character. Mother was to have a bottle of Nocino liqueur and a real sponge, my sister-in-law Italian table linen, and for my sister, who has a rich husband, two elegant houses and is moderately interested in cooking, I had found two large white truffles. The vendor had packed them most carefully in a little aluminium pan filled with rice to absorb the odour, sealed it with clingfilm, finished it off in the shop's exclusive paper and tied it with monogrammed ribbon. I had tucked the elegant package among my underwear, with the nefarious intention of not declaring it.

As I gulped my grey coffee, a Voice intoned on the tannoy in seven languages: 'Australia is an island, free of many of the pestilences that plague other lands, and insists on staying that way. Any fresh foodstuffs or vegetable material must be declared.' The Italian pilot sitting next to me warned that not only would my truffles be confiscated if the customs officers found them, I could be fined some enormous amount of money and even sent to prison. Italian flights are carefully inspected, for a single salami could introduce foot and mouth disease or anthrax or rinderpest. God knows what grim organisms infest a truffle. Rabid snot from the truffle hound or vesicular fever from a truffle pig. By the time I got to customs control I was ready to torch the truffles myself.

The cadaverous Friulian peasant in front of me was encumbered with two phony-looking mandolins. The officers smelt them, tapped them, rattled them, and for a second looked like smashing them, to see if anything was inside.

My customs officer was Vietnamese; I had chosen him because the Vietnamese, unlike the Australians, have one of the most sophisticated cuisines in the world. I unwrapped my precious parcel and exhibited two very dodgy-looking grey blobs, charm-

27

less as turtle testicles. The smell filled the entire customs hall. The supervisor was called. He poked at the truffles with the tip of his pencil. 'No, no, no,' he said, with the kind of extreme patience one shows to a child. He flicked a grain of rice on to a sheet of newspaper. ' You can't have that.' He rolled the truffles over with his pencil and flicked off every grain of rice, and he poured the rice out of the pans on to his piece of paper.

'You eat these, do you?' he asked, rolling the truffles with his pencil. 'All of them?'

I gave a quick lecture on the use of the white truffle in Italian cooking, wishing that the wretched fungi would pull themselves together and try to look worth the considerable sum I had paid for them. The officer was unimpressed. 'Take them,' he said and pulled away the paper with the rice. I looked at him stupidly. 'You weren't gunna eat the rice, were you?' Only then I understood; the uncooked rice was the prohibited import. (You are supposed to use the scented rice in a risotto but I had left that out of my lecture.) I scooped the truffles up and put them naked into my pocket.

This little episode struck me as seriously odd. I would have been more able to read the situation in the airport at Addis Ababa or Guatemala City than I was in my home town. I still felt quite disoriented sitting behind my Greek taxi driver, who chatted amiably in a combination of accents which I found considerably more difficult to understand than Greek. The roadscape was as anonymous as airport motorways usually are. To re-embody myself I spoke to the driver in Greek. The back of his hairy neck suddenly glowed with hostility. Did I think he couldn't understand English or something? Impossible to explain that it was I who couldn't understand Australian.

Ann answered the door wearing nothing but a T-shirt, which at our age and our weight looked rather like a sackful of puppies. I glanced at the driver expecting some Mediterranean reaction, especially when she bent to take my suitcase, but, half-naked himself, he seemed to find it unremarkable. I had yet to realise that in Australia my own dress or 'frock' with sleeves and a hemline below the knee was as obsolete as the bustle. To compound my morning's blunders I assumed from Ann's new bulges that she was pregnant and kissed and hugged and congratulated her. Though she forgave me at once, I trod warily thereafter, warily but not warily enough.

The easy part of my journey was over. I now had to fit in willy-nilly. The first thing was to change body-clocks; to do that I had to stave off sleep. To keep me moving we decided to go to the races; all that was available was a rather unpromising meeting at Sandown. In my day Sandown used to be a motor-racing track; turf has now been laid on the inside of the tarmac, and an ornamental pond, and beds of Sam McGredy roses and assorted bedding plants embellish the grassy flat. Sam McGredy roses also exhibit their leathery charms in hedges around the saddling paddock, quaintly renamed the 'mounting enclosure' or, with unconscious obscenity, the 'mounting yard'. The scattered groups of people which constitute an Australian 'crowd' or 'mob', in the same way that two cars abreast are called 'heavy traffic', displayed every sartorial extreme from draped gowns of shiny synthetic material, elbow-length gloves and hats with spotted veiling, to boxer shorts and pyjama bottoms. The ladies who had opted for elegance stood clutching their headgear, turning their faces into the hot wind blowing out of the centre of my electric storm. Years of such wind and the pitiless Australian sun had turned their cheeks the texture of a Sam McGredy rose petal; the vivid colour they had applied themselves. The wind flattened their draperies against their bodies and worked up so much static electricity between their tights and their skirts that they could not have walked about even if their stiletto heels had not sunk into the turf at every step.

The Sandown sumptuary laws, painted in four-inch letters on a large wooden sign, were difficult of interpretation. Gentlemen within the members' enclosure were required to wear a tie – unless wearing something called 'a neat safari suit' when the tie might be forgone. No cravats or turtlenecks would be tolerated evidently, although there was plenty of masculine thigh in evidence, besides the ubiquitous Australian knee. 'Ladies,' the sign continued, 'are expected to maintain a suitable standard in keeping with the dignity of the reserves.' The 'dignity of the reserves' was evidently not compromised by the presence of two very young women wearing cotton sunsuits so brief as to show chubby half-moons of buttock behind, and so wide in arm and leg holes as to allow pubic fuzz and most of their small breasts to be seen. Their unattachedness, and the conscious way they stood and sat about, watching the punters rather than the horses, suggested that they might be prostitutes, but in Australia it would not necessarily follow. 'Vice squad,' somebody said. It was not funny enough to be a joke.

The first race went well enough. In my day it was the Wenona Girl Handicap over five furlongs for two-year-old fillies; it was now the Mackintosh Motors Handicap over a thousand metres. I picked out a sprightly little grey in the 'mounting yard' and she won in sizzling time at better than eight to one.

In the second race, the horses were bunched up about half a mile out when one stumbled. Her head went down, the boy lost his irons, then she buckled and the boy began sliding off towards the rails. The jockey alongside him, Dinn by name, known of course as 'Gunga', reached across and grabbed the lad before he went down beneath the thundering hoofs. The race was a shambles; the punters howled in disbelief; the bookmakers looked for the name of the eventual winner on their boards, hoping they hadn't laid him and the jockeys came in steaming mad. 'Gunga' had thrown the race; he said afterwards that anyone would have done the same, but I can think of some champion jockeys who would have ridden past the falling boy without checking their horse's stride.

What had happened was only too obvious. The grass, which had been watered all day every day for a week, was long and slick, but the turves had not rooted to the baked clay beneath. The horses had been running on the equivalent of a stone slab spread with jelly. The day's racing should have been cancelled there and then, instead hundreds of men were pressed into service to move each rail nine metres out.

As the next race was delayed an hour, I thought it would be a good opportunity to celebrate my tidy win with a bottle of champagne. The bar was a dark, echoing concrete cavern under the main grandstand. The unwashed floor was the size of a cricket pitch; the idea was that you bought your beer or your whisky from an island in the middle and stood juggling race-book and field-glasses and change, trying to gulp it down in the middle of the floor, before going out to throw more money into the bookies' bags. The bar-tender thought they had no champagne; then they came up with a bottle of Seppelt's Great Western which has not improved a percentage point since I sipped my first coupe in 1957. They charged us only three times the high street price and we made for the door.

'Oi!' someone said loudly. An ancient individual festooned with medals of long-forgotten campaigns intoned again, 'Oi! You!' indicating us, 'Where do you think you're going?'

We boggled.

'You can't take drink out there,' he said.

Drink is, admittedly, a perfectly adequate way of describing Seppelt's Great Western. 'Why not?' I asked, a silly question, which got the answer it deserved.

'Because it's not allowed.'

I turned to sail out in a dowagerly fashion – I could almost certainly outrun him, I reasoned – but he called his superior, who appeared astonished and affronted by our insane determination to drink our champagne 'on the lawn'.

'People might sit on it,' he said; by people he meant, I suppose, the fashion plates in their acqua crimplene.

'We won't let them,' we said brightly, but he would have none of it.

Then I made my fatal error. 'You can drink champagne on the lawn on every racetrack in Europe,' said I.

Fury suffused his face until his eyes swam on the dark surface like jellyfish; 'Why don't you get back where you came from,' he shouted. 'I'll get you a vacant flight!'

Ann considered this offer to be evidence that the man was either drunk or suffering from the delusion that he owned Qantas. She was all for defying him, but I had suddenly lost my nerve and my sense of humour. No one in England has ever taken me for English, but here was an Australian unable to recognise me for a compatriot. I was used to drunken Englishmen (and Scots and Americans masquerading as Englishmen) ordering me out of the country and back to where I came from, but here was proof positive that I had no home, anywhere. The Australian passport I was so proud of, that I wouldn't surrender no matter how long the aliens' queue at Heathrow, meant nothing if my countrymen took me for a foreigner. We stood on the stained concrete in the dark hangar and hurriedly drank our warm champagne. The rest of the day's racing was rendered even more dire by the instant headache and acid indigestion that are the insignia of bad champagne.

Even after the whole track had been moved three metres over, wise trainers ran their horses dead; wise jockeys took their horses wide; wise punters went home. Dogged and doomed as usual, I didn't know when to give up; we clung on through the worst day's racing I have ever seen. On their way to the start in the fourth race, two horses suddenly went for each other. One succeeded in landing a damaging kick, unseating the other horse's rider, who was then trodden on by both horses. The clerk of the course, who ought to have seen to it that this sort of thing could not happen, dismounted to assist the fallen rider and then treated the punters to a slapstick display as he tried repeatedly to hoist his beer belly back into the saddle. Still we did not decide to cut our losses until after the second-last race, when Ann's husband had lost a great deal of money and all my winnings were gone.

We dined in a Chinese restaurant, where the waiters stared stoically ahead as they were treated with odious condescension by one member of our party. The same member of our party was anxious to have me know that stories of a Holocaust had been greatly exaggerated. 'Trouble with you fucking liberals is you haven't the nous to question ideas like the Holocaust. Six million Jews bullshit. Even if it was six million, more Australians per capita suffered worse at the hands of the Japanese than Jews did by the Nazis. Nazis are the excuse for all of it, for bloody Israel, for bloody Communism. Germans are all right. Compared to the fucking Japs.'

To my shame I bit. I owed it to Primo Levi who lived through Auschwitz, to Lisa, my Italian housekeeper, who was only fourteen when she was forced to stand by her mother and watch as her eldest brother was shot through the head, not to hear such crap without protest. 'Anecdotal evidence,' he sneered when I tried to describe the refinements of pointless brutality that these people and others had suffered at the hands of Germans simply carrying out orders.

'Take it easy,' someone said. 'Don't let him upset you.' But you must let it upset you, you can't not. It is intolerable that the kindest, richest and best-educated people in the world could allow themselves to be imposed upon by such lies. Australians never understand that I get shrewish with them because I think they are the best people in the world, every one of them a 'Gunga' Dinn. If they forget the lessons of history, who will remember them? Maddened with jet lag, exhaustion, monosodium glutamate, cornflour and coarse wine, I stood behind my chair screaming at my tormentor. We were celebrating the fact that he had just won pre-selection for the Liberal Party. I did not succeed in making an exhibition of myself, for none of the diners in the restaurant had ever heard of me, but this was small consolation as Ann tucked me under her arm and led me away.

During the night the hot wind sucked the storm clouds down to meet the charged sea air at the coast and rain burst forth in cataracts. I lay in Ann's daughter's narrow bed, under her forty square feet of Boy George posters, and listened to the unfamiliar roar. It really rains in Australia, I thought, not like the mizzle they have in England, wrung out of the sky like cold sweat. Still there was a resonance to the noise that I could not relate to the pitter on the slates of my house in Essex. I realised with another twinge of strangeness that the roof behind its Victorian balustrading would not be slate, of course, but tin. When I was an undergraduate I used to love to lie abed and listen to the drumming of 'huge rayn' but now it occurred to me that Chaucer's 'weder for to slepen inne' had a different sound and I must have got the atmosphere of Troilus's seduction of Criseyde quite wrong. In my warm cocoon I was suddenly chilled by the sense of not belonging, of never having belonged anywhere. Perhaps I had everything wrong, who I was, who my people were, what my language meant. My heart began to race as anxiety pulled out the choke, and I swung my legs over the side of the bed.

In the half light from the street the tiers of Boy George masks made the room look like the kind of Mexican catacomb where corpses are stacked against the walls. I switched the bedside light on and took up the Len Deighton paperback I had been reading on the plane: I was at page 312 before my revs had dropped and the sentence sprang off the page like neon: why were the protagonists so concerned about events in Berlin?

'For him and for me Berlin represented some part of our fathers' lives that we still hoped to rediscover.'

I am not so superstitious as to open a Bible, let alone Len Deighton's *London Match*, for guidance, but it was reassuring to know that the father search was not just my own soft-headedness; nobody could call Len Deighton soft-headed.

There was no time to be lost; as soon as I had decided to set off in the morning on the next stage of my journey, across Bass Strait to Launceston hoping to re-discover my father's boyhood, my motor stopped racing. As I pulled the covers up again and composed myself for sleep, outside on the verandah there came a scratching sound and something wailed.

Tasmania,
December 1986

'Prima di morire, vedete la Tasmania; e un paradiso eterno.'
Although I am a native of Launceston, I am told that our
native flora is in many respects similar to those of the
Fatherland. We have our moss-covered hills with tufted ferns
feathering deep little stony brooks, rosy prodigality of briers
and summer scented broom.

JOHN FITZGERALD

THE TASMANIAN writer C. J. Koch maintains that Tasmania
is different from the rest of Australia.

'The entire land-mass of Australia, most of it flat and very dry –
lies north of latitude forty. Tasmania, filled with mountains and
hills, lies south of latitude forty, directly in the path of the Roaring
Forties. It genuinely belongs to a different region from the continent: in the upside-down frame of the Antipodes, it duplicates
North-western Europe, while the continent is Mediterranean and
then African. So it was very easy, in what was once Van Diemen's
Land, for our great-grandfathers to put together the lost totality
of England.'

It is not clear to me at least why C. J. Koch's German ancestors
should have wanted 'to put together the lost totality of England'.
Australians might imagine a totality of England for the same
reason that Englishmen imagine a totality of Australia, sheer
ignorance. The exiles took their scraps of wilderness and did their
best to turn them, not into a simulacrum of a nation state, but
into home. They cleared the native trees and scrub, tried to grow
the food that they knew both how to grow and how to cook. If
they became prosperous they built houses like the ones successful
people inhabited in the regions they had left. The names the early
settlers chose were not connected with 'England', or even the
home counties or Cockney London, but with provincial Britain,
the depressed areas which supplied not only the convicts, but the

35

soldiers who guarded the convicts, and the free settlers and the miners. The map-makers went by superficial similarities of topography and climate; if an estuary reminded them fleetingly of Devon, they called the river the Tamar and the new town above the estuary they called Launceston.

Most of the settlers had small reason to love something called 'England', their first colonial master; one of the reasons they hated England was that its draconian economic policies had driven them into exile from Devonport and Bridport, from Swansea and Melton Mowbray, from Sheffield and Derby, from Deloraine and Queenstown, and they brought the names and their provincial accents with them to the far south side of the world. C. J. Koch plays down the predominant Scots-Irish-Welsh character of the life they tried to build. Australia was not principally 'another Kent, another Dorset, another Cumberland for the free settlers': it was a mosaic of tiny bits of Ulster, Wales, Cornwall, the Scottish Highlands, Norfolk, Lancashire, Yorkshire and Derbyshire. It was the later suburbanites who called places Brighton and Beaumaris and Dover Heights.

Australians like to pretend that Tasmania is their Norway. They go there to eat venison and buy smoked salmon, and call Tasmanians Taswegians. It is in the interests of tourism, Tasmania's only growth industry, to pretend that Tasmania is exotic and antique but any real differences between Tasmania and the mainland are minimal. While it is true that Tasmania lies south of latitude forty, it is also true that the effect of the Roaring Forties is felt on the southern shore of the mainland, where the climatic type of southern Victoria, called 'cool temperate west coast' in the geography books, is the same. Cape Otway and Wilson's Promontory, like King Island and the Furneaux Islands, are tassels on the end of the chain of the Great Dividing Range.

A Tasmanian who abandoned Tasmania for Sydney might be impressed by the contrast, but no Victorian facing into the Tasmanian wind has any feeling of novelty. The seal-grey clouds that roll across the sky are the self-same ones that cancelled most of the tennis when I was at school in Melbourne. The wind has the same rawness; it delivers a slap like a wet towel, with no hint of the crispness of frost. I knew well the massive blue-grey sea

36

that shifted its surface like sliding plates of rock, uneasy to the horizon and beyond. I remembered the old shiver, when I read

> *Great waves looked over others coming in*
> *And thought of doing something to the shore*
> *That water never did to land before.*

I have stood on the coast of New England where those lines were written and felt nothing like the coldness that creeps into the bowels when looking south from the western Victorian coast towards a heaving horizon beyond which there is only Antarctica and the dark blue sky. The polar ice-cap only has to warm up a fraction of a degree and that vast indifferent water whose temperature never changes will in its huge inertia do something to the shore. It will not be like *aqua alta* in Venice, slopping over the mosaic floor of San Marco; it will be dark, implacable, dreadful. This, with its grinding shift of dark water by the ton, is not a sea to swim in; instead I waded in the rock pools with the other creatures that sheltered from its thumping roar, or dug myself a hole in which to hide from the stinging sand spray and read my inevitable book. I learned to swim in Port Philip Bay, practically land-locked and warmed with sewage; on the blue-black ocean on the see-saw slopes of the westerlies I learned to fish. And, like all fishermen, I learned to fear the sea.

Tasmania and the remoter parts of southern Victoria show the same pattern of attempts at intensive agriculture and sporadic mining activity, now mostly abandoned. The eastern half of the island is the same rolling parkland cleared of native vegetation and striped with massive bulwarks of spreading conifers planted a hundred years ago for windbreaks, now dense black arcades sucking light from the air.

The conifers are *Cupressus macrocarpa*, native to Monterey, California, like that other arboreal scourge of Southern Australia, *Pinus radiata*. Once the settlers had realised that the cypresses, first identified in 1838, grew rapidly and were unbowed in the very teeth of the gales that batter the Californian coast, they could not wait to import them. As fast as they ringbarked, burnt and grubbed up the native tree cover, they propagated and planted out long lines of *Cupressus macrocarpa*, to stop their newly naked soil from blowing away. They planted them round their

37

houses, and alongside the home paddocks. They defined drive-
ways and entrances and boundaries with fast-growing walls of
fresh green, lemon-scented when crushed. The trees grew fast,
and kept on growing fast, upwards until they reached their full
height of forty metres or so, and then, ominously, outwards. As
they spread they turned a darker colour, a bitter green, atrabi-
lious, the black of the vegetable world. The lateral branches
pushed sideways and kept on pushing, until the great black base
of the tree was broader than the tree was high.

Nobody could have imagined that in their new environment,
suckled on the sweet water borne on the southwesterlies, unscor-
ched by frost, the cypresses would grow so enormous. They
engulfed houses, knocked over walls, squeezed cart tracks out of
existence, and created tracts of desert strewn with their shed
scales. The native eucalypts are leggy and shallow-rooting but
these titanic trees have their tap roots sunk in the bedrock;
nothing can uproot them nor can their sawn stumps decay. They
never sprout or coppice but stand impenetrable as stupas for a
hundred years. The native birds avoid their funereal branches.
No orchid, no mushroom, no climber will grow in this driest of
dry shade. Here and there householders tired of living in the
roaring darkness underneath them have assaulted their flinty
branches with chain saws, laying open the creaking skeletons
beneath their green-black raiment. The amputated arms do not
bud but display their nakedness like a curse.

In a cemetery outside the western district town of Birregurra,
I was trying to read gravestones for someone else's family with
the wind that always accompanied me whipping my wet hair
into my eyes, when a groan came from somewhere under my
feet and a limb of one of these black trees crashed to earth a few
feet away. The tree was one of a double file which had originally
marked the road to a little stone church, which now lay in ruins.
Left to themselves the trees will soon uproot the headstones and
crack open the graves. Most of the farmers are long gone; the
village schools and churches and church halls that they built are
ruinous, but the black trees will be there forever.

The Australian belief that Tasmania is unlike the rest of Australia and very like England is rather like the impression that most
people had of my father, namely that he was English. He did not

trouble to deny that he was English, although he was careful not to overdo it, chooms being fairly universally detested. He was English, born in South Africa, brought up in Tasmania. This scenario combined all that was acceptable about Englishness without the negative elements of whingeing pommery. A man with this quaint insular background would be more charming, more olde worlde than a brash mainlander. This corresponds with the view that Tasmania takes of itself, as a tiny, picturesque, friendly sort of place. In fact Tasmania is dirt poor and struggling to survive. The centrifugal pull of the great cities of the mainland is, has been, and will always be, too much for it.

The free settlers and the emancipists shared a dream of rich farmland serving pleasant market towns, each with handsome churches, a library, a couple of schools, a shire hall and a mechanics' institute, and the usual flotilla of shoemakers, clothiers, jewellers, pastrycooks, saddlers, fodder merchants, blacksmiths, a lawyer or two, all within easy distance of their farms. It was not to be. Although the churches were built and still stand, because they were built with love and lavishness of real stone or solid brick, the towns have collapsed around them. The farmers could not generate enough economic activity to sustain such an infrastructure. The land was simply not productive enough. If the cropping was good, Australia was too far away from the great markets of Europe and there were not sufficient ships to carry the produce there in time. Tasmanian apples sold in London until they were pushed out by cheaper and better American produce. Anything Tasmania could grow, Victoria could grow and sell, without the expense of crossing Bass Strait. Though the settlers may have had a dream of becoming a sturdy yeomanry, the historical epoch for such a development was over. Only commercial farming of cheap foodstuffs for the urban masses was to be viable. The small farmers of Australia struggled for generations. Even today, one in three of all Australian farms is without income of any kind.

When I was born Australia had one of the most urbanised populations in the world; since then centralisation has intensified. More and more the countryside becomes a resort for trippers from the capitals; as the motorways streak out from the cities, the city dwellers travel further and further to create 'sophisticated recreational lifestyles'. On remote Cape Otway, after half an hour driving on a sand track, I came across a kind of private zoo for urbanites, where houses made of glass and western red cedar were to be tastefully hidden among the stringybarks and heather, affording an unimpeded view of wombats and blue-tongued lizards, as well as the golf club tucked away at the end of the drive. We may scoff at the settlers who broke their hearts trying to turn this ancient, implacable continent into a granary, and we may execrate their memory for inflicting upon us sparrows and rabbits and blackberries to destroy the native flora and fauna, but at least they did not use the countryside as entertainment. They did not trifle with it, but gave it all they had.

When my father was a boy in Launceston, it was still a live city, supporting two good newspapers, churches of every denomination, two public schools for rich boys, half a dozen local primary schools, half a dozen clothing and drapery stores, a number of cricket clubs, rowing clubs, a football league. There was hardly such a thing as 'leisure', let alone a mass of people 'leading sophisticated recreational lifestyles'. Everyone was busy at school or at work, for long hours; once a week at the end of their ten-hour work-day, all the boys had to do cadet drill.

The Launcestonians created their own entertainment, and were not simply spectators of entertainment generated in faraway Sydney, or further-away Hollywood. In their spare time they went to church, and then trained for the sports events which happened every week, rehearsed for the church choir, the band, the annual concert, the amateur theatricals, the Gilbert and Sullivan, the smoking concert. They arranged fêtes, bazaars, raffles, contests, made cakes, garments, bibelots, etcetera for the fêtes, bazaars and so forth, attended race meetings, cricket matches, regattas, football, cycling, hockey, rifle shoots, lectures on theosophy, hypnotism, spiritualism, exotic religions, gave parties for engagements, weddings, anniversaries, visitors from the mainland, retiring dignitaries, grew things, cooked, embroidered and preserved things for the local show, and competed in practically every human activity including rabbit-skinning, sheep-shearing and the wood-chop. The Launceston newspapers carried long lists of names of everyone who took part in anything, including parties given for visiting or retiring clergymen in outlying districts; obscure indeed must have been the individual whose name never appeared in any such list.

Reg Greer's name does not appear in any such list. Neither does any Greer except W. who won some of the cycling races at the annual Caledonian Games on New Year's Day in 1910. I was sure I had found Daddy's elder brother.

Doubtless the entertainments thus provided were rather rustic; the dresses at the parties and the race meetings were probably years behind the Paris fashions, and more beer was drunk than claret, and the singing and dancing and acting were probably downright laughable, but everybody on the street had somewhere to go and something to do, and people to appreciate it when it was done. With such satisfactions there was hardly any reason to go in search of more sophisticated (and costly) professional entertainment. The advent of the movies changed all that.

Launceston was a port, and the principal supply depot for the miners of the north-west. In 1871 James 'Philosopher' Smith had found the greatest lode of tin ever at Mount Bischoff, eight miles from Burnie on the northern coast of Tasmania from where it was shipped to smelters in Launceston; by 1889, under its manager H. W. F. Kayser from the mining town of Clausthal in the Harz mountains, the Mount Bischoff Tin Mining Company had paid £1,000,000 in dividends. More tin was found in Scottsdale and Ringarooma to the east of Launceston together with zircons and sapphires. Then gold was found in the vicinity of Beaconsfield, on the Tamar estuary north of Launceston, and silver at Zeehan and gold at Mount Lyell. The population of the town grew from 20,000 to 60,000.

The mining boom of the eighties relieved twenty years of depression; the see-saw kept moving. Speculation was repeatedly followed by inflation and collapse. The great days of Tasmanian tin, gold, copper and lead were followed by the spasm of Tasmanian scheelite, but the lodes could not compete with more accessible lodes in other parts of Australia and money ceased to be available for development of Tasmanian mining. Tasmania is now permanently depressed. Most successful Tasmanians, like C. J. Koch, leave Tasmania and go to the mainland. Unsuccessful Tasmanians also leave. Gone are the days when Tasmanian mining shares were quoted on the stock exchanges of the world and when Tasmanian apples were shipped around the world to London, the only apples available in the early English spring. The damp air and low cloud brought on by the incessant westerlies do put one in mind of Somerset, and apples used to be the result, but when I drove all around the eastern part of the island in December I saw not a single apple tree. Instead I saw tiny towns of a street or two of recognisably Victorian houses, some built in stone, with signs begging rich mainlanders to visit them, although their souvenir shops were closed and only the pub stood open for the convenience of a drinker or two. I passed dozens of tiny churches and dozens of graveyards full of surnames that had vanished from Tasmania, one of which was Greer.

A William Greer died in Tasmania in 1832, and a James Greer in 1849. A Mrs Greer lived at Perth in 1881, a James Greer farmed in New Norfolk in 1896-7, and a Frances Greer died at Longford in 1895, unmarried, aged sixty-five, of dropsy of the lungs. In each case the trail ended right there; none of these people had issue living in Tasmania. As I was looking for Greers who arrived in Tasmania in 1907 or 1908, I gave no importance to the Perth-Longford-Campbelltown Greers. However, one Greer family kept turning up like King Charles's head. They were three brothers from Maghera, who emigrated in 1854. All the brothers used their mother's name Shaw as well as their surname Greer. The first to be associated with Tasmania is the middle brother, John Shaw Greer, who was born in Maghera in 1834. In 1863 John Shaw Greer entered the Methodist ministry. He married a girl called Elizabeth Bennett, who bore him a son, Mansley John, in Deloraine in 1873. He was based at Campbelltown from 1875 to 1878, and his baby daughter, Millicent Laura, died there in March 1878 of teething and diarrhoea. By 1880, when his son Claude was born, the family was living in Launceston and appears in Manning's Directory for 1881-2. Some time after that the family moved to Victoria, and never came back to Tasmania.

The primal elder's curse made sure not only that I brought my bad weather with me to Tasmania, but that, when I opened my spectacles case to read on the plane, it was inexplicably empty. Although the Sunday evening was damp and blustery, I explored the tiny grid of streets lined with two-storey shops in the hope of finding an optician; there was no one about. The cinema was closed; all the cafés and fast-food bars were closed. The shop façades were supplied with metal awnings, on which hung illuminated signs advertising the 'House of this' and 'exclusive that'. I saw a tiny boutique (pronounced bo-teek in Australian) that advertised 'Pret a Porte'; another was the home of Comfoot-Plus Footwear; Casa Mondé sold lamps, a few doors along from the Lets-B-Crafty Craft Shop. Only the pharmacy was open.

In twenty minutes I had walked the length and breadth of the town centre, where there were almost no office buildings; it was no more than a shopping centre after all. I was amazed at the number of opportunity shops which sold cast-offs in aid of the Salvation Army, St Vincent de Paul, and the Red Cross. It seemed hardly possible that the people of Launceston had so much clothing to discard; I wondered if the clothes had been shipped from elsewhere to the poor of northern Tasmania, for the other shops were thinly stocked and the goods shoddy. In the centre of the noughts-and-crosses grid of one-way streets designed to force the motorist to pull up and pay attention to down-town Launceston, there was a pedestrian plaza. Its two telephone boxes had been vandalised. Over the whole lay the smell of frying beef dripping which characterises Australian cities, where fish-and-chip shops are more often encountered than stockbrokers.

Launceston is potentially a pretty town, with the wide river moving sleepily to its serpentine estuary, kept snug by tight blue hills. The few thousand houses nestle in the river valley like sugar crystals in the cupped palm of a hand. Launceston is but a mill town after all, but a mill town tormented by the dreams of avarice. Boom threw up the huge churches and Romanesque emporiums, and built tall houses with intricate gables and barge boards, sweeping stairs and elaborate verandahs. Bust sold off the gardens of the big houses for sub-division. Launceston has neither the poetry of workmen's houses marching in egalitarian rows up and down, nor the leafy elegance of a spa town, but an uncomfortable mixture of the two. Clots of suburbia have coagulated in the valley and grabbed the heights, with wasteland and pasture cropping out in between. Cheap brick veneer cuddles up to the great Victorian houses, compromising their dignity, revealing them as simply monstrous. Flowers splurt out of gardens too small to hold them, spilling on to streets absurdly wide, up which

43

cars occasionally wander, adrift on a sea of tarmac.

Poor and draggle-tail though it is, Launceston has charm. When the town woke up the next morning I discovered that, though the telephone boxes might be vandalised, traders are happy to offer the use of the telephone. The optician could not sell me magnifying spectacles, but he lent me a pair of heavy hornrims without asking for a deposit. Nobody stared, nobody badgered, nobody bullied or hurried.

In the Local History Room at the Launceston Public Library a lady in rose consulted the biographical index and handed me a clipping. It was the death notice from the Launceston *Examiner* dated the 24th of August, 1908, of William Lyons Shaw Greer. (My father would have been nearly four years old.) It carried the imposing addendum 'Interstate papers please copy'; among the personal notes on another page was a longer account of how William Lyons Shaw Greer had 'died suddenly early on Saturday morning' at his residence, 'The Hollies', in Youngtown. 'The event cast a gloom over the district,' wrote the anonymous correspondent. William Lyons Shaw, or W. L. S., as I quickly came to call him, was the youngest of the three brothers. He had been in Tasmania about twenty-five years, for most of them as resident Secretary of the Victorian Mutual Life Assurance Association. He had abandoned his Methodist religion and was lay-reader at St Leonard's Church of England, superintendent of the Sunday School and church treasurer. He had eight children, who were listed as Arthur, Harold, Millie, Olive, Clara, Kathleen, Gertrude and William. No Reg. No Eric. No Eric Reginald.

The rose lady (whose name turned out to be Mrs Rosemann) did not doubt, and neither did I, that we had found my family. It was only a question of finding the missing link. My father could have been the child of Arthur or Harold or William. I didn't take to the picture of the patriarch in the weekly pictorial. He seemed short and bumptious to me, with his round bald forehead surrounded by a black froth of beard and whisker and a smug little smile laying round his mouth. I liked him even less when I discovered that he had died intestate. Over the weeks that followed I got to know W. L. S. better and to dislike him more.

W. L. S. went originally to the Victorian goldfields at Maldon; there he married another member of the Methodist congregation,

Christina Symons. She gave him four children, the Millie, Olive, Clara and Harold of the announcement, before she died in 1884. I gazed at the photograph of Harold William Greer for a long time. He was dressed in the uniform of a lance-corporal of the second contingent of Imperial Bushmen which had sailed for the Transvaal on the *Chicago* in 1901, when he was nineteen. It may have been simply his youth, but the face that gazed out of the photograph was artless, finer than his father's smug and shining bonce, more like my Daddy I thought.

At the time of his father's death, Harold William was a school-teacher on King Island in Bass Strait. I could find no indication that he had ever been married, or fathered a child in South Africa. Upon hearing of his father's death he resigned and left the windy isolation of King Island for Launceston, confident, I daresay, that he was his father's heir and the years of drudgery in one-room schools were over.

Harold William was the first-born son, but he had two half-brothers and two half-sisters. W. L. S. re-married very soon after the death of his first wife, when Harold William was still a baby. The second wife, Annie Elizabeth Martin, came with him to Tasmania in November 1883 and bore her first child, Arthur Edmund Greer, in March 1884. Her second, Kate, was born a year later; her third, another boy, William Martin, was born four years after that, and her last, Gertrude, was born in June 1893, eighteen months before her mother's death from 'tuberculosis and con-vulsions' at the age of forty-one.

After Annie Elizabeth's death, W. L. S. had resigned from his position with the insurance company, although he was offered promotion to company secretary when it amalgamated with another society. He justified his early retirement for 'family reasons', but it seems likely that the hapless Annie Elizabeth had brought money with her and had left it behind. In 1888 he had acquired the finest house in Franklin Village, on the south side of Launceston. It had been built as a speculation in 1838 by a brewer, in the best, if already outmoded, Ulster Georgian style with Australian cedar panelling and marble fireplaces. W. L. S. called the house 'The Hollies' and planted a cherry orchard and brewed cherry wine. He and his wife were patrons of the little church of St James which stood like their own private chapel just across the road. He sent Annie's boys to public school. In 1895 he acquired Clifton Park, 1,200 acres on the Supply River north of Launceston, with a further 262 acres adjoining. In 1899 he bought an allotment of three and a quarter acres at Wivenhoe as a speculation.

The day W. L. S. failed to wake up his empire fell apart. Harold William had to appoint the Permanent Trustees' Association executors of his father's estate, which was, unknown to the children, encumbered with a large mortgage. Nobody seemed to want to stay at 'The Hollies'; Harold William took over immediately and charged the Trustees ten shillings a week for the eleven weeks that he stayed. Then a Miss Greer 'minor' took over and did the job for two and six a week until April 1909. 'The Hollies' was becoming dilapidated when in 1910 it was sold for £500 to a Mr Hughes to give to his daughter for a wedding present. The allotment at Wivenhoe went in 1913 for £200.

Harold William applied for another teaching job but was refused. All the children, except Clara, Mrs Bryan, who stayed in Bismarck, and Gertrude, who lived all her life in Tasmania, keeping herself by teaching school, and died unmarried in 1963, left for the mainland. I considered the possibility that my father might have been the illegitimate son of one of the Greer girls, two of whom went nursing after their father's death, but no trace of an illegitimate birth could be found for any of them.

Clifton Park was no colonnaded mansion standing in rolling parkland with woolly sheep safely grazing. The only building on the land was a 'paling house of four rooms with iron roof besides kitchen, pantry and storeroom'; the pasture, dry in summer, flooded and cold in winter, was considered 'unsuitable for cattle or sheep'. It needed clearing, fencing, ditching and draining. In December 1908, the surveyor was already recommending a quick sale before the property could deteriorate further. Instead it was leased, but the lessee was unable to make his crops pay. In 1911 he had to sell his engine and his wagon to pay the rent. In 1917 the crops failed altogether and the tenant farmer defaulted on his rent. The property was split up and separately occupied by various farmers of the neighbouring district until in 1933 it was sold to pay costs. The children got nothing.

The first of the Shaw Greers to leave Tasmania seems to have been Arthur Edmund, whom I found after a long search, managing a station in western Queensland. Harold William also tried his luck in Queensland but after seventeen years he gave up and came south again. He stopped in Melbourne where he died, aged fifty, of a brain tumour and was buried in Burwood Cemetery, in June 1932. He had never married.

William's name is entered on the honour roll in St James's, Franklin Village, as having been wounded in the Great War. In 1933 William came to the Trustees' office to collect the family bible, so it seems that not only his half-brother but his elder brother too was dead. He married and went to New Guinea, probably when cattle were introduced there. Eventually he retired to Launceston where he lived from 1943 until he shot himself in 1968. He like his brothers had no child.

The trail was cold. I hired a car and drove out to Winkleigh, to look at Clifton Park for myself. The road wound northwards along the western bank of the Tamar estuary, which lay shimmering and tranquil in the lee of the hills to the south. At first I drove among suburban gardens choked with rampant blossoming plants. Hot pink and iridescent orange pelargoniums tumbled down concrete escarpments and frothed on to the road. Alyssum crawled out from under fences and rooted in the tarmac.

Gradually the suburban phantasmagoria faded away and rolling green paddocks took over, horses, cows, a few sheep, hobby farming country. I turned west from the estuary in the direction of Beaconsfield, driving through dappled sunlight under tall stringybarks. Cattle dreamed in the shoulder-high grass of the Supply River flats. In rolling fields above them on the other side of the river tractors were mowing or turning the cut grass over in long satiny swathes, filling the air with the scent of new-made hay. A sign creaked on the breeze, suddenly grown gentle, 'Clifton Park Hereford Stud' it read. Someone had done the ditching and draining, and poisoned the bulrushes. Someone had built calving sheds and grain stores and hay-ricks. I passed several old weatherboard houses with tin roofs, but the long drive of Clifton Park led to a red brick something I felt too shy to look more closely at. I dreaded being hailed by one of the tractor drivers, so I quickly turned and drove away. I was glad poor Harold William had been spared the sight of what nearly was his.

47

The only other thing I wanted to see was W. L. S.'s grave in Franklin Village. At first I couldn't find the village which seemed to have been shouldered aside by the main north-south motor-way. I was driving back southwards along a road I had travelled on my way from the airport and several times since, when my eye fell on a green sandwich-board on the pavement. 'The Hollies' it read, diagonally, 'Tea-room'. I pulled up with a bump and ducked into a gravelled parking space, which turned out to be the car park of Franklin House, the first property acquired and restored by the Tasmanian National Trust. I was hungry and thirsty so I made for the tea-room called 'The Hollies' and ordered a salad and a cuppa.

'Is there a house called "The Hollies" hereabouts?' I asked, with a face red as fire.

'You're in it,' said the manageress. 'Franklin House used to be called "The Hollies" so they used the name for the tea-room.'

I didn't want to say that it was my forebear who had called the house by that name, or that it was simply someone with the same surname as mine. And I didn't want to explain my absurd situation, prying as I was into matters that may have been none of my business. But, like most Launcestonians, the manageress was expressing a kindly interest, so I told her of my miserable state of not-knowing.

'Take a look around,' she said. 'You never know. There might be a clue.'

I walked up the wide cedar staircase, and looked out over what used to be W. L. S.'s six-acre garden with its cherry orchard, and the gravelled sweep round to the stables and the carriage house. Except that all was just as I myself would like a house, there was nothing. None of the books or pictures in the house had been given by a Greer although there were pictures of the Hawkes family who had lived in the house before them, sent by their descendants from New Zealand. On the street side the house looked over a busy highroad; the once-salubrious residential area around it had been taken over by the noxious trades. Tanks of solvents and lakes of grease stood amongst chain-link fences, which crowded the island of sick yellow grass on which stood the tiny pink stone church of St James.

The manageress gave me the key to the little church, and I

48

poked in the cupboards looking for the parish register, but it was not there, being in fact lost. The church is still used for baptisms, marriages and funerals of the descendants of the old parishioners, but none of the Greer children had chosen to be buried there, although W. L. S. lay alongside Annie Elizabeth under an imposing headstone. The old schoolfriend who collected William Martin's ashes was buried there. The man whose family firm lent the money on W. L. S.'s mortgage was buried there. But the children of William Lyons Shaw had spurned the family plot. I eventually traced every one and replaced it in its order, with its affines and its progeny, but even as I worked I knew my father was not a Shaw Greer.

There was nothing for it but to go to the Registrar-General's office in Hobart. I pointed my rented car towards the South Pole and set off under lowering skies.

In Hobart everything was different. A bitter wind knifed through the streets, forcing the citizens to scuttle from shop to shop. Everyone I spoke to seemed fractious and hurried, and I found myself becoming fulsomely apologetic. Thoroughly cowed, I crept into the Registrar-General's department, expecting to see something like St Katherine's House, where anyone may consult the index to the registers in privacy if not in peace and quiet. Instead I found a counter with booths, like a pawnbroker's shop.

'I should like to consult the index to the register,' I said to a blue crimplene lady.

She gave me a look that asked plainly, 'Who does she think she is?' 'Well, you can't,' was what she said.

'Why not?'

The silly question got the usual answer, 'It's not allowed.'

In the interests of people with something to hide, the indexes to the registers are closed to the public, by law. What I could do was, I could pay the staff of the Registrar-General's department ten dollars to search on my behalf. 'Give us a name, and we'll search for the entry for ten years for ten dollars.' On a system like this I could have been haemorrhaging ten-dollar bills. I demanded to see Mr Christie, the Registrar.

'That's been the law since the thirties. We can't make the records from 1900 onwards public, no, even though virtually all the people concerned are dead. That's right. Yes, the law probably

49

does need to be up-dated. Well, no, I'm not exactly sure it's a law. What's the point of marriage registration if it doesn't make the marriage public? Yes, I see your point, but no, you can't see the indexes, and yes, I know it's a few minutes' work to check a relatively uncommon name over a ten-year period but that's what it costs.'

He withdrew behind his safety barrier. He had not said that his office would withhold the information I was seeking if they thought it bad for me, but if they didn't demand the right of censorship it was hard to see what justification their interference could possibly have had. Unless of course it was merely a way to squeeze money out of the public that was already paying their salaries. The message was plain; I could only have verification of information if I already had the information. In half an hour I could have done the work they were offering to charge me a fortune for; now it would take months and probably hundreds of dollars just to verify the fact that no member of my father's family was born, married or buried in Tasmania. And even then I couldn't be sure that the search had been done properly, or that information had not been withheld. If every other keeper of public records in Australia was to play the same game, my search for my grandparents was going to cost thousands of dollars. And so in fact it proved.

The Archives Office of Tasmania is a small and uncomfortable place. Here there was no lady in rose to take an interest or make helpful suggestions; a series of irritable young women and one languid young man vied with each other to avoid dealing with enquiries from the counter. I was not surprised that the librarians were sick and tired of tourist family historians anxious to prove that their convict ancestors came out with the first fleet. Their evident desire to discourage the spread of the craze, which had led to a massive increase in their work-load and no improvement in pay or conditions, had all my sympathy, but their coldness, boredom and rudeness, on what must have been a fairly slack day, for there were fewer readers than counter staff, diluted my sisterly feeling.

The system of delivery they had devised to protect the microfilm records from the far-fetched possibility of theft was cumbersome and difficult to understand, especially as they explained it so perfunctorily. Each of my mistakes produced noisy sighs and eye-rolling; every time I asked for a new microfilm, a wave of hostility surged over the counter at me. 'Are you sure you know what you're looking for?' one of them asked with a sneer.

'My grandparents,' I answered with the usual surge of shame. I wanted to ask what bloody business it was of hers, but I needed the feeble remnant of whatever good nature she had been born with, so I struggled on, determined to leave no record unturned, for I hoped fervently never to have to go that way again.

By the time they threw me out that evening my borrowed hornrims had worn a bruise on my nose and my head ached roaringly from eye-strain, so the next day I gave up the search through the records and drove by a roundabout route back to Launceston. For much of the way I drove through high banks of Shasta Daisies naturalised from some settler's long overgrown European garden. Their silvery-white stars and yellow buttons were pretty, but all wrong. Every now and then the tiny car was blasted off the road by the yodelling sirens of American-style timber lorries, carrying the forty-foot columnar trunks of Tasmanian hardwoods. I crept in among the daisies and watched sick at heart as the rigid load swung around the bends, carrying all that Tasmania has left that anybody wants.

The conservationists are all leading sophisticated recreational lifestyles elsewhere. Tasmanians have to live somehow, or leave. Perhaps they too are under a curse. For forty thousand years this tiny shield of rock supported forty thousand blacks, hunting and gathering in small, intricately woven kin-groups; in forty years they had been all but exterminated by the Cornishmen, the Irishmen, the Scotsmen, the Englishmen and the miners who came from everywhere. Beside the coast road near Triabunna I found a dead Tasmanian devil, still soft and warm in his glossy black coat with its clergyman's collar of shining white hairs.

'Forgive us,' I said to his dead smile full of needle-sharp teeth. To myself I said, 'We have no business here.'

Melbourne Again,
December 1986

What seas what shores what rocks and what islands
What water lapping the bow
And scent of pine and the woodthrush singing through the fog
What images return
O my daughter.

T. S. ELIOT, 'MARINA'

THE HALL I sat in was long, three times as high as it was wide, and yellow, with an arched ceiling of corrugated iron, which once perhaps was glass. Opposite me was another counter, not so much a pawnshop this time, more like a bank.

The young people behind the counter were very cheery and relaxed as they went about the work of protecting Victoria's public records from the public who owned them and might wish to consult them. They knew little of the protocols governing the collection of these records, but they were expert in getting money out of their nervous clients. For the exorbitant sum of $18 they would agree to undertake a search, but such a search would need at least five working days to complete. None of their clients knew enough to know that if the search took half an hour, it was already unusually long. I watched as people who had made the initial visit, paid their $18 and now returned to collect their documents were told to wait on the hard bench beside me. The hum of lazy chit-chat on the other side of the barrier would be momentarily stilled as a clerk would get languidly to his feet and stroll out of sight. This barely perceptible movement signalled in fact the beginning of the 'search', which was after all only a flip through a microfilm. For $18 the client bought an artificial wait and the privilege of making another visit. For an extra $19 the clerks would graciously consent to look out and copy the documents 'today'.

Family history is said to be already the most popular hobby in the United States, and the number of enthusiasts continues to grow exponentially; what happens in the United States invariably presages what is to happen in Australia. As long as the demand for replicas of official documents came principally from lawyers there might have been some justification for high charges; most family historians are pensioners, who are as poor in Australia as they are elsewhere in the English-speaking world. The Registrar-General's department is fast hauling back the pittance doled out to retired people by the state. What they could be doing with the money was more than I could guess, sitting on a hard bench in the makeshift hallway, waiting for a piece of paper that had cost me $37.

If I had only known, they were already extending to me a degree of privilege, for Australian children are not entitled to see their parents' marriage certificates upon request. In Australia the only people entitled to see the official record of a marriage, as of right, are the parties to the marriage. The purpose of such legislation (if indeed the practice is enshrined in law and not merely the rule-book of the Australian civil service) seems to be to allow bigamists to bigamise without fear of discovery. There is no stigma on illegitimacy, which is at least as common in Australia as in all other English-speaking countries. The regulations hark back to a more hypocritical and neurotic era when Australians were less interested in their family history than they were in claiming a respectability their families had never had.

Despite the atmosphere of casual kindliness, I could not stop the flutter in my chest. If compiling family history was now the favourite pastime of retired Australians, it was not mine. The old ladies beside me on the bench kept up a running chatter about their grandfathers in the Victorian goldfields; I listened enviously as they discussed the whereabouts of the mining claims their forebears had filed, parish records in Daylesford and a certain Mary who may or may not have been white and may have been wife to more than one man at a time. For them it was all a wonderful adventure; for me it was the primal elder's curse all the way.

I distracted myself by trying an ethological study of the genus 'Victorian Civil Servant'. The uniform adopted by almost all those I could see was stretch jeans, trainers and windcheaters, for male

53

and female alike. The windcheaters were insulation against the chill south-westerlies funnelling down the city streets; the jeans were sexual display; the trainers did not noticeably speed up the pace of the individuals who chose to cross and recross the hall with files clasped to their windcheaters, but they did allow a slow motion version of a walking racer's provocative hip-roll.

I tried guessing which windcheater was pressed against my family record. I heard a microfilm being rewound and my heart wound itself up tighter. One of the old ladies at the counter was pleading, 'This is my third visit. On my pension I can't afford all this travelling.'

The beardless bureaucrat gave her the classic response, 'Insufficient information. You'll have to pay another search fee.'

'The surname could be spelt without the "e", and sometimes it's "ea" or "ie",' ventured the old lady.

'Then you'll have to make applications in the different names.'

The old lady took some forms and turned back to the bench.

'And you'll have to pay a search fee for each name.'

The old lady put the forms back and walked away down the hall.

I wanted to talk to someone. I wanted to ask why the indexes to the records could not be made public, so that anyone could search and find out if a document was held. Concern for privacy could come into operation when permission to see the document was requested. The system that allowed them to screw money out of us all was cruel and idiotic. I longed for good old St Katherine's House, where we all toiled through the indexes side by side, lawyers' runners, family historians and searchers for missing persons alike. If you wanted to read all the Greer births from 1850 to 1950 you could. I had. After a morning of heaving bulky volumes and fighting for space at the reading benches, while my ankles swelled from standing with my bag on my feet so nobody could walk off with it while I made notes, I had the names of all the Greers born in England and Wales between 1900 and 1910, whether in Aberystwyth, Alverstoke, Ashton Park, Aston, Barnet, Barrow-in-Furness, Barton Island, Bethnal Green, Birkenhead, Brentford, Camberwell, Canterbury, Cardiff, Chorlton, Devonport, Edmonton, Epsom, Fylde, Gateshead, Godstone, Grimsby, Halifax, Hendon, Holborn, Kensington, Lambeth,

54

Lanchester, Leeds, Lewisham, Liverpool, Manchester, Medway, Middlesborough, Milford, Neath, Newcastle-upon-Tyne, Oldham, Ormskirk, Paddington, Poplar, Portsea, Portsmouth, Preston, Prescot, Prestwich, Romford, Runcorn, St German, Salford, Settle, Sheffield, Shoreditch, Southwark, South Shields, Swindon, Stoke-on-Trent, Tonbridge, Toxteth, Tynemouth, West Derby, West Ham, Whitechapel, Whitehaven, Wigan, or Woolwich, 266 Greer babies in all, 139 of them boys, and none of them an Eric Reginald.

By lunchtime I knew for sure that wherever Eric Reginald Greer was born, and my grandparents were born and married, it was not in England. Simply to confirm that my father was not born in Australia would cost a search fee to each of seven state record offices, and would not eliminate the possibility that his birth was registered under a slightly different name or guarantee that the relaxed young persons entrusted with the job had done it with due diligence, or checked possible alternate spellings.

This time I did not make the mistake of suggesting that Australians adopt the English system. I waited cowed and obedient. During the time I sat on the bench I saw only one person come away from the counter with the document she had paid for. As my face burned under the stares of the clerks who came out from the inner office for a look at me, I scribbled desperately in my notebook. *What if it was all an act? What if Daddy's dignified, standoffish manner was all invented, modelled on some movie hero, some member of the royal family, or the Saint by Leslie Charteris? They called him the Toff, a fictional title for a fictional man. What if he pretended to be upper crust, top drawer, and invented the kind of past for himself that could never be checked? Perhaps he stayed in his dead-end job among advertising men because he was unlikely to meet anyone who would see through his act? If Daddy had ever claimed an ancestry or hinted at a claim, I would find it easier to believe that he was a phony. He said nothing, after all. He wore no old school tie. He made no attempt at social climbing. His toffishness was evinced mostly in his reluctance to hobnob with hoi polloi, and his treating himself to a bespoke tailor.*

To be a Greer is not to be just anybody. Greers are not Smiths or Browns or Greens. The name has a history and a meaning, whether it is encountered in England, Scotland, Ireland,

DADDY, WE HARDLY KNEW YOU

Australia, Canada, South Africa or the United States. Or the Isle of Man.

The Greers can trace their line back to the Scottish kings. The Greers who care about such things (of whose number Daddy was not) believe that they are descended from the ancient Highland clan McAlpin, via the third son of King Alpin, who was called Prince Gregor. Prince Gregor's elder son, Dongallus, married Spontana, sister of Duncan, one of the Irish kings, and their first-born son, Constantine, married his cousin Malvina and they called their son Gregor. Gregor, standard-bearer to his uncle, Malcolm I, was killed by the Danes in 961. His wife Dorigelda had given him a son John, who married Alpina, daughter of Alchaius, brother of Kenneth the Great. The line continues through the seventh generation with Gregor, Laird of Glenurchy, who married the daughter of Lochow, ancestor of the Dukes of Argyle. His son Gregor was Bishop of St Andrew's. The line continues through Sir John McGregor, Laird of Glenurchy, one of whose sons, Gregor, was Bishop of Dunkeld and Lord Chancellor of Scotland in 1157. His eldest son, Sir Malcolm McGregor, married a kinswoman of the king, and his heir, Gregor, married and had a son Malcolm, whose second son, Gilbert Gregorson, took the name Grierson and on 17 May, 1410, received the lands of Lag, Dumfries-shire, from his cousin, the Earl of Orkney, which were inherited upon the death of his eldest son in 1457 by his second son, Vedast-Grierson. His son, Roger Grierson, married a great-granddaughter of Lord Darnley, and by this alliance the Rockhall estates came into possession of the Griersons, who hold them still. Roger's son, Roger, a member of the Scotch parliament in 1487, was killed at Flodden in 1513. The line continues through Sir John Grierson who died in 1566, and his son Roger, who died in 1593, to Sir William Grierson of Lag and Rockhall, and then things get a little muddled.

In 1593 Sir William married Nicola, daughter of Sir John Maxwell, fourth Lord Herries and second son of Robert, fourth Lord Maxwell by Agnes, his wife, who was Lady Herries in her own right, daughter of William, third Lord Herries, and a grand-daughter of Archibald Douglas, fifth Earl of Angus. The sons of this alliance were called Grier. Sir James Grier, of Capenoch, Dumfries-shire, and Rockhall, and Alnwick in Northumberland,

56

married a clergyman's daughter, Mary, who was the widow of Thomas Grier of Barjarg Tower, Dumfries-shire. By this time, 1626, there were Greers in Ireland as well as other Griers in Scotland, descended from junior branches of the family. The stock was tough. Despite religious persecution and exile, and for many of the junior branches of the family, grinding poverty, they hung on.

The Greers are amongst the oldest of the Ulster Scots families. In 1622, there were 70 British families, 60 of them Scots, in that proportion of the Barony of Fews which then belonged to John Hamilton, brother of James, first Viscount Clandeboye, many of them Greers. Hamilton bought a thousand acres in Magharyentrim from Sir James Craig in 1615 and he exchanged land in Cavan with William Lauder of Belhaven, Kilruddan, Fews. The muster rolls of 1630 show many of the Greers as having survived Irish attacks that had decimated the settlers.

Once the clan had been parted from its heartland the wandering went on. Ulster was not the end for these rebel Scots, from there they embarked again to America with the Quakers, to South Africa and Australia, fleeing famine, following gold. Where the traumas fell, memories were obliterated. Teenagers arriving illiterate in the new world put their shabby gentility behind them, rolled up their sleeves and set to work, unmindful of the antiquity of their line. They were conscious only that famine and destitution make nonsense of crests and mottoes. For generations the matter was forgotten, until now genealogy has become the hobby of their prosperous descendants.

The motto of the Greers descended in the direct male line from King Alpin is *Memor esto*, 'Be mindful of your ancestors'. My groaning files bear witness to the fact that many a Greer follows the motto to the letter.

My father would have called it all 'guff'. He wore no ring on his little finger showing the crest of an eagle displayed ppr., charged on the breast with a quadrangular lock. If he knew who the Greers were, he gave no sign of it. He chose no blue-blood for a wife and he made no inquiry about her ancestry when he chose her. Her name was in fact more ancient than his, but neither he nor she had any notion of how she came by it and neither cared.

57

And nor do I. It was hard to convince the genealogists, riding on the crest of their international wave, that I was not anxious to prove my descent from the kings of Scotland. Librarians assumed when I crept in to continue my father-hunt through the electoral rolls and newspapers in their custody that I was playing family history. They could not grasp what I was saying when I told them that I had no family to write the history of. 'Where is your grandfather buried?' they would ask, with exaggerated patience. Or, 'What does it say on your father's birth certificate?'

One of the reasons I did not order a heavily embossed copper plaque with the Greer arms, 'On a field azure a lion rampant or, armed and langued gules between three antique crowns of the second, on a canton argent, an oak tree eradicated, surmounted by a sword in bend sinister, ensigned on the point with a Royal crown, all parti per rect' to hang in the den, or 'embroidered in gold and silver bullion wire thread on a velvet mat blazer badge' is that Daddy would have sneered at such foolishness. Another is that I have no den to hang it in or blazer to sew it on to. Yet another is that the Great Greers might descend on me and trash me for my insolence. I had not even established my right to the name, let alone the arms.

The instructions to family historians are plain; before undertaking any research you must interview all the elder members of your family and write down all they can tell you. You must acquire certificates of births, deaths and marriages, in order to verify the information you have been given. You should try to find the family bible which would have been kept by your grandparents and their parents, if not by less godly generations, and you should locate the family graves. You should consult parish records. In Australia it is essential to do all this, because you cannot search the official records until you already know where to find what you are looking for, so you can then pay someone else an exorbitant sum to look where you tell him.

The genealogists and registered search agents could not understand that I had no one to ask. The only member of his family that I had ever met was my father and for him I had not a single document. I possess nothing of his except a copy of the studio portrait made on his retirement. I did not know the names of his brother and sister, or the name of the school he went to. I had never met anyone who knew him before he was in his late twenties.

I was luckier that day than usual. My thirty-seven dollars paid for a photocopy of the certificate of marriage of my parents made on special paper with an all-over pattern saying 'State of Victoria' a few thousand times. On 27 March, 1937, Eric Reginald Greer, bachelor, newspaper representative, married Margaret Mary Lafrank, spinster, milliner, at St Columba's Catholic Church in Elwood. That much I more or less knew. He was thirty-two; she was (barely) twenty. That too I more or less knew. What I had paid my $37 for were the sections 'Birthplace' and 'Parents' Names'. My father's birthplace was given as 'Durban, Sth Africa', his father as 'Robert Greer Journalist' and his mother as 'Emma Rachel Wise'.

At last, I thought, irreducible fact; economical with the truth though he may have been, I would never have believed that my father would say the thing that was not. Surely he would not have lied to the woman he was marrying, who trusted him enough to give her whole life into his keeping. He was after all a Houyhnhnm. I was (I had to be) sure of that. He looked like a Houyhnhnm with his long ruminative face, and, more to the point, he behaved like one, 'looking with a very mild aspect, never offering the least violence' of word or deed. Like a Houyhnhnm he had 'not the least idea of books or literature' as far as I could tell. Gulliver found it difficult to explain the idea of improbability to his Houyhnhnm master:

'And I remember in frequent discourses with my master concerning the nature of manhood, in other parts of the world; having occasion to talk of *lying* and *false representation*, it was with much difficulty that he comprehended what I meant; although he had otherwise a most acute judgment. For he argued thus; that the use of speech was to make us understand one another, and to receive information of facts; now if any one said *the thing that was not*, these ends were defeated; because I cannot properly be said to understand him; and I am so far from receiving information that he leaves me worse than in ignorance; for I am led to believe a thing *black* when it is *white*; and *short* when it is *long*. And these were all the notions he had concerning that faculty of *lying* so well understood, and so universally practised among human creatures.'

(If I had read my Swift aright, I should have known that it was impossible that my father should have been a Houynhnhnm, especially as I know myself for Gulliver's sort of naked Yahoo. But in those days I was still nursing the prelapsarian fantasy that I had escaped the common human lot. I know now that my father's whole life was a lie, yet we were quite correct in thinking that Daddy hated lying, told fewer lies than most people, in fact, said nothing rather than something insincere. The pity of it, to think that a man who hated lying was obliged to lie so hard in order to survive! His heroic lying made it possible for his children to tell the truth.)

I was surprised that I had got my grandmother's name so nearly right, for I had virtually convinced myself that I had invented a Jewish grandmother called Rachel Weiss. Emma Rachel Wise was not quite the same thing; her name was as likely to be Irish or Cornish as Ashkenasy. One thing it was not likely to be was Northern Irish; a marriage between a green Wise and an orange Greer would have been virtually unthinkable in the old country. Although I saw no reason to doubt my grandmother's name as my father gave it, 'Robert Greer Journalist' struck me as a phony. Nevertheless I spent the next month looking for him.

Perhaps the parish priest had asked to see documentary verification of these statements. After all he was not supposed to take the groom's unsupported word for it that he was who and what he said he was. When I looked at the information given about my mother on the certificate I was not reassured about Dr Greenan's thoroughness. My mother was still a minor but consent to her marriage had been given by her mother, as if her father was dead or unreachable, neither of which he was. She had been given away by my uncle, her elder brother. I asked him later why he hadn't got more and better information about the man who was marrying his little sister and he said, ruefully, 'I was only a kid myself'. There cannot have been many virtuous girls so unprotected in Melbourne in 1937.

Because of Daddy's resistance to our attempts to recruit him into the church, we children decided that he must have been true-blue, dinky-di. Nothing would have been easier than to have acquiesced and given lip service. We thought that, though he mightn't say much about anything that mattered, what he said would be true. He would not encourage false intimacy, would say less than he felt rather than more, but what he said would stand. Jack Tosh, an old business associate, who knew him better than I did and saw him often during twenty-seven years, told me over a bottle of rather good claret that Daddy wasn't an obviously friendly type, hail-fellow-well-met; Daddy was aloof, even stand-offish, but 'You knew you could trust him.'

'I never heard a really nasty word about Reg. He wasn't one of the boys, but everybody liked him – or rather nobody disliked him.'

(Ah that I could say the same! I thought.) 'Lots of people thought he was English. Did you think he was English?'

'Can't say I did. I thought Reg was, you know, posh. Public school, definitely. I left school when I was twelve, so I really felt the difference.

'He'd stand on rank, mind you. If I called him because of some cock-up about an account, he'd always put me on to his secretary. "What's that? Just an account query – my secretary'll handle that." If he rang up with a query he'd always ask for the principal. He'd never talk to me when I was a humble accounts clerk. Much too grand.

'But I got to really like Reg. He was stiff, a bit pompous sometimes – you know he'd say things like, "As I was only saying to Sir Lloyd Dumas the other day . . ." We'd take the piss out of him for that kind of thing, but he was completely genuine. He'd never tell you what you wanted to hear, if he wasn't convinced of it himself. Most of the reps used to go for lunchtime drinks at one particular pub, pandering to the media managers who regularly drank there. Choir practice, we used to call it. Reg never went. Never.

'You have to imagine what these people were like. Your father was far too good for the job he was doing. Most reps are boozy lightweight boys. His opposite number, on the rival paper, was best mates with everybody. Bit of a spiv really. He'd worm his way into your confidence and then use it against you. Reg'd never do that. Your father wasn't a drunk, for one thing. Never saw him drunk. We all thought he was a family man. He never hung around to get pissed with the boys; always off home.'

Actually, he was off to the St Kilda Cricket Club, but the main point was incontrovertible. Daddy was no maltworm. 'Do you agree with those who say Reg Greer never worked an afternoon in his life?'

'You mustn't think of your father as selling anything. He didn't have to. That job was automatic. All the agencies knew they had to take space in the 'Tiser and they all did. The most your father'd have to do'd be to tell them that they'd have to pay more for the space because of newsprint rationing or something, and that didn't happen very often.

'He must have had an expense account but he never bought expensive lunches. The other reps wined and dined each other all the time, but not Reg. The reps didn't get much of a salary you know, but they made it all up on the exes.'

Somehow it seemed typical of Daddy that he would have left his expense account virtually unused. Neither of us thought for a moment that he would have swelled his meagre salary with phony expense claims, although such lying is so commonplace it is hardly seen as immoral. His job was dead-end, dreary. He considered himself superior to most of the hustlers doing it, but he had what he wanted. He had organised his life for maximum leisure, minimum strain; I remembered that one of the distinguishing characteristics of a gentleman is that he is never, ever, in a hurry. He may be poor but he must never bustle. Daddy was certainly poor, but he lived the leisured life of an English gentleman. Like many of the ilk he had no library, no cellar, no music, no pictures; his wife had no clothes and no car for a long time and he was mean with his daughters.

'When your book came out, you know, they must have given him a hell of a time. Your father wouldn't have liked that one bit.'

'Did you all know that I was Reg Greer's daughter?'

'Oh, yes, we knew that all right. Only have to look at you. You're the spitting image of Reg.'

In the drawer of my writing desk there are a dozen or more letters from Greers who say that the moment they first saw me on television they said, looking at my narrow forehead and long jaw, 'She's a Greer of the Greers.' I am the spitting image of a dozen Greer aunts and grandmothers. Greers tease their rebellious daughters, asking what could be expected of tall girls called Greer with fly-away hair. When I begged for help in finding my kinfolk, they sent pictures of themselves. 'You're definitely one of us,' they said, and added photographs of the family coat of arms, watercolours of houses in rolling Ulster landscapes and photocopies of the Greer pedigree.

Among all the indicators of kinship none is more misleading than physical resemblance. It can be so strong as to cause a physical shock and yet be nothing more than a coincidence. As I had no information about my father's family whatsoever, I followed any lead as far as it would go. Among the leads I found was a photograph of a man who looked so like my father that I yelped, and disturbed two lilac-haired ladies peering at a microfiche just behind me. I was holding an illustrated book, put together at the height of the anti-imperialist agitation after the catastrophe of the First World War, when Australians felt very bitter, and the Irish led by Archbishop Mannix were protesting against possible commitment to serve in any other British war. As a red rag to an already enraged bull, the book was called *Australia's Fighting Sons of Empire*; on page 177 there was a portrait in the uniform of a pilot of the first Australian Imperial Force of Henry Reginald Greer. It shook me, as Daddy would say.

He had Daddy's long chin and narrow nose, with a slight furrow at the tip, and he had the same small mouth, with its tight upper lip, but it was the way his hands were loosely clasped around the swagger stick that gave me a turn.

I found out what I could about Henry Reginald. He was twelve years older than my father, and born in Bellingen, northern New South Wales. He was third-generation Australian, for his grandfather, Isaac Greer, came to New South Wales in 1842, when he was fifteen; in 1849 he married Ann Nicholson at Shoalhaven, and established a farming dynasty, but as far as I could tell Henry Reginald's father, Colin Pollock, had no kinsman called Robert who married an Emma Rachel, and neither did Henry Reginald. He survived training on Salisbury Plain, and active service on the Somme, at Bullecourt Ridge, Polygon Wood and Passchendaele, and came home to take up farming again at

Fernmount and then Wingham and Tweed Heads. He died in 1955.

He had to belong to me – he had my face – but he does not. He ought to have been something closer to my father than a cousin, but he is not even a second cousin. This Greer family has been trying to identify their Ulster ancestors without success. I, who could penetrate no further into the past than 1933, envied them so much their ancestor born in 1827 that I visited Shoalhaven churchyard and walked disconsolate among the stones, but no whisper came forth.

The only source of hard facts for the Reg Greer story had to be the Veterans' Affairs building in leafy St Kilda Road, a few blocks south of the War Memorial, which looks like part of a set for *The Magic Flute*, Sarastro's temple perhaps, being half classical with a sort of sawn-off ziggurat for a roof. I walked from the sun-dapple into a car park under the building which is raised on stilts. A utility truck was drawn up hard by the front entrance so that semi-naked men could toss bags of papers down the steps and into the back of it. More such bags choked the doorway. As I dodged among the bag-heavers I savoured the sharp tang of their body-odour.

Inside the glass doors there was no receptionist, no com-missionaire, no porter, no directory, just a bank of elevators. The way to the heart of the Veterans' Affairs administration lay wide open to any combat psychotic with an M-16. The people standing around carrying brown-paper bags full of food, smoking, chewing and recounting the excesses of the festive season, were mostly too scantily dressed to be hiding even a hand grenade. 'Jeez Ize wrecked,' one said. 'Took me till t'is mornin' t'find m'car.' He smiled beatifically, as befits one who has reached the summit of human bliss, to be blind drunk in Australia.

I had been advised by a well-wisher to go to the third floor, which was as well, for without this hint I could have wandered around the building for hours. Facing me as I walked out of the lift was another pawnbroker's counter. In all but one of the bays there was no functionary to be seen. In the one inhabited bay, a woman and two girls were pleading with a woman official. I stood at a respectful distance behind them, but the official looked over her clients' heads and said loudly, 'Are we in your way?'

I stared at her, too shocked to answer for an instant. I began to stammer, 'So sorry . . . no idea . . . didn't mean—' in just the way that used to irritate me so when I heard the British do it. Surely I had committed some appalling offence against Australian etiquette.

The woman said, again loudly, 'Can I help you?' By this time I was smirking and bowing to the clients before me, and noticing with horror that the woman's face was wet with tears. 'I've an appointment with Rob Coxon,' I answered, gesturing ineffectually to signify that there was no hurry and I had not meant to jump the queue. The official walked away from her clients, who settled down at the counter as if it was their second home.

Mr Coxon appeared with a stack of files. He was unusually amply dressed in that the legs of his shorts were quite long and his T-shirt had something like a collar. He took me to a tiny, stifling interview room and sat me in a rather soiled armchair.

'Under the Freedom of Information Act,' he intoned, 'you are entitled to see your father's files. A précis of his case was made when your mother's pension was being considered, and you will find that easier to read because it has been typed out.' He leafed through the file, describing the contents. He seemed to have read the whole thing. Then he handed the file to me, and sat on the low table by my chair, watching my face as I turned the yellow leaves.

My heart was bouncing round my chest like a frog trapped in a bucket. The narrow room, like a confessional, and the closeness of the man peering at me, made the heat come into my face. Dark patches kept appearing on the paper. I was terrified that I would faint. I tried to take deep breaths, but my ribs were crushed tight. I could only pant. The palms of my hands were running with sweat. I laid the typewritten précis by and lifted one by one the brittle originals, RAAF Forms P/M 8, First Medical Examination, Certificate of Service, RAF form 39 (2), RAAF form 45, Forms NZ 376 and 377, RAAF Forms P/M 54, 43, 41 . . .

RAAF form 41 contained my father's own précis of his pre-service life: 'School – Secondary Senior Public Aet 15 and a half years Tasmania. Average amount of sport. Free mixer. No especial worries or problems. Occupation – Newspaper work – Reader –

Reporter – Interstate Representative – Manager. (7 years last job) Home – Married 7 years. W a & w. 1 child four and a half a & w. F[ather] died aet 58 years. 1 year ago – Heart trouble. M[other] died aet 53 years. 3 and a half years ago. Influenza. Collaterals 1 Brother aet 42 years a & w, 1 Sister aet 36 years a & w. Childhood days happy – well cared for – no home discord.' This brief statement of his background was the most comprehensive Reg Greer had ever uttered; for a year I struggled to verify it. In my hurried first reading I didn't notice one obvious untruth; Reg Greer was not a manager when he enlisted. He was not a manager until shortly before his retirement, nearly twenty years after the war was over.

Every document in the file seemed to me unbearably sad; I longed to lay it down and rest between each harrowing vision of Daddy being examined and re-examined by men half his age, judged and found wanting. He told them of his nightmares. I fancied they were laughing at him, when they quoted him saying of his recurrent nightmare of being run down by cattle, 'Fierce-looking things, you know'. The worst came upon me without warning. One of his nightmares was of 'danger impending for his daughter due to cars rushing at her at incredible speeds'. A howl leapt out of my mouth before I could stifle it.

I clapped my hand to my mouth and struggled to get back in the air that I had so thoughtlessly expelled. I was literally winded by the sudden intimacy. I wanted to grab the man in shorts and tell him, 'You see! He did! He did! He loved me!' Instead I heaved and spluttered, like one choking on her own spit.

Mr Coxon leaned forward. He was satisfied. 'You can have a copy of that,' he said and took the file out of the room.

All I knew was that I dared not cry, for once I started I would never stop. The thought of being led sobbing past the counter and the other people whose lives were in this bureaucratic mincer boiled my tears dry with embarrassment.

Mr Coxon came back with the file. 'How much is that?' I asked.

'We make no charge,' said Mr Coxon. He meant it as a kindness, I am sure. I would have paid him a thousand pounds to have been allowed to read that file in private. Perhaps he thought I might deface it, or steal it. Surely Daddy's next of kin should have the right to do both, I thought. In the land where the information gathered for the census is ritually destroyed, why should this stuff stay on file?

For the rest of the day the vision of my father standing naked before the medical officers would not leave me. He would have made light of it himself, joked about the short-arm inspection and his own embarrassment. I have only once seen my father naked and then for so brief an instant that I cannot remember what I saw. Now I saw him like a prisoner stripped before his jailers, and my heart ached for him.

When he was old and frail and soon to leave this world, I nurtured a fantasy that I would have time and he would have time for me to nurse him, to bathe him and groom him and feed him and hold him close so that he did not find his way out of the world alone. I have done as much for total strangers but I was not to get the chance to do it for my father. He went so fast and so far away that I couldn't catch up. If I had but once held him unprotesting in my arms, I could have survived that dreadful afternoon unscathed.

Still in Melbourne,
January 1987

Always we have believed
We can change overnight,
Put a different look on the face,
Old passions out of sight:
And find new days relieved
Of all that we regretted
But something always stays
And will not be outwitted.
ELIZABETH JENNINGS, 'DISGUISES'

WHEN I was fourteen years old, imprisoned in a bookless house, bored at school and double-bored at home, the Public Library of Victoria was my Valhalla. I would travel 'into town' from the sea-side suburb where we lived, on the train, with something for my lunch hidden in my briefcase, most often a jar of mussels I had gathered and brewed into a mouth-crinkling vinegary mess and a wholemeal bun. I'd walk fast up Swanston Street, chastely averting my eyes from the shop-window displays. They were in fact about as elegant as the average Oxfam shop, but I knew as little about that as I did about preparing mussels. The walk was uphill; I processed towards it as reverently as any Greek to the Acropolis, although standing on its mound of green grass it looked rather more like a miniature version of Belfast Town Hall. As I walked past the statue of Joan of Arc, I always remembered my grandmother's joke, the first time she took me to visit the Art Gallery, which used to be housed in the same building.

'What's Joan of Arc made of?' she asked.

'Bronze?' I ventured.

'Orleans!' she yelled and hooted with laughter.

Through the revolving door I'd go, out of the blue-white blaze of the sun into mahogany, pietra dura and green baize. I strode confidently, hoping no one would challenge me for being no more

68

than fourteen. My fears of discovery were probably unfounded; my face was so grey and drawn with adolescent misery that the average bar-tender in any of the lavatorial pubs that lined Swanston Street would probably have poured me a brandy without missing a beat, judging me nearer thirty than twenty. I'd take the staircase in a busy little tripping run, as if I did it twenty times a day, and stroll loftily into the reading room. Convinced, as all adolescents are, that everyone was looking at me, I dared not stop and peer. Too proud to hiss a question and scared that my question might give me away, I never quite got the hang of the system.

As in the British Museum, the circular reading room was domed in glass, with long tables radiating from a mahogany core towards the book-lined walls. I used to take a turn or two round the perimeter just to get the feel of bookish gloom, the patina of polished wood and leather, and my heart skipped with suppressed excitement. Although the supervisor in his pulpit at the hub worked away at some librarianly task without raising his head, I was sure he kept a fingertip on each spoke like a spider. I knew that if I should dare to chew or fart or drop a book, or blot it with my cheap pen, he would dart down and paralyse me. So I would quickly get a book, which was never quite the book I wanted, edge my behind onto a slippery chair, and take notes the way I saw others doing. So the habit of a lifetime was formed. More of my waking life has been spent in libraries, with a pen in my hand, than anywhere else.

My dream was to live in this heavenly building and know all its secrets, to have the right to put cards with my writing on them into the catalogue file, to be allowed to go behind the curving book-clad walls into the stacks and have keys to unlock the cabinets of bookish rarities. They didn't give university scholarships with a living allowance for librarians, however, only for teachers. Although she had seldom seen me without a book, and must have known perfectly well that I read most of the nights away with a candle hidden under the blankets, my mother thought I would soon get bored with books, and want pretty clothes and good times. To be a librarian was not a serious ambition. To learn tennis, now, and get to meet nice boys at the tennis club, that would have been a serious ambition. No girl in her right mind could want a job behind the scenes in a library, long hours, bad pay and all that whispering, when she could have a little nine-to-five tedium in return for a tidy pay-packet, lunch-time shopping in town, pretty clothes and boys. That was normal, that was healthy, that was life in fun-loving suburbia. These were the fifties, and I was a freak waiting to be born. Waiting in a library, with a brain stuffed with dreams of *luxe, calme et volupté*.

There are libraries where you hang like a fly on a window against a curtain wall of glass. There are libraries so over-heated and so dry that walking across the carpet and putting your hand out towards a steel bookcase makes a spark leap the gap with a crack like a bull-whip. There are libraries like the Bibliothèque Nationale in Paris where if you leave your seat to go to the lavatory someone else will take it, and libraries like the Wren Library at Trinity and Duke Humphrey at the Bodleian which have not changed in three hundred years. There are libraries where you may not rest your hands on the books, or lick a finger to turn a page, or use anything but a pencil to make your notes, and then, never, never with your note-pad on the open book! In such libraries you can read the original muster rolls that list the Greers who struggled and survived in the first of many grim chapters of English colonialism. They were sent to a fair and fertile country of green hills and full streams that had been depopulated by a long and vicious war of attrition under Elizabeth. Like all colonials they were exiles from their own land, forced to steal the land of others and to defend their stolen property with their lives. If my father had been born three hundred years ago, the libraries of Britain would have yielded up to me all his tragedy and all his glory in a matter of weeks.

Libraries are reservoirs of strength, grace and wit, reminders of order, calm and continuity, lakes of mental energy, neither warm nor cold, light nor dark. The pleasure they give is steady, unorgastic, reliable, deep and long-lasting. In any library in the world, I am at home, unselfconscious, still and absorbed. It was inevitable that I would begin my search for my father in a library, although I would reckon that my father was never inside a library in his life.

When I got to the Public Library of Victoria this time, I

discovered that someone had built a sort of box around it and I had to run a gauntlet of wobbly planking and scaffolding to get in. Though only a stripling among libraries it seemed this one was falling down, but I could see no workmen on the scaffolding, nor did I in any of the weeks that followed. I pushed the swing-door the wrong way, as being left-handed like my father I nearly always do, and walked into deafening, smelly chaos. The smell, and a good deal of the noise, came from a dinette which had been installed in what used to be an exhibition gallery. A makeshift plywood counter had been built half across the foyer; for a panicky moment I wondered if I was going to have to pay the people on the other side of it to read the books for me, but they wished merely to take my bag. Being very used to libraries, I hadn't a bag with me, which rather flummoxed them. I wondered if I shouldn't leave them something else, a shoe or an earring, as a hostage.

Instead of running up the curving stone stair, I was now directed to go in under the staircase, to a part of the building I didn't know existed. I recognised the old catalogue drawers marooned in the middle of an expanse of cheap carpeting. A few steel bookshelves stood about at odd angles. The people sitting at the large tables were not reading or making notes, but gazing at something over my head. I turned and saw that they were watching a board with winking numbers, as if they were playing librarians' bingo. Underneath the board was a small wooden counter, rather like a cocktail bar, and behind it stood four young men talking animatedly in carrying voices.

As I was taking this in, two schoolgirls gingerly approached the bar and one of the young men handed over two slips of paper.

'Sorry,' he said, 'Can't find either of these. Any others you'd like?'

The girls tendered two more slips, went back to their table, and fixed their eyes on the board again.

Clearly, librarians' bingo was weighted in favour of the house. Nobody won the jackpot while I was looking. Not only were the library staff unlikely to be able to find any particular book in the stacks, the readers had little chance of finding any book they wanted in the catalogues, of which there were several, all compiled on different principles. None of the catalogues was kept up to date and none was exhaustive. Books missing for the last fifty years had yet to be entered as missing and whole collections donated to the library had yet to be mentioned in any catalogue.

One of the attendants at the counter saw the expression on my face and called cheerily, 'Terrible, isn't it? This place is a real dump. What are you looking for?'

'The local history collection.'

'Oh, that's in the Latrobe Library.'

I stared at him in horror, thinking I had to go to Latrobe University which was out in the sticks somewhere.

'Through there,' he waved me off to the left. I followed my nose out into a lofty corridor which led to one of the side doors of the building. The massive timber portal, where once great canvases and statues were loaded and unloaded, stood open to the street. The corridor was screened from the bleak south-westerly which blew the sweet-wrappers and crisp-packets up Latrobe Street by a plate-glass partition with a smaller door in it. Every inch of the glass was covered with greasy marks, even thirty feet up, dribbles and slobbers of dried this and that. Burnt rubber, lead, perhaps salt from the sea-breeze. Such ancient grime is to be expected in countries like Cuba where detergent is in short supply and rubber squeegees and chamois leather are not to be had, but in Australia! Home of the twice-daily Lifebuoy shower!

Through another equally dirty glass partition, which formed the wall of the Latrobe Library, I could see the pensioners at play amongst the archives, chatting gaily as they fed microfilm and microfiche into a motley collection of elderly machines. By the time I had found anything among the dog-eared volumes that lay higgledy-piggledy on the shelves of the Family History Section, only the worst machines were left, the ones that had worn patches on the lenses and screamed and rattled and banged as you wound the films on and off, which mostly had to be done by hand, the switches being worn out. Within hours I had the names of every Greer born, married or dead in Victoria before 1900. And every Greer listed as a householder in every directory. I had found W. L. S.'s daughters, and John Shaw and his sons. But no Robert and no Emma Rachel. I needed the electoral rolls, which were upstairs.

This time, the room that I could see through the smeared glass partition was uninhabited except for a semi-clad male lolling half under a small table a few feet from the glass. I went to push the glass door open and bounced off it. It was locked. The man on the other side seemed not to have heard the impact of my body and did not look up. I knocked. The man lifted his head, looked benignly at me, and looked away again. I knocked again, this time with my wedding ring. 'It's locked,' the man mouthed. 'So open it,' I mouthed back. He got to his feet and to the door in one seamless and very slow movement, as if doing Tai Chi, and opened it a crack.

'Whaddya want?' he asked.

'I want to look something up.'

He seemed surprised. 'What?'

'What do you mean what?'

'Whaddya want to look up?'

'Electoral rolls.'

'Which?'

'Several,' I thought it best not to startle him by saying, 'All.'

'Where's y'card?'

Card. This was the first I had heard of a card. The librarian downstairs should have issued me with a card. The librarian downstairs seemed irked but she scribbled me a chit and sent me back upstairs.

The sleepwalker let me in, chose me a table and brought me an electoral roll, in another of his continuous movements, in which the aim seemed to be to lift the soles of his thong sandals from the floor as infrequently as possible. Two minutes later I had the Greers out of that roll, and asked for another. He had not chosen my table at all well; try as he might he could not reach down the book and swivel it round to me while standing on one leg. His rooted objection to walking finally overcame him and he sank down behind the little table, giving me to understand that I could fetch and carry for myself. And so I discovered that no Robert Greer journalist had voted in Victoria during the time my father was growing up. There was a Robert John in the directories from 1908, but he was a farmer. There was a saw-miller in Gembrook, an ironmonger-cum-fruiterer who moved about in the Oakleigh area, an operator in Albert Park, labourers in Camberwell, South Yarra and Dartmoor; none was married to an Emma Rachel.

This exclusion exercise completed, it remained to try to trace Robert Greer journalist through the newspapers. They were yet further upstairs. This time the room was thronged with people, standing, sitting and lying about among stacks of tattered volumes, which leaned this way and that like the towers of San Gimignano. The noise, and the grime, and the makeshift partitions put together out of bookcases, and the smell of newsprint made it seem more like a printing shop than a library. Behind one partition sat a man with a flat-iron, ironing newspapers. By the door stood a photocopier, for the use of the public, who used it I noticed with a commendable disregard for the law of copyright. As I came past, a woman was making a copy of a book on do-it-yourself divorce, while two toddlers who had evidently come with her jumped up and down on a wooden bench and screamed like macaws. The next table was crowded with men reading the news from the Aegean in Turkish and Greek, who were too busy muttering, bristling and glaring at each other to resent the row the children were making.

At length I managed to distract the librarians from an animated conversation. 'May I see the Launceston *Daily Telegraph* for 1928?'

The librarians looked at me, and then at each other, each trying to stare another into dealing with my request. The loser in the contest slid off the desk they were all sitting on, fetched the check list of newspapers and stood holding it, without opening it. 'Do we have it?' he asked the others. They looked at each other and then by common accord looked at me. 'Bedder look in the main catalogue,' one of them said.

Down six flights of stairs, there was no sign of the Launceston *Daily Telegraph* in the main catalogue, or in any other of the catalogues. Eventually a librarian produced the check list I had seen upstairs.

Back up the six flights, the librarians were sceptical. I showed them their own accession number in their own check list.

'Bedder get the librarian,' said one.

'Yeah,' said another, 'get the librarian.'

Again the wordless contest to see who would weaken first and actually go to get the librarian. After a long minute one of them put down his coffee mug and, after bumping around the walls like a blowfly for a bit, disappeared from view.

His place was taken by the most spectacularly under-dressed individual I have ever seen anywhere but on a beach or in the Amazon jungle. He wore nothing but very short shorts with a split at the side, of the kind called 'stubbies', a thread-bare T-shirt, thong sandals and a fringe of dusty-looking curls. Although he seemed near-sighted, he wore no spectacles. He moved my request slip back and forth a few times, and then gave up any attempt to focus on it, and asked me what I sought.

'Oh, they're not here.'

I opened my mouth as if to scream. The librarian waved away my distress, 'Nah, nah, they're y'know in P'ran.'

'Must I go to Prahran?'

He shook his head as if to calm my unhealthy haste. 'Nah, nah. Somebody'll be driving.' It sounded as if Prahran was half-way up the Birdsville track and we were waiting on an Afghan camel train. 'Tomorrow, prob'ly. Whaddya reckon?'

One of the loungers came momentarily alive. 'Back around four. Tomorrow.'

Not bad going really, seven hours to go four miles or so to Prahran and back. A day with the library van to yourself could only be spoilt by people like me asking for newspapers.

'D'y'know what date y'want?' asked the naked librarian.

'I thought I'd just read through from the beginning of the year. 1928, that is.'

'Go for it,' said the librarian kindly and withdrew.

And I went for it. I had to find where young Reg Greer had started his newspaper career as 'reader', and gone on to be 'reporter'. Nowadays such a progression would be impossible, but in the twenties new recruits to the newspaper business were often employed long hours at night reading and correcting copy brought in by the leg-men. Some of Reg Greer's old colleagues were certain that he had been employed by a Tasmanian news-paper that closed down, whereupon he went to the mainland. The newspaper that fitted the bill was the Launceston *Daily Telegraph* which closed down in 1928.

If I had been given to suspecting my father of mendacity, I might have realised that journalism was one of the few professions, as distinct from jobs, in which an individual could operate with virtual anonymity. Clergymen, bankers, lawyers, accountants, shopkeepers, publicans, doctors, can all be traced through one list or another, but journalists are a different matter. Until well into the 1930s reporters considered their anonymity to be an important aspect of the freedom of the press and refused to publish over by-lines. Pressure for the use of by-lines was first applied by politicians anxious to identify the authors of editorials which materially influenced readers' votes. The newspapers responded with an angry defence of their editorial freedom, and refused to expose individual journalists to discrimination and reprisals.

In the twenties the only by-lines appeared on articles dealing with specific and limited fields; 'The Poultry World' in the *Daily Telegraph* was written by 'Utility', bloodstock by 'Bingen', rifle-shooting by 'Sighter', trotting by 'Mauritius', the turf by 'Valais', tennis by 'Top Spin'. The noms de plume sometimes concealed well-known local characters, like Sir Ray Ferrall who was 'Uncle Sunbeam' and 'Agricola', but equally juniors standing in for the experts sheltered behind them. If Reg Greer was on the literary staff of the newspaper, he would probably have been reporting sport which remained his particular field of expertise all his life, but if he was 'Top Spin' or 'Valais' there was no way of telling. The duty books of the *Daily Telegraph* have long since disappeared.

I read on steadily hoping for a sign. The Launceston Coursing Club advertised for live hares. I noticed that thirty-five-year-old Donald Kerr of Adelaide had slashed his wrists and gassed himself. In 1914 he was Stow prizewinner at the University of Adelaide; he had enlisted in 1915 and fought in Egypt and France. He won the Military Medal and was wounded at Pozières. They must have thought that he had got his life back together again when he graduated Doctor of Laws in 1919 but they were wrong. Nine years later he made sure that he did not have to see another day. Perhaps he needed Chamberlain's Tablets. 'A Co-lonic can never be happy,' sang the advertisement. 'Take one tonight, tomorrow you're right.'

The paper soldiered on until the very end; only on the last day of publication did it admit that it was closing down:

And now the little army of workers who were the *Daily Tele-graph* staff will go their several ways, many of them facing the uncertain future with misgivings, but withal maintaining the cheerful spirit of hope and courage born of long association with the hazard of the 'inky way'. Yesterday's entries in the duty book of the *Daily Telegraph's* literary staff included the following observations:

'Peace declared.'
'Be it known: on this day ceased the war waged between the sub-editor and the foreman printer. No more the angu-ished yell for early "Brev's" and the scream of "no Space".'
'Time off (indefinite): the Staff.'

For hundreds of hours I put together the history of the Laun-ceston *Daily Telegraph*. I knew the names and addresses of all the owners, managers, editors, journalists, columnists and reporters the paper had ever had. I knew the names of their wives and the composition of their households, which I studied to discover if there were any foster-children or step-children who might have been called Greer. I read the records of the Australian Journalists' Association, and found that no Greer had ever been a member. I talked with the two survivors of the crash of the *Daily Telegraph*, who still live in northern Tasmania. Neither of them had ever heard the name Greer in connection with Tasmanian newspapers. I went to Canberra and studied their list of Australian pressmen, which includes details of the provincial newspapers, their owners, managers and staff. No Greer appeared anywhere in their lists. There was something seriously wrong somewhere.

The only possibility was that Reg Greer's parents had indeed left Australia, as I had soon to leave it. All was not well at Mill Farm, where the inmates had begun to drive each other crazy, under the influence of the primal elder's curse. The winter was cruel; as one person crept around the house turning heaters off, another was creeping around turning them up. The greenhouse heater burned out completely and eighty daphne seedlings and a few hundred other laboriously propagated odds and ends were dead. Besides I was expected in India, where I was to combine attending a conference in Delhi with investigating the Doolally connection.

The day before I left Australia, I came across an entry in the Tasmanian marriage register. I had stopped searching Greer names, for by now I knew them all, and had started on Wise. I found an Emma Wise who got married in Launceston in 1889. The town was right, the name was nearly right, but the date was all wrong. I looked up the marriage certificate to see whom she married, on 26 March in the Manse of York Street Baptist Church. Her husband's name was Robert Greeney. There were too many coincidences by half. All but three letters of their surname, plus their Christian names, were right. If this illiterate labourer born around 1863 was my grandfather, every word of the history my father gave the interview board of the RAAF was false, including his name. I was not so disloyal as to entertain such a suspicion; I scribbled the details in the margin of my notebook, and did my best to forget them.

India,
February 1987

Destiny is beyond the range of experience:
it can be adored only by meditations and prayers.
But father is living-God and it is not proper to slight him for
an unknown destiny.
By worshipping the father, one in fact worships all,
and wealth, virtue and objects of desire are gained by it.
There is no higher sacred duty than this.
Devotion to truth, charity and sacrifice are not equal to this
duty.

THE RAMAYANA OF VALMIKI

*D*ELHI. My suite on the seventh floor of the Ashok Hotel is larger than most Indian houses. Tall dark chairs upholstered in deep purple stand about like mourners, attended by squat tables as gloomy as themselves. They are borne up by a magenta carpet with flowers of the most unhealthy blue, pink and yellow wriggling all over it like chorionic villi. I have turned off the glacial air-conditioning, so that the warm air can bring the happy-sad scent of India through my open windows. It is the smell of life in death and death in life, of rottenness and ripeness, of promise and denial. I love this country so much that my sides ache with it. Round every corner there is more wonder, more sumptuousness, more anguish than I could ever have foreseen before I walked that way. Every time I am in India I am astonished at human ingenuity and endurance and nobility. Nothing less like the suburbia of my childhood could be imagined. Poor Daddy; he would never have understood my rush to squalor from the even tenor of suburban ways.

There is to be a wedding in the hotel garden; huge garlands made of millions of marigolds are being hung on the dyed calico walls of vast open-air rooms. Persian carpets with designs of fantastic vegetation are being stretched over the tattered reality of grass. Long tables are being arranged round the swimming

pool like stripes on an enormous serpent. The silken dais erected
for the musicians is being festooned with chains of frangipani
flowers, and another dais is being canopied in cloth of gold.
Within hours the dusty gardens of the hotel will be transformed
into an earthly paradise where two divinities, Radha the bride
and Krishna the groom, will be united and for an hour or two
the world will make sense. The servants behind their bamboo
partition are chopping, mashing, mixing, slicing, releasing gusts
of fragrance, ginger, coriander, turmeric, tamarind, asafetida,
that mix with the scents of the flowers and mount up to my room
as aromatic smoke. The maker of rumali rotis has arrived on his
bicycle and is arranging his braziers and iron pans with all the
absorbed self-consciousness of a genius.

If I turn to my other window I can see a roof-top where two
little girls are playing cricket with their brother. They take turns
to stand up in front of a red wicket painted on the pink wall and
endeavour to block their brother's fiendishly acrobatic bowling
with a home-made bat almost as tall as they are. The ball will be
made of paper, rolled and flattened, plaited and mashed and
bound with string in a roughly spherical shape. If you can hit
one of those soggy objects off the top of an Indian tenement
building, you can definitely sky a six at Lords. The red bows on
the ends of the little girls' braids flip round their heads as they
dash back and forth along the roof, avoiding the stretched saris
and the kari bush. Their brother shouts 'Howzat' with every
other ball but, as there is no umpire and the little girls cannot
bowl well enough to interest him, they stay in.

The air is as usual thick with smoke and dust. Australians
would find it hard to realise that most of the people in the
world never get their lungs quite free of either. They complain of
pollution without the faintest idea of what it really is and who
really suffers by it. The children's father has appeared on the roof
and is clapping. A grey pigeon comes to ask me for something to
eat. He stands diffidently at the end of my window sill. I give him
one of the sugary biscuits the hotel management left for me, and
he leaves me a turd in exchange. The hotel balconies are all
fouled by pigeons and the ventilators are all stuffed with nests. If
I open my bathroom window, there will be a storm of fluff and
wings and straw as the nesting pigeons take fright. Pigeons are

supposed to be Brahmins in the transmigratory exchange.

I am still in Limbo. Daddy is still unknown to me, more unknown than ever, since I can find no corroboration for the account that he gave of himself to the Repatriation doctors. It is becoming important for me to feel that he didn't lie, not to me or anyone, however economical he may have been with the truth. This business just has to be lived through, if I am to grow up to the point where, as my friend Bauci says, I forgive my parents. Some people are so afflicted by anxiety spasms that they can't make their legs work, can't open a door. Daddy couldn't seem to clear his throat, couldn't eat. I can eat alas, but a cold blanket of something is creeping over me like a pigeon-coloured cloud. I find myself sighing heavily, dragging stale air into squeezed lungs, like an unwilling charlady climbing stairs.

I turn away from the window and stare into the darkening room. My heart has swollen up until my ribs feel stretched to bursting. My gut is painfully coiling and uncoiling upon itself. 'Touchy tummy,' Daddy called it. I have it, my brother has it. My nephew Peter Marcus has it. We got it from Daddy, but where did he get it from?

By the time I emerge from my vast marble bathroom, the wedding guests have arrived and the garden is ablaze with Benares silk. Jewelled filigree twinkles in the glow of the fairy lights; great ropes of jasmine swing against tool-smooth hair. Somewhere a brass band is playing. It marches around the corner into my line of vision, and behind it on a white horse, with his little sister mounted behind him, rides the bridegroom. In another corner of the garden the bride, dressed in red and gold, shimmering like a flame, moves surrounded by her gopis towards the dais. Two huge families are about to become one.

Bombay. In my obsessional way I have become hypnotised by the father-daughter relationship. Just now, between the galled ponies and the piles of green coconuts, a bespectacled man passed by, carrying on his crooked elbow a little girl. She is dressed in a burst of petticoats and a red nylon dress with a frill. He is kissing her round cheek as if he could not get enough of it, and she rests her head in the hollow at the base of his neck, using his tall body for a palanquin. Her hair is oiled and curled, her eyes darkened with kohl, and small knobs of gold stand in her ears.

81

There are no flowers in the house if there are no daughters.

Where the silk surface of this flat sea heaves up the water is brown, but the foam as it breaks on the flat sand is as white as anywhere. This sea brings not plastic bottles, plastic bags and plastic twine, but ropes of decaying flowers, bound together with cotton. They are the flowers brought down from the puja rooms to be thrown in the sea where no creature can step over them. This is not a sea to swim in, or to wind-surf across, still less to churn up with motor-boats and skis. Under the palms the cows chew the cud, watched by their saddhu cowherds, resplendent in tattered saffron. Another saddhu walks the beach with a python sleeping round his shoulders.

Occasionally a plump businessman passes by, doing his best to jog, as if he were in America or Australia. Otherwise Juhu beach is happy to be India, not California. The sea is for worshipping, not for swimming in. The beach is for strolling, for socialising, not for tanning or physical jerks. Brightly painted pony carts bowl up and down at the water's edge, plastic pennants flying, avoiding the camel swaying along with a wide-eyed child clamped to the pommel, and the Himalayan bear trudging along behind his young master, who is annoyed when I give the bear a banana, not I think because he wanted it himself, but because the bear will not do his tricks if he is not hungry.

Another father-daughter ikon passes by. This time the little girl is wearing a black frock with gaudy floral insets. Daringly her mother hoists her sari all the way to her knees and walks in the water.

The beach is very wide, eighty yards at least, yet every man who walks along it comes within two yards of where I sit writing in my notebook. Some of them, emboldened by their smart western apparel, tight nylon shirt with huge collar, flared synthetic trousers and high-heeled plastic shoes, dare to sit down and stare fixedly at me. 'Move. Go. Be off. At once,' I say in a piercing mem-sahib voice. They pretend they have not heard, look away for a minute or two, and then, face saved, casually saunter off. I put my head in my notebook, anxious that they should not see my grin.

Why is it, I wonder, that all men are confident of their attractiveness and so few women are? Why would any tatterdemalion

Mahratta imagine that a foreign tourist lady of apparent wealth would welcome his attentions? I think it is not simply a matter of her being alone, which is certainly unusual in Indian society. I think it has something to do with the difference between mothers and fathers as lovers of the young. Mothers carefully, diligently, constantly build the confidence of their sons. Fathers give only fitful testimony to the lovability of their daughters.

Nasik. Why did Daddy hate kite-hawks so? Shite-hawks they called them although they shit neither more nor less than most other birds. They have a curiously unaggressive cry, timorous and mournful. I can understand that the vultures would have shaken a man as ill as Papa, but the kites are harmless. Even the Indian crows, though they get everywhere, ride on horses in the carousel and pick the noses of the cows, are far less horrible than English crows, while no crow on earth is as despicable as an Australian crow, with its penchant for removing the eyes from new-born lambs or unconscious humans. Indian crows have a silly walk; they jump about with both feet and never seem quite to get their balance. Teetering back and forth in their neat grey hoods they hardly look like crows at all.

Daddy was offended by the cows too, the most benign of all the sights of India. Whether eating waste paper in Calcutta or the petunias of the Bombay Parks and Gardens Department, they are deeply inoffensive. The first time I saw a 'sacred cow', as my taxi was lurching and bouncing through the solid human mass that is Calcutta, her eye met mine at the same level, as she sat on a traffic island, munching multi-coloured excelsior with all the appearance of enjoyment. She looked at me under her long eyelids, with fronds of pink paper dangling from her wet nose, as if to say, 'Only the roughage counts. All else is illusion.' I longed for her to be miraculously transported to Piccadilly Circus, by way of showing that there is more to life than corporate slavery. I had been terrified of Calcutta, because of the stories Daddy had told us about India. Somehow I imagined that he was talking about Calcutta, because I knew he was quite wrong about Delhi, Agra, Benares, Bombay and everywhere else I'd been. I had been peering out of my taxi expecting the abomination of desolation, and instead I saw a cow munching paper froth. I wound down the window and started to enjoy myself. Reg Greer was still alive then; sacred cows became just one more thing I couldn't talk to him about.

Daddy belonged to the vast mass of westerners who believe that if people are poor and hungry it must be their own fault. He always spoke of India as if all its inhabitants were superstitious morons. He believed that the suppliers of fuel and dahi, the drawers of the carts and ploughs, that wandered round the streets eating rubbish, should be farmed and slaughtered for food, in the Australian way. The Australian way seemed to him sensible, the right way. If I had told him that I have come to see cattle farming as a major abuse of the ecosphere, and of cattle, he would have been convinced that I was quite barmy. One day perhaps there will be signs and slogans saying 'Beef is bad for you', but by then the world will be all brown, and Reg Greer's nightmare will have come to pass.

Of course Reg Greer did not have the option of getting to know my India, for a soldier cannot get to know the country he is in. He sees only beggars, prostitutes, camp-followers and thieves, only the society as it is distorted by his presence. Daddy never had the privilege of staying in this house or any other Indian household.

A minister in Mr Gandhi's government, concerned that I should not encounter difficulties because Nasik is off the tourist track, has confided me to the care of his friend, Mr Vaishampayan, whose elder son collected me at the airport. When I arrived I was shown every room in their house. All are open to the outside with small balconies. All have cement or marble floors and the worn look of rooms that are cleaned every day by servants, like railway waiting rooms. There is no personal clutter, only beds with railings of light metal alloy, to carry the mosquito nets. The bare floor will be swabbed every day by one of the servants, who may enter the room at any time. It hardly matters when, for no one sleeps naked, or spends any significant amount of time undressed.

Two beds have been made up in my room at the top of the house. One of the daughters-in-law will keep me company each night, leaving her husband to sleep alone. The three little boys sleep with their grandparents, except if their father is away when they sleep with their mother. It is assumed that nobody would

84

willingly sleep in a room by herself. I succeed in persuading the co-sisters that I have always slept in a room by myself and reluctantly they give in, only asking me several times if I am sure that I will not be lonely. I do not bother to explain that I do not wear night clothes and will suffer greatly if obliged to sleep dressed.

Daddy would have noticed that the house is shoddily built and shabby, from the stained purplish white distemper on the walls, to the rusting electric conduit, the bare fluorescent tube, the hard beds, the thin mattresses, the clumsily cobbled curtains. The grandest things in the house are the huge vinyl-covered settees in the sitting room, where forty people of Indian dimensions can be seated at once. Against the dreary background, the women move like jewelled moths. The sound of their laughter wells up the echoing marble stairs.

To me all seems exactly as it should be. This is not a house to be worshipped, bedizened and beautified at the expense of all who live in it. There are no emblems of conspicuous consumption here. The best silks are the oldest; the car is as old as I am. There is no lavishness, no waste. The only luxuries are the smell of fresh masala being ground for lunch and the gold and silver of the puja room. The lady of the house, the babis' mother-in-law, cleans the puja room herself. Every morning she goes into her garden and picks the blooms that have just opened. Freshly bathed, barefoot, she brings them to the devi and arranges them before her in an intricate pattern on a flat salver of pink-tinted marble, until the whole room fills with the scent of zafar and roses. The devi is an eight-armed dancing Durga, attended by most elegant handmaids. Around her stand figures of Shiva, Brahma and Krishna, all old, precious and exquisite.

When the babis are bathed, they too come to the shrine with offerings of flowers, and standing before the devi sing the morning canticle, keeping time with finger cymbals, not the dreary tramp that westerners associate with religious music, but a skipping, gliding music that floats through the house. The goddess exists to glorify and be glorified. When her flowers have faded the servant will gather them in the corner of her sari, walk to the river and throw them in, for no creature must ever step over them. All of life in this household is a dance; the aim is beauty, grace and harmony, not what Mrs Thatcher calls 'an increased standard of living' or the Australian 'sophisticated recreational lifestyle'. From my room at the top of the house, I hear the babis' laughter, and smell the spices and flowers, and the little boys' treble chatter and for the first time in my life understand the meaning of the word 'glory'.

One of the co-sisters, Kunda, is plump and golden-skinned, with a merry laugh, which is quickly answered by the other, Alka, who has one son to her two. When Alka bore her son in Poona hospital, she suffered an abdominal infection, for which she was given too much medication. Since then she has had trouble with her eyes and there have been no more children. Before her son was born, Alka had written three novels in Marathi, two of which were published. Her husband brought her to meet me at Nasik airport, and told me about her novels. From the way he looked at her when he told me, I could have sworn that he loved her better for being so extraordinary. Since the damage to her eyes Alka does not write any more; when I asked her why she had resigned herself to damaged vision and given up her writing she said, 'I do not want to struggle. I want to be a happy person.' She had purged her discontent like a sin; her grace and light laughter, the singing that made the house glorious, were the triumph of discipline. She had succeeded; she was happy. The girl who went to the arranged marriage with the Vaishampayans' elder son thin, large-eyed and nervous had become this sleek, tranquil, genuinely light-hearted woman. Even if Alka had been a great novelist, there would have been no regrets.

Kunda was different. Her energy was of a more restless kind, and she was plainly ambitious for her husband and sons. The calm Brahmin household allowed her her competitiveness, let her make a more vivid impression, sparkling momentarily on the strong tide of their spirituality. When Mr Vaishampayan should die, the brothers will set up households of their own, and Kunda will have to learn the subtle discipline of a mother-in-law. Her own mother-in-law moved noiselessly about the house, clad in the simplest cotton saris, guiding the household through its hours like a convent. When the little boys came home from school, shrieking and tumbling over the great black settees, in noisy mock fights that too easily turned into real ones, one inaudible word from Mrs Vaishampayan hushed their hysteria. She was not well; her face was pale and her eyes shadowed with pain, but she was happy. I struggled to find the right things to say to her, for her English was not good. When I succeeded, and we made contact, her drawn face became young again and she laughed like a girl. The little boys adored her.

The strenuous discipline that results in such structures of spiritual elegance and calm is called by people like my father, fatalism. It is blamed for everything that is wrong in India. If the tap drips, a Hindu feels that it is better to surmount the irritation than to tear the house apart trying to mend the pipe; therefore every tap in India drips. It's enough to drive a Reg Greer crazy.

Mr Vaishampayan took me to the library in Nasik, so that I could pursue my researches into Devlali in wartime. He was also anxious that I should see the collection of Indian artefacts that he had given to the museum, 'curios' he called them. The librarian came to meet us, louting low, so that we saw more of his dyed head than of his gleaming face. Throughout the visit he kept up a loud ingratiating chant, exclusively addressed to Mr Vaishampayan, turning his back on me in a manner too pointed to be rude. He was obviously making a desperate pitch of some kind, possibly for a salary on which he might be able to pay his bills. Mr Vaishampayan listened courteously, as birds flew in and out of the window grilles. The librarian, and the walls and the chairs and tables, were all copiously stained with betel juice. I pointed to a line of droppings more substantial than the bird-dirt to be seen all around.

'Bats?' I asked.

'Owls,' said the librarian unhappily. He pronounced it to rhyme with 'bowls', logically enough.

As the spines of the books were neither lettered nor numbered, it hardly mattered that the glass of the bookcase doors was opaque with dirt. I took up a volume at a venture and the pages erupted in a cloud of red dust and cascaded on to the filthy floor, leaving me clutching a pair of warped boards.

'Perhaps they had kept a file of the local newspaper?' I suggested. The librarian shook his head; all paper went for recycling. Given the humidity, and the dust and the super-phosphate and rat droppings all over the library, newspapers would not have lasted more than a few months.

As Mr Vaishampayan took me in to see his 'curios', a pair of extremely skinny men in filthy pyjamas scuttled past us and began to enact a music-hall routine involving a glass-topped display cabinet and a tape-measure. Inside the cabinet, a rather good miniature was lying half-hidden by decaying newspapers, together with a spent light bulb and some boxes of Indian playing cards. As one man measured the cabinet, the other ceremoniously entered the measurements on the back of a tattered notebook, nodding and bowing to Mr Vaishampayan as he did so, evidently to reassure him that proper storage facilities for his treasures were even now in process of construction.

There was even more filth silted over the objects inside such display cabinets as there were, than on the pieces lying scattered about on the floor. Wonderful South Indian bronzes were so encrusted that they seemed crudely fashioned from iron or terra cotta. The silver and gold idols were shrouded in blue and black oxides. Only a sumptuous natraj still wearing his diadem of red and vermilion kum-kum glimmered with all his old glory, safe in his own glass case. Mr Vaishampayan stepped over idols pocked with stone disease and ancient wood carvings, occasionally directing the custodian to clear away debris so that I could see. He seemed not to mind that his treasures were decomposing, but I felt some sympathy with those grave robbers who say that they steal the cultural heritage of others to save it from destruction. The Government of India would prevent me from taking any of Mr Vaishampayan's pieces out of the country, but it could not force the citizens of Nasik to preserve them.

I could feel Reg Greer's disgust with India gnawing at my heart as I looked at Mr Vaishampayan's paintings on glass, fifty or more of them propped on a high picture rail where only the birds would see them. The birds preferred to sit and shit on them. The damp of the plastered walls was lifting the pigment off the back of the glass before my very eyes.

'Corrupt, incompetent, useless . . .'

Then I came to my senses. 'Yes but.' Poor Daddy. All he ever heard from me was yes but. 'Yes but, museums are for tourists, Papa, not for makers. Not for dwellers. They're for people passing through. Every Indian makes art every day. It's the process that is important not the product. The activity is the end in itself. Happiness is happening. Indian women make paintings with flowers every day. On special days they make patterns in the earth outside their houses with white lime and when the guests come the pattern is destroyed by their feet. Living art is bio-degradable. When the idols are not worshipped they are only brass or stone. And then they are fit only to be collected by anal fixates. India does not struggle against time; time is the essence of the dance.'

Next door to the library the Sri Vivekananda primary school was conducting its annual prize-giving and display. In the gloomy interior of the concert hall a thin miasma of dust, cow-dung, smoke and car exhaust drifted slowly in the dim light of two fluorescent bars. The dirty plastic seats were crammed with people sitting two to a seat, with children on laps, knees, shoulders, arms. Children giggled, wailed, scrapped and raced up and down the aisle. I was surprised to see how many fathers had come to see their children perform. Many of them carried their little daughters, heedless of their dribble or the smears of kohl that menaced the immaculateness of their safari suits.

I sat at the edge of the crowd, observing the audience more than the tiny performers. A squad of children with breathtakingly skinny legs performed something that purported to be the Hokey Pokey, but it seemed likely to me at least that neither they nor their teachers had understood the words, for they put their hands in when the words said they were putting them out. Their motion of the main step was a kind of abrupt knee bend and momentary dislocation of the pelvis. The next dance was performed by tiny girls in huge saris stiffly encrusted with lurex, to the words of a song bawled from the wings by a lady accompanying herself on the tabla. Little boys in soldier suits standing at the back of the stage unconsciously copied the girls' movements, and gave a much better account of the dance than they, but their attempt at military formation marching ended in pointless milling around. The audience roared and applauded like mad. Great waves of love rolled up and lapped around the children, and only the teachers, whose fault it all was, looked less than utterly gratified.

As Mr Vaishampayan's car wriggled through the throngs of people and animals I wondered why Reg Greer never came to

89

any of our speech days or speech nights. We three children all supposed that it was because he was too busy or too tired. He was his own boss, unlike the civil servants, and council employees and clerks and salesmen who had been so happy to put on their best suits and sit for hours in the dark hall listening to interminable speeches and watching other people's children singing badly and dancing worse.

Reg Greer was even less likely to have risked being a guest at the Vaishampayans' than he was to have enjoyed the Sri Vivekananda primary school speech day. His conviction that India is some kind of madhouse would have been borne out by the constant obbligato of pye dogs' barking, owls' theatrical screaming and donkeys' braying that punctured my dreams all night. The practice march-past of the police band at six in the morning would have been interpreted by Reg Greer as utter lack of consideration, and the passing-by of the saddhu, mad-eyed and gaunt, babbling tantric prayers and incantations among which the word baksheesh figured rather prominently, would have crowned the whole idiotic panoply.

Reg Greer would have been incensed to see the elder Mrs Vaishampayan come reverently out in the dew to wash the marble of the garden shrine this morning and disgusted to hear her soft singing of the hymn as she worked, a hymn with a throb as clear as the thumps from the Devlali gunnery range over the hill. Her piety would have seemed to him mere superstition, even hypocrisy, for were not the Vaishampayans rich and their servants poor? He would not have seen that the Vaishampayans lived pretty much as their servants did. They ate the same food and slept on the same beds and wore the same clothes most of the time. They treated their sweepers and washers-up with the same quiet courtesy that they showed to each other and they paid five people to do the work of one.

The road to Devlali rises slowly as it goes southwards from Nasik. You know you're in Devlali when rows of sanatoria appear on each side, mad Gothic bungalows with steeply pitched verandahs under roofs of tile. Hindu, Muslim, Jain and Sikh sanatoria, sanatoria built in memory of this functionary and that, all exactly alike. 'The climate here is very great,' said one of my escorts. And one of the Indian Army officers elaborated, 'This is a no-fan station.' There was no sign of kite-hawks; only pigeons nested in the red temple blossom trees that glowed in the dappled shade cast by immense deodars. I was mystified. Where could Reg Greer have got his tales of monsoonal squalor from, when he had spent two months, not two years as I had mis-remembered, in this idyllic hill-station with one of the best climates in India? Summer in Devlali is marginally less uncomfortable than summer in Melbourne.

My guide was the youngest Mr Vaishampayan, who had thought it best to bring along a Brahmin friend who had married a Parsee whose father was a trader in Devlali. 'The Parsees were always close with Britishers,' he said. Another friend had come along apparently for the ride. The three of them learnedly discussed my mission. The man who married the Parsee assured me that the military hospital was 'top secret'; what he thought Indian army personnel could be suffering from in peace-time that would be top secret, he didn't say. In fact neither he nor his friends knew anything whatever about Devlali, or they would have been aware that the cantonment hospital, like every other military hospital in India, treats civilians as well as military.

Courtesy obliged me to allow them to set up my interviews in Devlali, and that meant getting hold of the Parsee father-in-law who knew nothing of our visit and was nowhere to be found. My escorts left me to wander around the market set up on the temple terrace. Vendors were stringing marigolds into garlands to be offered in the temple, together with platters of kum-kum and sugar crystals. Behind the temple, Marathi women with huge mango-shaped nose rings of thick gold and orient pearl were selling vegetables with the dew still on them. No women in India are more dazzlingly clean in their saris of printed wash cotton and no skin in India is a lovelier colour. To produce that clear golden burnish little girls are rubbed with a paste of turmeric, mango and mustard oil, but it has more to do with health and hygiene than beauty care. A Marathi woman would no sooner allow her skin to be dimmed with dirt or her hair to stand up in a bush for lack of oil than go out without a flower in her hair. Marathi women, who pull the palu through their legs and wear their saris caught up into breeches, had swept the great stone slabs of the market floor clean of every trampled leaf and cigarette butt before the farmers arrived with their produce in the morning. Having done their day's work, they set out their wares and sat in the shade, chatting softly and smiling at me. No one pushed or shoved or hawked her wares. How could Reg Greer have hated this place?

My honour guard returned, with the Parsee gentleman, and beckoned me to fall in behind them. Inside the compound they collared a clerical officer, and gave him some garbled account of my quest. Then they pulled me forward and introduced me to him. I began to tell my tale for the tenth time that day. 'I am looking for someone in authority at the military hospital who can tell me if any records have been kept of Allied personnel quartered in Devlali during the Second World War.' The man's eyes swerved in a manner that I have come to associate with ignorance of English. Ignoring my escort, who seemed altogether bewildered by the military environment and the proliferation of stripes, pips and badges, he led me through a curtain into a consulting room, where two very beautiful women were dealing with a rather haggard mother and child. I was in the Devlali cantonment family planning clinic. My four companions came stumbling in the door behind me.

Both women wore forest green safari shirts and saris, with the palu held by their left shoulder tabs. One carried on her tabs the three red pips of a captain, the other the red three-headed lion of a major, of the Indian Army Medical Corps. I was impressed. This time when I told my story two pairs of brilliant dark eyes followed every word.

'Please write down your father's name,' said Captain Mathrani, and pushed her prescription pad across to me.

I wrote, 'F/O Eric Reginald Greer, seconded to RAF from RAAF, No. 254280.'

'Put your name also,' said Major Chibbha.

'Germaine Greer,' I wrote. Captain Mathrani picked up the paper.

'Oh my God!' she cried. 'Oh no!' She held the paper out to Major Chibbha, who fell to crying 'Oh no!' and 'Oh my God!' as well. My four male companions rushed the desk, thinking that I had committed some appalling solecism and we were all about to be flung in the stockade.

'Is it really you?' said Major Chibbha. 'This is really wonderful for us.'

'Very wonderful,' said Captain Mathrani.

'Why do they know you?' asked my escort, mystified, as they handed me into the front seat of the car this time.

'Women's business,' I said indistinctly. I was shaken to think that Captain Mathrani and Major Chibbha should have been so honoured to help me.

It fell to the youngest of the three Mesdames Vaishampayan to drive me back to Devlali next day to meet the commanding officer. Sitting majestically behind a froth of printed silk she gazed genially upon the struggling crowds and assailed them with loud fanfares from the Ambassador's brand new electronically amplified horn. Like a conquering devi with conches blowing before her she sailed through the wobbling, darting, stumbling, foot, bicycle, tricycle and ox-cart mêlée and cut her noisy way to Devlali.

Mrs Vaishampayan had evidently been taught never to use first gear, in the interests of fuel economy, I suppose, and never ever to change down once she had achieved top gear. She was completely innocent of the concept of clutch control, which was not surprising in view of the fact that she could barely find the pedal amid the yardage of silk that foamed around her feet in their gilded mules. The only part of the car that she fully understood was the horn. The instruction to be found on the backs of trucks in Maharashtra, 'Horn please', was by her followed to the letter. She horned us from our garden suburb into Nasik and horned us out again. Even inside the vehicle the horn was so loud that it juggled my bridgework; what it did to the unfortunate bearers who struggled past with heavy loads on their heads, only to receive a blast clear into the ear-drum from a foot away, Mrs Vaishampayan certainly could not imagine. 'My husband does not like this horn,' she said. 'He says it makes us seem something we are not.'

I supposed it was misleading if people walking in front of the car took it to be a bus because of the extraordinary loudness of its horn. Certainly we had noticed some of them hurling aside their loads and leaping into the ditch.

'It's not that,' answered Mrs Vaishampayan. 'It makes us seem

93

rich. He doesn't like to appear rich. He is very complicated, my husband.' She beamed over her pearl necklace, with a large cabochon ruby at the centre. I said I found his reaction quite straightforward, for I too was not enjoying our masterful progress, which would have shamed the most arrogant aristo on the eve of the French Revolution.

'Yes,' said Mrs Vaishampayan. 'He is very straightforward,' and her trusting smile assured me that being straightforward is the most complicated thing in the world.

Unwisely, after we had taken several corners and a row of speed bumps in top gear, I ventured to suggest to Mrs Vaishampayan that she might change down from time to time, whereupon she took to doing so at the most unpredictable moments, crashing from top direct to second. The Ambassador being the only car in the world that will travel in top at speeds of less than 5 kph, this advice was quite uncalled for. I had nobody but myself to blame if I shot through the windscreen during any such maneuvre. As she horned deafeningly along, Mrs Vaishampayan kept up a lively conversation, mostly about her installation as President of the Nasik Sita-Jaycees. The ceremony had consisted of an endless series of awards offered by one splendidly silk-clad lady to another, much giving and taking of huge nosegays of flowers and sheaves of long-stemmed roses, and a number of charming and rather adroit speeches in English.

'I was very appreciated at my installation,' said Mrs Vaishampayan. 'Everyone appreciated me. But my husband, he did not appreciate me.'

'Doesn't he like you being in the Jaycees?' I asked.

'Oh yes,' said Mrs Vaishampayan proudly. 'He said to me, "Others appreciate you now. At the end of your term, if you have done well, I will appreciate you then." ' She smiled as if to say, 'Men will be men.' I tried to think of any man of my acquaintance who would say something so challenging to his own interest, and failed.

'My husband is very severe,' she went on, 'If I apply lipstick he says, "I shan't kiss you today." He says I am beautiful without.' This was obviously true. Mrs Vaishampayan glowed with satisfaction.

'Does he tell you you are beautiful only to stop you wearing make-up?' I asked.

'He says, "I married you because I found you beautiful. I don't have to tell you every day."'

In fact Kunda met her husband when they were both students at college. There being no obstacle of caste or community, they asked their parents if they could marry, and permission was given even though their elder brothers and sisters were not yet married. The result was that Mrs Vaishampayan the younger was treated more like a western wife, while her sister-in-law had experienced the traditional Indian love story. As a shy and nervous bride, Alka had been courted after marriage; never a day passed without her husband giving proof of his love and admiration.

As steering interfered with horning, Mrs Vaishampayan tended to keep it to a minimum, especially as she was fond of mysterious hand signals, one of which clearly invited those behind her to overtake as she turned right. Her fellow motorists understood her a good deal better than I did and we arrived in Devlali in no worse shape than when we set out, except that we had acquired some minute attendants, called chiltas. At first I thought that I had worms and they were merely spots dancing before my eyes, but then I caught sight of spots dancing round Mrs Vaishampayan's eyes and realised that they were actually tiny flies trying to snack off our eyeballs.

At Devlali we were told to go in search of Lieutenant Colonel Sardana at the Art'y Association Museum. Mrs Vaishampayan set off down the metalled road past libraries, gardens, messes, clubs, all in apple-pie order, past the army farm acquired from Major Wellman, down Haig Row, and all over the place, for we were soon quite lost. Everywhere immaculately uniformed Sikhs gave us new directions and snapped a salute as we jerked and freewheeled away. At one point Mrs Vaishampayan backed the Ambassador into a ditch and within seconds a tribe of giants with navy turbans and black beards had lifted us bodily back on to the road.

'Oh,' cried Mrs Vaishampayan, returning their salute by flapping her hand out of the window, 'don't the sadarjis realise how much we love them? Why do they want this Khalistan thing?'

Lieutenant Colonel Sardana warmed to the task of describing Devlali in wartime. He divided it into South Devlali, where the Americans were, the centre which is now North Devlali and etcetera and so. 'Sometimes there was as many as 50,000 men billeted at Devlali, and things got rather difficult.' The present commandant's house was the surgical ward of the old hospital and the present hospital was the old officers' mess. Most of the buildings have been as he put it 'swept away', but four of the hospital barracks remain. There is also a Tower of Silence for the Parsees at Devlali, and a cemetery of Turkish prisoners who died during the Great War, which the Turkish government still pays to maintain.

'There has been a TV show in England about Devlali,' said Lieutenant Colonel Sardana. 'This has shown Devlali in wartime, tents and everything, but I am unable to see it. Also there are maps and plans of Devlali from the British time, and we have not seen those either.' I promised to send copies of anything I could find and went my way. If Reg Greer had had medical treatment in Devlali, it would have been recorded in his file. Actually he did what everyone else did in Devlali, he sat around and waited. There was no brain-washing; there was just bad food, poor sanitation, and unending tedium.

If Mr Vaishampayan was surprised by my declared intention of paying my respects before I left Nasik to the mother goddess at Sabtashrungi, he was too courteous to say so. As one of the trustees of the shrine he was keen to see it become better known as a place of pilgrimage. He lent us his car and driver for the trip and sent a message ahead that the infidel was to be allowed to visit the inner shrine as his guest. I wore a long kameez and loose salwar, in case the goddess should be offended at the sight of my legs, and a broad dopatta to cover my head; Alka was wonderful in apple-green silk. Kunda brought fresh flowers to scent the car, including zafar that smells sweeter as it fades.

The driver drove up the steep zig-zag road through the seven peaks in all the wrong gears. Where great black boulders had crashed down from the heights they had simply been painted white so that we could more easily avoid them. At intervals we passed rocks bedizened with vermilion paste, which marked where the pedestrian route crossed the road. There the footslogging faithful stopped to rest, to drink water from a holy spring, and to pray.

At the foot of the great stone staircase that leads up to where the goddess looks out towards the cave where Markundeya Rishi lived that he might gaze every day on her majesty, we slipped off our sandals and, barefoot, began our ascent. Each of us was burdened with a massive garland, embroidered blouse pieces, rice, kum-kum and agarbati. The five hundred steps were so steep that we sometimes staggered, and had to pause and pant, looking about us at the eagles that tumbled into the air from their nests on the ledges above the shrine, wheeling over and over in their spiral mating flight. Halfway up we passed Ganesh, the gate-keeper of the gods, and rang his bell to warn the goddess of our approach. We avoided treading on his tortoise carved in the middle of the path.

The temple was tiny, no more than a closet hewn in the rock. Inside it the stone idol wheeled her eighteen arms, rocking on vast feet, gazing at nothing with perpetually astonished eyes. One huge hand cupped her ear the better to hear the song of praise that Markundeya Rishi sang to her from the opposite hill every morning of his life. A blouse piece of woven gold thread was fastened across her breasts; on her head a three-coloured bindi showed the Indian swastika, sign of power through wisdom, in the middle and on her huge feet lay scarlet kum-kum an inch thick. She was barbaric, gross, garish; she was wonderful. The priests of her sanctuary were slick with coconut oil, casual in their manner, conspicuously well fed, as usual. Reg Greer would have found their naked torsos and grey hanging nipples extremely distasteful. They were not exactly delighted to find that they had to allow me to touch the idol. I drew my veil over my head and waited.

A sweet-faced boy took the puja offerings. Reverently he received the padi that the old lady ahead of me poured from her unknotted shawl, carefully he hung up our garlands and the roses from Mrs Vaishampayan's garden. Then he opened the gate of the Holy of Holies and I passed inside. I knelt and laid my head on Durgadevi's great hard foot.

The purohit watched me impassively. Sweat dripped down my back under my kameez. The boy anointed me with kum-kum, so

97

copiously that it dripped down my nose; I must have looked as if I had been hit on the head with a hatchet. He gave me prasad, a paper of kum-kum, and a coconut, and tied a scarlet and gold thread about my wrist.

Alka had been fasting all day; after her bath she had stayed in the puja room, singing her prayers in her low sweet voice, and keeping time by clapping. Now she moved out of the sanctuary and sat in the lotus position in front of the shrine and began singing and clapping again. Our driver sat listening, clapping in double time. As Alka prayed, absorbed, a monkey with a new-born clinging about her neck stole the temple kum-kum out of her basket and bit into the paper. Before she threw it down, the fine scarlet powder had painted a broad smear across her face. A goat walked down the perpendicular rock face and through the sanctuary to nose at the coconut shells. Our fellow pilgrims were breaking their coconuts on a spike set in the ground and handing around the sweet coconut meat. They were mostly poor people, thin and harassed, limping old ladies, and a pair of newly-weds. The bride stood proudly by her husband, for her presence was essential for the proper performance of puja, with the tinsel-laden palu of her red sari drawn over her head.

Why did I go to Sabtashrungi? I went to draw strength, to turn my face away from the dark past. By performing this puja, spending money, veiling myself, abasing myself before a painted rock, herself only an image of the mountain itself and the power that pushed its volcanic core up through the plain, I was doing penance for defying the laws of life. Durga is time, the now, the immediate. By digging my father out of his grave I was flouting her. She is the lady of destruction, the queen of cannot be. As I laid my head upon her stone wedge of a foot like an anvil, I accepted my destiny, the dharma of a woman with neither father, husband nor son. With Durga's help I could pass among the rakshasas of my father's night unscathed.

'Why do you go so far into it?' asked Alka. 'Why do you want to know so much about your father? He borned you, that is the great thing.'

'Bored me rather,' I thought but did not say. I had tried to convey to Alka and Kunda just how little I knew of my father, but it was beyond their imagination. They simply thought that

98

they had understood my English wrong if I said that I did not know my grandparents or even the names of my uncle and aunt. They did not believe me if I said that I had little idea what my father really thought about anything, except India, which I knew he hated. Hated in a silly, racist, stereotyped way, not as Indians themselves hate it when they yearn for the bliss of non-being, an end to the endless anguish of rebirth. I was beginning to realise that Reg Greer did not really experience India. Most of the things he claimed to hate so much were things he had heard of and never seen. The shite-hawks, the Towers of Silence, the sacred cows, the fakirs, the burning ghats, he had never seen any of them.

Essex,
March 1987

I thought the road led to a splendid city,
   Noble and bright.
Love did I love, nor feared the touch of pity:
   I walked in light.
'I shall be there,' Hope whispered, 'ere the night.'

Others I see arriving, enter gladly,
   But in my face
The gates are shut. I may not enter. Sadly
   I run my race
I know not whither. Night draws on apace.
                    MARY COLERIDGE, 'DELUSION'

IN MY March notebook I wrote: 'Another blue day. It is not hard to believe that yellow feathers will pop out of the seamy bark of the acacia on such a duck-egg-blue day. The winter-flowering irises are wearing crowns of melting snow and the witch-hazel is carrying dangles of white and silver on its tassels of gold; only the hellebores seem to be enjoying themselves. I have hardly slept at all, through the silent snowy night; my little red cat stopped snoring and watched through the night with me.'

When I began to write this book, I knew that my only hope of finishing it was to try to keep one of my feet firmly in the now, which is now of course the then. When I realise that, I feel a slight panic, as I used to when we discussed that old Philosophy I conundrum, can one step in the same river twice? The answer, if I remember rightly, is no. That is the sort of thing you can remember rightly, the only sort of thing you can remember rightly, like the date of the battle of Naseby and the name of Leonardo's birthplace, or how to prove that the square on the hypotenuse is equal to the sum of the squares on the other two sides. This is the lure that draws so many of us into the academy, the prospect of escape from the myriad dancing shadows of our real lives into the linear simplicity and elegance of eternal truth.

When an academic turns her face from the solidity of her text, black characters on a lit page, to look at the man sitting next to her in the dark, his face perpetually turned away, she is asking for trouble in mind. It is not wise to insist on an answer to the unutterable question, 'Did you love me?' The inevitable, eternal, unanswerable woman's question, with its flotilla of implied questions, 'Did you respect me? Why did you never ask my opinion? Why did you never spend time with me? Why did you never confide in me?'

It is to avoid such questions that men give us presents on the days set down, and buy overpriced trash at the airport on their way home, scent and sexy nighties. Not, mind you, that I remember much in the way of gifts from my father. He used to bring me the foreign-language selections published by the Readers' Digest, *Das Beste, Selection* and *Selezione* which one of his colleagues probably gave him for me. He brought home all the special book offers made by the Herald and Weekly Times newspapers as well, but they were English and anyone in the house could read them. *The Collected Plays of Bernard Shaw* I remember, and the speeches of Sir Keith Murdoch. They jostled in the tiny bird's-eye maple bookshelf with Negley Farson, *The Way of a Transgressor*, and Gautier's *Mademoiselle de Maupin* and *The Countess of Rudolstadt* in translation, with *A Tale of Two Cities*, and O'Flaherty's *Famine*, the dictionary and the encyclopaedia both covered in fake morocco leather, and an old Shakespeare with steel engravings and Alan Moorehead's *The End in Africa*. I have no book he gave me, not a single thing that was his, except his face and half of my genes.

Up on the white hill the hares are capering in the snow. The greenfinches are fat and greasy from eating my peanuts. I own a stake in this beauty, a wedge of second-rate land, all chalk and masonry rubble, dotted with gnarled gobs of flint shaped like spat-out chewing gum. By that land alone those who come after would know me, even without the millions of words generated by my own literary activity. Land, any lump of it, confers immortality. It gets you into the gazetteer, into rates and rent records, onto lists of householders, whether you've got an unlisted telephone or not. People who can't find me anywhere else can find me at Mill Farm. If I had descendants they would be suffocated

with information and disinformation. They would have to prac-
tise incuriosity in order to survive. Perhaps it is better that I have
none to be so troubled by the ersatz phenomenon of Germaine
Greer, celebrity. Anything I have forgotten someone else will
remember for me; much of what they remember never happened.
Anyone who feels a passing tickle of interest can find me in any
of dozens of biographical directories, while I cannot place my
father, my father(!) in his background, amongst his own kin, his
schoolfellows, the friends of his youth. Eric Reginald Greer, where
did you come from? How did you get here? What did you bring
with you?

On this blue day a letter finally arrived from the Departement
van Binnelandse Sake in Pretoria in answer to my request for a
copy of my father's birth certificate. I had had one before: a form
letter in Afrikaans and then in English setting out the regulations
governing the issue of copies of the records, most of which had
two lines drawn criss-cross over them and the words 'gekan-
selleer/cancelled' written over them, and the form I was supposed
to fill in. The form demanded his *Identiteitsnommer*, which did
not, I thought, apply to persons born in 1904, and his *Bevol-
kingsgroep*. I considered putting Caucasian/ Aryan/ Ulster Scots/
Jewish/ British/ don't know, and then put down White. I learn
now that South Africans prefer the locution 'European' whether
true or false.

I tore open the letter. It contained the form I had filled out, and
another form letter, Afrikaans on one side, English on the other.
'With reference to your application, I have to inform you that
with the particulars furnished by you the registration of the birth
of Eric Reginald cannot be traced in the Department's Records.'

What did it mean? Did it mean that they had looked up the
wrong name? Did it mean that birth registration was not compulsory in Natal in 1904? Did it mean that yes, my father was
born in Natal in 1904 but no, his name was not Eric Reginald
Greer? It meant the primal elder's curse.

I had not meant to place great store by the birth certificate in
the first place, thinking that my father and his family would
surface through school and employment and voting records in
Tasmania, but although Tasmania is a tiny place, no Greers were
findable in it. No Greer was listed as a householder between

1910 and 1920 in any directory. No Greer passed any public examination in that time.

We had always believed that when my father was born the family was passing through Natal en route to somewhere else; from England to Australia, maybe. The port of Launceston had lost its records in a flood. None of the lists of passengers arriving at Fremantle, Port Adelaide, Melbourne or Sydney between 1904 and 1920 shows a Greer family travelling into Australia out of Durban with two children, or for that matter any Greer family, but steerage passengers are not usually listed. I worked my way backwards through the passenger lists just for interest and on the SS *Agenoria* in 1849 found a William Greer aged twenty-seven. On the SS *Augustine* in 1841 I found James Greer, eighteen years old, of Balty Bay, Monaghan, a Presbyterian who could read and write. The next year Jane, twenty-one, Thomas, twenty, and Hannah and James, both nineteen, Protestant farm workers from Antrim, arrived on the SS *Elizabeth*; they could all read but only Jane could write. A Greer was named in the *Morning Herald* as the builder of the Mariners' Church at Soldiers' Point in Sydney in 1844. At first I had no reason to do more than note these names in passing but, as lead after lead petered out, I researched every one of these Greers backwards and forwards, and no Eric Reginald born in 1904 could I find.

If we are descended from Old Australian Greers then Daddy did rather a good job in misleading us, for he knew we believed that he was born of 'English' parents passing through Durban on their way to a temporary sojourn in Australia. Certainly my mother thought that and continues to think it. This is only one of the many things we might have had all wrong. On the other hand, our vague notions may all be correct as far as they go, and only the name is wrong. My father seems to have lived his whole life without a birth certificate or a passport; this in itself is something of an achievement, but why should he have done it?

No one had ever mentioned Ireland in connection with my father, but while Greer is a name relatively rare in England it is common in Northern Ireland. No Ulster-Scot living in Australia would call himself Irish because the vast majority of settlers from Ireland were Catholics from the south. The middle-class adventurers who came to Australia from Northern Ireland were quite likely to call themselves 'British'. The records for all of Ireland before 1912 were held in Dublin where they were destroyed in a fire caused by an IRA bomb in 1922. The possibility still exists that Robert Greer met and married Emma Rachel Wise in Ireland sometime around 1900 but, unless I have some idea of the parish where the marriage took place, I cannot find any record.

English Greers do exist, and none of the English Greer families can be excluded. Thirty-five babies Greer were born in West Derby between 1901 and 1910, twenty-eight in Prescot, twenty-six in Salford. Melvyn Bragg, holidaying in the Isle of Man, sent me slides of Greer graves he had found there. One of them was fairly easy to read, 'In Memory of William Greer of Douglas, painter, who died 17th of May, 1875 aged 56 years Also in Memory of Jane Greer, of Strand St. Douglas, relict of the above, born August 9th, 1812, who fell asleep March 28th, 1882.' Nothing remarkable there, except perhaps that my sister is called Jane, which was not when she was christened a popular name, and I was born with a facile talent for drawing. The other gravestone was at the wrong angle to the sunlight; holding it up to the desk light didn't make it legible, even with the magnifying glass from my compact Oxford English Dictionary. I rigged up another stronger light by turning a spotlight upside down and putting a sheet of paper over it. 'Robert Greer of Douglas,' I read, 'something who departed this life on the tenth of, was it October? aged something and Elizabeth Greer, something, beloved wife of the above, something, who departed this life the something of something, and Coultry Greer (Tom) youngest son of the above' ... The sunlit graveyard scene framed in my square magnifying glass suddenly darkened. The conjured spirits of Robert Greer and his kindred vanished with a confused noise. The slide had melted to treacle.

Melvyn had said in his note that Manxmen were great seafarers. I could have told him not only that many of the Greers are greater wanderers, but that when they go they never return. There was no return to Scotland for the scions of McGregor stock, but their Quaker descendants who went west to Pennsylvania in the seventeenth century, and those who turned southwards to South Africa, New Zealand and Australia in the nineteenth, never came that way again. They sent back no antipodean gold to found colleges and hospitals at home; the better I knew these Ulster Scots and their unforgiving ways the less likely I thought it that my grandparents had tried the new world and 'gone home'.

My quest had travelled many miles before I discovered in the Melbourne Probate Index notice of the will of Rachel E. Greer, late of Ireland, widow, died on the 26th of May, 1931. I scribbled the reference and tore out of the library and up the hill and round the corner and into the probate office which was on a building site, and was promptly sent out again to run to the post office and buy a slew of duty stamps to pay for the 'search' and back through the building site. They wanted me to make a second visit and tried to pretend that finding the documents would be a long and tedious business, but they were on the point of closing for the Christmas break and didn't they understand that if this was my grandmother I would know where not to look at least and ... So five minutes later the slim packet tied with the pink tape always miscalled red, just as huntsmen's red coats are always miscalled pink, was on the table before me.

Rachel Elizabeth Greer died at a house called 'Wharparilla', after a township near Mildura, in Portaferry, County Down. At the end of the day I knew the precise value of Rachel's estate in Victoria, and I also knew that she was not my grandmother who had returned to Ireland leaving her son to fend for himself. I went to Northern Ireland and read every Greer will I could find, visited Greer graves in dozens of country graveyards, Church of Ireland, Presbyterian, Wesleyan and Quaker, and deciphered dozens of mossy Greer gravestones. And the sum total of my inquiries, into the Greers of Portaferry, Derrynoose, Ballyhalbert, Donaghadee, Drumbo, Knock, Killyleagh, Tullylagan, Ballyculter, Downpatrick, Moira, Strangford, Ballylesson, Dromore, and Greerstown itself was a pair of wet feet and a memorable meal of Irish oysters. I tried more desperate measures, appealed on TV chat shows for a sign from my kinsfolk, published my father's picture in mass circulation newspapers.

The more I repeated our childish scenario, that Reg Greer's parents had finished what they came to do in Australia, and returned to the old world, the less convincing I found it. There was never any hint in my father's behaviour that he remembered a different way of life. He only drank fizzy Australian beer, and he drank it half-frozen. His beer, beer glasses and silver beer mugs were all kept in the refrigerator so that no tittle of the deep chill could be abated in the pouring. So ubiquitous is the Australian preference for ice-cold beer in glasses so cold that water condenses on them in a white rime that I could never find any tumblers in Australian hotel rooms. My god-child Hannah would click her teeth and say, 'Where are glasses kept in Australia?' and sure enough there they would be, in the frigo-bar.

Though Reg Greer never went to the beach, and was so unused to the sun that he got blisters on the tops of his feet if he wore sandals without socks, he began to seem to me less and less English and more and more Australian. His conviction that there was no better place on earth than Australia was never rationally propounded; beyond a fleeting encounter with North Africa, Malta and India, it seemed to me that he knew nothing whatever about any other country, beyond a grab-bag of assorted clichés. If I suggested that he travel to Malta or to England, his reaction was not so much that of a man who had seen it all, as of a man who was terrified of 'abroad'. He would not like the food, the drink, the climate, the people; he would be incapable of adjustment. A boy who had been brought up by newcomers to the country could hardly have viewed the world from such a perspective. Little by little the notion that he was the child of British migrants or *Gastarbeiter* or whatever faded away, until I could hardly believe, unless I read my notebooks, that I had ever believed it at all.

In the missing persons game there is no substitute for luck. Even Philip Marlowe and Lord Peter Wimsey have to have luck. It never occurred to me in setting out on the father hunt that I would be dogged by super-bad luck. Or that I would spread it around me like a foul smell. Omens proliferate. If I thrust my stainless steel fork into the stiff cold earth, lo, I have pierced a toad through the belly. He flings his arms wide and opens his mouth, spread-eagled by me, who love toads better than flowers. I have to shut my eyes and push his body off the fork before I have time to register what has happened, before my knees go weak. I bury him fast, hoping he was still in his winter sleep before my steel icicle transfixed him. If I turn my car out of the drive on to the road I find one of the hares I have just been watching as they leapt and caracoled in the plough, mashed on the road. The wind lifts one black-tipped ear and flutters it, a reminder of past frivolity, and on the other side of the hedge a lone hare goes March mad on its own. The silver cat brings in a shrew and loses it under the kitchen bench where it dies slowly until I draw it out with the broom. The cat, Shanghai Jim by name, flicks it from the broom with a paw and bites its face off. Christopher, the red cat, meanwhile concentrates on rolling a new-laid egg to the edge of the table, so it will smash on the floor and he can eat it. I pick a horse to run in the Grand National and it falls at Beecher's and breaks its neck. It was second favourite, so it wasn't just my luck that day. If I become so arrogant as to think all these disasters a judgment on me, I shall have become completely, instead of just fairly, irrational.

> Oh, let me not be mad, not mad, sweet heaven;
> Keep me in temper; I would not be mad.

(Oh, Papa, I would be your Cordelia, but I'm afraid I shall prove a Goneril or a Regan.)

Every day, in every way, it is demonstrated to me that there's nae luck about the house, but I cannot go backward. I've spent too much of the advance; I must blindly struggle forward but I need some energy harnessed on my side. Somebody out there knows my story and doesn't know he knows it. I decided to send stronger signals so I agreed to do 'Wogan', for 'Wogan' is watched by millions all over the British Isles.

Impossible with ten million viewers that someone somewhere hadn't connections with South Africa and Australia. Before the programme was over a gentleman rang; the television workers were wildly excited. This was it, this was the breakthrough. This was the power of television to bring people together.

I had been to the dead end of so many promising leads that I found it hard to share their excitement. In fact, I'd got to the point where I thought that my very expectations were blunting the needle of my compass and preventing my coming to the truth. I took the number but I waited to return the gentleman's call in privacy and calm.

First of all I had looked in *Burke's Irish Families* and there they were, a distinguished family of Greers, going back to the Quaker linendraper Thomas Greer whose account-books are a major source for the history of the linen industry in the seventeenth century. Many of his descendants had turned Church of Ireland or taken their Quakerism to Pennsylvania. There were members of parliament, soldiers and judges galore, canons, prebends, bishops and lepidopterists.

One of the descendants of this family, the Great Greers, I call them, had fought with the Australian Imperial Forces in the First War. My heart leapt when I beheld Nathaniel Alexander Staples Greer, and sank as suddenly when I found that he had died unmarried. If Daddy had been the son of a remittance man sent to cool his reprobate heels far from the sight of his offended family, his reluctance to claim the connection would do him no shame. Perhaps Nathaniel Alexander Staples Greer had issue that Burke's wotted not of. It was a forlorn hope. I found Nathaniel for myself; when he arrived in Australia he went opal-mining for a few years in south-western Queensland, but he did not make his fortune. After the Great War he drifted from town to town; when he died, he was a labourer in a fruit-growing town called Yenda, in the Murrumbidgee Irrigation District. His grave in the local cemetery is unmarked.

The name Robert Greer that my father gave as his father's name on his wedding certificate seemed to me to hark back to the Scotch origins of the Irish family; it was a name to be expected of the Presbyterian Greers, who had never swerved from the faith that caused them to be driven out of Scotland by James Stuart. The Great Greers arrived in Ulster forty years after the Presbyterian Greers and came from Northumberland; they seemed to be at pains to distinguish themselves from the Presbyterian Greers and called themselves names like William and Frederick.

Those who kept the Quaker faith were usually called biblical names but the Robert Greers who arrived in New York in 1804 and Philadelphia in 1827 were probably Quakers. I longed to find that Daddy was originally a Quaker. His antipathy to organised religion, and cant and hypocrisy of all kinds, would have taken on a positive character for me, if it had been grounded in the democratic traditions of the Society of Friends. I could have understood how the disciplines of Quakerdom might have been irksome to a young man, and how he might have run away from them, and lost the baby along with the bathwater. There was a Quaker school in Hobart, and a strong Quaker presence in East Africa; perhaps that explained his parents' wanderings.

At St Katherine's House I had found ten Robert, Robert Somebody or Somebody Robert Greers married between 1890 and 1904, two on the Isle of Man, and one each in Runcorn, Portsea, South Shields, Basford, Birmingham, Neath, Newcastle-on-Tyne and West Derby, but none married to an Emma Rachel Wise. I found a Reginald Ernest, too, born in Hampstead in 1875, and married there in 1898, but not to an Emma Rachel Wise. In the births I found a Robert who was born in 1880 and seemed not to have been married in England, from Middlesborough. After many weeks of struggle with genealogists amateur and professional helping me in South Africa, in Australia, in Ireland and in England, no one had found anything. One old hand wrote, 'Depend upon it, if your father didn't tell where to find his parents, it is because he had something to hide.' In my first flash of indignation, I tore the letter up, fancying it had been prompted by malice and superciliousness. I see now it was a warning, and well-meant I'm sure, but I had no choice. My hand was on the plough, and the apparently solid ground was already gashed. There could be no stopping until it was all laid open. Time then to tend the wound.

I wrote in my notebook: 'The day has turned dark now. Snow is whirling through the bare branches. A wicked little draught is licking at my ankles with an icy tongue although the heating is full on. I feel as if my heart itself is turning hard and failing to pump warmth into my body. I am afraid that my father is a liar, not just economical with the truth, reticent and unwilling to disabuse others of their cherished fantasies, but a deliberate liar. I am afraid that he married an uneducated child woman, with none to protect her interests but a brother barely older than she and a gullible mother, impressed by my father's sang-froid and savoir faire and tailored elegance, and deliberately told lies on the register. I am afraid "Robert Greer" does not exist, never existed. "Thou shalt not uncover the nakedness of thy father," says the commandment. Daddy forbade me to search; perhaps he told me I would find nothing and I disbelieved him and so forgot what he said. I have no one but myself to blame.'

Everyone asks me the same question, 'Doesn't your mother know who she married?' I don't know if she even cared. Perhaps she had been systematically misled, or perhaps, like me, she misled herself. Daddy was so affable, so genteel, so well-dressed, so nicely spoken; we would be doing violence to our own capacity for judging people to have taken him for anything less than a public-school man. Why would anyone doubt the information he gave for the Register? Of course, his parents were overseas if he said they were. But where did he say they were? Most people thought he was 'English' and he seems to have wanted them to. The reasons they thought him English were bizarre: 'He always wore gloves when he went out of the office, even on the hottest day,' according to the man who worked beside him in 1933, 'so we assumed he was English.' I thought his family were in England; when I suggested making contact when I left for Cambridge, he didn't tell me I couldn't or wouldn't find them; he told me not to.

There were many reasons for not searching for my father through my mother. There would have been ways of interrogating her over time that would have built up a picture of what she knew without knowing that she knew it, but such a proceeding seemed to me impious and brutal. At a lower level lay another motive: I wanted to find my own father, not my mother's husband. I did not want simply to adjust my mother's fantasy to fit myself. My mother was sure that he had loved only her; any evidence that he may have loved me she would have suppressed or distorted. I will always remember a particularly grim moment during a family conference not long before his death. Daddy was already making his shaky way to the place I had made for him beside me on the sofa, when Mother came up and pushed him at it. 'Oh, go on, Reg, sit next to her!' she said, crinkling her face in a parody of earnest persuasion. As he sat bewildered, she shouted, 'Oh, go on, give her a kiss!' as if cajoling him to take cascara.

Though I could not make Mother party to my search, I had to go through the motions of consulting her. She was waiting for me on her sun bed, her head wrapped in a towel to protect her skin and scalp from the perpendicular sunrays.

'I can't find your parents-in-law,' I said.

Said Mother in a little girl voice, 'He told me he was an orphan.'

'Mother, if he told you he was an orphan, what are those names on the parish register at Saint Columba's?'

'What names?' asked Mother.

'Father: Robert Greer, journalist, and mother: Emma Rachel Wise.'

'Oh, those names,' said Mother.

'Who brought Eric Reginald Greer from Durban to Australia? Why would the South Africans send an orphan boy to a place where he had no kin? We're all orphans when our parents die; he seems to have known who his parents were. It's just that I can't find them. They don't pan out.'

'They went back to England,' Mother said patiently, 'when their job was done. Finished the assignment and went back. There's nothing so very unusual about that, is there?'

'Mother dear, that assignment took as long as it takes a child to grow up to be old enough to leave him behind. What do you think it was?'

'Oh, his father was an editor, of a newspaper. Wasn't it the *Examiner*? The Launceston *Examiner*?' I gazed out of the window at the row of houselets each with a door and a window and a little verandah that had somehow supplanted our neighbour's garden. All the glass doors and windows seemed to be staring into our emptiness.

'I know all the names of all the journalists associated with the *Examiner* and with its rival the *Daily Telegraph* which went broke in 1928. There is never a Greer among them. There is never a Greer who was a member of the Australian Journalists' Association, Mother. Australian newspapers were not graciously set up by foreigners and edited by foreigners for the benefit of foreigners. They were an intrinsic part of their communities. The Launceston *Examiner* was owned by W. R. Rolph and his associates; the editor was Prichard, the father of Katherine Susannah Prichard, and then Stanley Dryden; you could have found that out by looking in any *Who's Who in Australia*.'

Mother looked mildly non-plussed. 'But his father was an editor. He made him work long hours, and travel all over the place, getting copy, so that his health broke down.'

Poor Mother, it was all wrong. I did not tell her that I had written to the doyen of Tasmanian newspapermen, Sir Ray

Ferrall, who replied as soon as he got my letter, 'I wish I could remember a Robert or a Reg Greer as one of my comrades, but sadly I can't . . . if you would like me to follow up any clues please let me know for I will gladly do so.'

I had no further clues; Sir Ray's letter was the last of the many stones I had to turn. As I lay sleepless in my bed that night a greasy sweat of embarrassment collected under my chin and on the nape of my neck. Sir Ray, clever, solid, distinguished, courteous Sir Ray, knew my bizarre secret, that I had a phony grandfather, 'Robert Greer', and a mother whose family cared so little how she fared in the matrimonial lottery that they did not even bother to check whether the bridegroom's account of his background was true in any respect. In the stressful weeks that followed I slept little and when I did I ground my teeth to ruins.

It was only possible for Eric Reginald Greer to get away with these nebulous forebears because my mother's father was not consulted in the matter of his nineteen-year-old daughter's marriage. At the end of May 1935, my uncle, Bernard, left home because he was constantly at odds with his father, whom he considered unreasonably strict. The 'old man' as we all knew him was half-Italian; he wouldn't let his daughter paint a big blood-red bow where her mouth ought to be, or cut off her glossy braids, or stay out late. He was furious when she gave up her scholarship to Windsor Convent and went out to work in the fashion business. He lurked in wait to attack the boys who brought her home from a date. She and her mother had dreams of a glamorous future for her. Some weeks after Bernard moved into his own lodgings, his mother appeared on the doorstep, with his sister and little brother.

A few months later the little sister was tripping down Collins Street in her lunch-hour when she saw and was seen by a handsome well-dressed man, standing chatting with his cronies. She turned and came back for a second look. The man detached himself from his mates and offered to buy her a cup of coffee, and so my parents' courtship began.

Reg Greer was big in advertising and it was probably through his offices that Peggy Lafrank got her one big modelling job, the job that in hindsight became a brilliant career that she gave up when she became pregnant with me. One of the rapidly forming advertising agencies devised a campaign for Swallow and Ariell Ltd, the Uneeda bakers, based upon an antique theme, principally to dispel prejudice against factory-made foods. On the back cover of *Table Talk*, for 6 February, 1936, appeared an advertisement, which averred that 'They lived well in 1854. They knew good food and liked it – even as you and I. Certainly they used more home-cooked food those days, but there was one delicacy they always bought ready for use, Swallow & Ariell's Biscuits. They knew these could not be improved on, and they wanted the best – even as you and I.' By way of illustrating this series of contentions, a fat, bald actor was leering at a young woman dressed in what passed for an olde worlde gown who was offering him a plate covered with a doiley, from which he was taking a biscuit. The young woman, her bobbed hair inexpertly curled and her eyes gluey with mascara, was my mother. Beside her on a table covered with a lace cloth stood a cut glass decanter with a four-inch-long decorative stopper and two champagne glasses full of some dark liquid. Mother's arm, emerging from under a rather clumsily draped fichu, was still rounded with puppy fat. She was eighteen.

'I never thought of myself as a beauty,' said Mother, who all her life has thought of little else, 'but no one else had such a neck, such a line of head, neck and shoulder.' This one example was the sum-total of Mother's career as a photographic model which was part of the mythology of my childhood. Perhaps the truth about Daddy would be as insignificant.

The lack of curiosity about my father's background would have been much less understandable outside Australia. Australians detest snobbery and insist that a man is to be valued for what he is in himself, and not the stock he may have come from on whatever side of the blanket. Migrants are special people who have the courage to venture into the unknown in order to beat the systems of inequality and limitation into which they were born in the old country; the process of making 'a new life' is long and fraught with danger of failure, destitution and death. There is little point in going through it all if you are still unable to escape from the fact that your grandfather was a smith who couldn't pay his debts or a country parson whose weaker children died of the diseases of malnutrition. Father's marriage to my mother was no rush job; her mother and brothers thought they had got to know him for 'a good bloke' and that was all they needed to know. Why, oh why, did I need to know more?

Mother was not disposed to jettison her illusions simply because I could not substantiate them. 'Well, perhaps it wasn't Tasmania,' she suggested.

'But, Mother, he said it was.'

'When?' challenged Mother.

'It's in his repatriation file. It's on the record. You went to the trouble of getting a copy from the Department of Veterans' Affairs. Didn't you read it? I'll show it to you. Where is it?'

Mother went to the cupboard under the sink and foraged among some plastic bags stuffed with papers. A blocked S-bend and we could lose the whole family archive, I thought gloomily. I found the page of the file for her. 'There, you see?'

Mother read wonderingly: 'Pre-service life. School – Secondary Senior Public Aet fifteen and a half years Tasmania. What's Aet?'

'To the age of. He went to school in Tasmania until he was fifteen and a half, or so he told this trick cyclist here. I'd like to know what Secondary Senior Public means. Is it an exam he would have taken or what?'

Neither of us knew. I read on. 'Average amount of sport. Elsewhere he says that he played football and cricket and rowed. Look what he says about his occupation, "newspaper work. Reader – Reporter – Interstate Representative – Manager." '

'What's wrong with that?' asked Mother.

'Well, he wasn't a manager, was he?'

'He was when he retired.'

'Mother dear, this is more than forty-five years before he retired. We're talking about 1944. He certainly wasn't a manager in 1944.'

'Well, I'm glad he wasn't more ambitious,' said Mother. 'Alec McKay got that job and look what happened to her.' Those used to my mother's mental processes would have realised that she was talking about the abduction and murder of the wife of the man who took my father's old job in Adelaide and went on to become Rupert Murdoch's second-in-command. I gave up the half-hearted attempt to call one of my father's lies to her attention.

'Mother, didn't you think he had lost all contact with his family by the time you met him? Then what's this? "F." Father, okay? "died aet 58 years. 1 year ago – Heart trouble. M. died aet 53 years. 3 and a half years ago – Influenza." That means that Daddy's mother died three and a half years before September 1943, early in 1940. Did you know about this? Did you know his father died in 1942? How did he know these things? Who told him?'

For the first time Mother actually looked surprised, and not pleasantly surprised at that.

'Don't worry, Mum,' I said wearily. 'It doesn't add up in any case. See here he says he has a brother forty-two; Daddy had just turned thirty-nine. And yet if his father had been alive he'd have been fifty-nine; that'd make him seventeen when he fathered his first surviving child, according to Daddy's figures. Doesn't sound much like "Robert Greer Journalist".'

'Do you think he was lying?' asked Mother. She liked the idea as little as I did: besides it didn't seem to fit what we knew of his character.

'I think he was trying to get this part of the interview over. Perhaps he didn't want the trick cyclist to realise that he was estranged from his parents and answered without giving himself time to think. Or perhaps the interviewer wrote it down wrong. I saw the original; I know this is what was written at the time. He didn't have to say all this, you see. It would have been easier just to say parents alive and well, see, a & w, as it says here about his brother and his sister, three years younger again. "Childhood days happy – well cared for – no home discord." So what went wrong?'

'You can't put too much reliance on what somebody says to a doctor,' said Mother soothingly.

'Don't think I don't know; it happens to be all I've got.'

The cats had had their morning milk; the hens were tucking into their laying pellets; the bird-feeders were filled and Livingstone the parrot had rather noisily watched 'Good Morning Britain', before I climbed back into bed with the red cat and called the number the caller to the 'Wogan' show had given. Would he say, 'I was at school with Reg Greer ...' or 'I knew a Greer family who lived in Tasmania ... ' or 'My wife had a brother Eric in Australia somewhere ...'

'Oh, yes,' said the man, 'I was wondering if you knew about the International Genealogical Index compiled by the Mormons, you know, with details of births, marriages and deaths all over the world.'

That was it. The break-through. Of course I knew of the International Genealogical Index. Without grandparents or a firm place and date of birth for my father there was no way I could use it. Thank you, very kind, goodbye. The red cat heard disappointment in the cadence, walked up my chest and put his white mitten on my cheek. Sometimes I understand the people who leave all they die possessed of to their cats.

I jumped out of bed and went to the study. There were three hundred or so Greers listed in the Belfast telephone directories and five hundred or so in the Australian directories, and heaven knows how many in the American directories. I would write to them all, telling them my story. Somebody somewhere must know something. If none of the details meant anything, I wrote, 'please forgive my intrusion and simply throw this letter away.' Replies are still coming, with photographs and great scrolls of family trees and kind words of acceptance and encouragement. I could hardly have made a bigger fool of myself.

When a Girl Marries

•

Each word
had been tried over and over, at any rate,
on the man who was sold by the man who filled my plate.
ANNE SEXTON, 'AND ONE FOR MY DAME'

THE DAY Reg Greer's eye was caught by that striking, snappily dressed girl as he stood chatting in Collins Street, the most elegant street in Melbourne, many thought Australia, he was pretty well able to call the world his oyster. He had more offers of jobs in the expanding world of advertising than he knew what to do with. When the girl turned around and came back for a second look at him, Reg Greer made his move. He raised his hat and asked her if she would like a cup of coffee. Brazenly, she said she would. He asked her where she would like to go to have it, and she said the basement of the Manchester Unity Building, because she knew you could get a cup of coffee for thrippence and there was a band and a dance floor. The distinguished stranger was amused.

'You're very young, aren't you?' he said as they sipped their coffee. My mother was eighteen.

'Of course, he rubbished the place,' said Mother. It was a shop-girls' hang-out after all.

In a letter my mother explained her attraction to the mysterious stranger like this: 'When I was at the vulnerable age of looking for someone as dapper as my father and about half his age (at that time the bespoke tailor was out of the question for a man on the basic wage) the great majority wore factory made suits and even with the two pairs of trousers supplied the coat was so "near" that what with the lean times and all, the view from the back was all depressing sag.' Australia was at that time unique in the world for having a 'basic wage'; men on the basic wage have

117

never been able to afford a bespoke tailor and in mid-1935 times were less lean than they had been for ten years. Nevertheless Peggy Lafrank's description of the impression Reg Greer made is probably spot on.

By her own admission Peggy Lafrank at the ripe age of eighteen was looking for a husband; Reg Greer happened to be looking for a wife. He called on her family, and discovered that the role of father figure to the three children was vacant. My grandmother was only too happy to cook for him and launder his shirts, in return for his charming presence and avuncular concern for her boys. Reg Greer visited every weekend, and he did not fail to notice that Alida Lafrank had brought up her daughter to believe in a strict division of labour, for all the samba and lipstick. Men do all the work outside the house, women all the work inside. Simple, but crushing. Peggy Lafrank was exactly what Reg Greer was after, a highly decorative and utterly innocent supermenial. Under his expert supervision she learnt to 'make the best' of her face and figure. Other people thought she wore rather too much make-up, but Reg Greer liked it. The more attention she attracted as they walked down Collins Street together, the happier he was. We used to have a photograph of Mother peek-a-boo under a tiny hat with veiling, clopping along in peep-toed sling-backs, her skirt whipping around her long brown legs, clutching my father's arm, and laughing a huge, painted, gleaming film-star's laugh.

Although she had no pretensions to be anything but a sales-man's daughter and a milliner's apprentice, Peggy had the refined and modest manners of a Catholic girl educated by nuns. Reg Greer had no difficulty at all in persuading the little family that he was their social superior. He took over the role of father and elder statesman to Peggy's mother and brothers. He advised the older boy to drop a girlfriend who was trying her hardest to drag him into bed, because her aim was forced marriage as soon as possible, and his advice was taken. The fatherless Lafranks were impressed by this worldly, distinguished man from a cosmopolitan background, and never dreamed of quizzing him.

They did not see how like their own father he was. Their father too dressed beautifully and spoke well. Like Reg Greer he was a crack salesman, but he came from a rough and tumble back-ground. His mother was said to have had so many children that she couldn't remember their names. At mealtimes she would plonk a pot in the middle of the table and shout 'scran's oop!' and leave the children to fend for themselves.

Albert Lafrank did not waste his charm on his family but kept it for his clients. Reg Greer was different. His refined manners and gentle, almost lost air went straight to Peggy's mother's heart. He said he was tired of wandering and living in hotels. He was looking for a family to belong to. When he asked Peggy to marry him everyone was thrilled. If Albert Lafrank had heard of it and come for a look at his son-in-law, the outcome would have been very different. The questions would have been asked, and failing satisfactory answers no marriage would have taken place. Not that Albert Lafrank was well-connected; his parents had run away from their respective spouses and children in New South Wales and set up house together in Victoria. Probably Albert Lafrank no more knew of his parents' adultery or the informality of their union than his own children knew that the eldest of them was born out of wedlock, but he knew salesmen. Reg Greer would never have been allowed to put a ring on Peggy's finger, until he had given a pretty comprehensive account of the thirty-two years of his life that had passed before he met her. The 'Old Man' was not consulted in the matter of his daughter's wedding. The questions remained unasked for fifty years. Now try as I might I cannot push back into my father's past any further than 1933, when he was twenty-nine.

In early 1933, Arthur Searcy, out of a job, with a wife and young children to support, succeeded in landing a job as a space-seller at *The News* in Adelaide. His boss was a rather punctilious man called Perce Messenger, who was so mean that he would not even use his expense account to buy dinner on the train when he went on inter-state trips. He was famous for saying that he'd 'hop off and get a cup of tea and a scone on the station at Seymour', when all the other reps were wining and dining each other in the restaurant car. He was the sort of man who worked hard and wore his glasses lop-sided, the diametric opposite in fact of the other member of the advertising team at *The News*, Reg Greer.

Reg Greer was then living in the best room at the Victoria Hotel in Hindley Street. The best room was the first-floor corner room, with a fancy bay that commanded a view not only up and down the main business street of Adelaide, but also down the alley to the *News* building fifty yards away.

Every morning at nine o'clock, Perce Messenger held a nugatory conference with his salesmen, just to make sure that they were out of bed. Reg Greer always arrived at the last minute. No matter what the weather, which in Adelaide can be quite unbearably hot, he wore an elegant belted raincoat and a blue and white spotted silk scarf round his neck. It took Arthur Searcy, who was a serious sort of chap, some time to realise that under the raincoat Reg Greer was still wearing his pyjamas. The conference over, Reg would stroll back down the alley to the Victoria, and shower, shave, dress and breakfast at his leisure. He would then work, selling more space in an hour on the telephone than other men could do in a day on the hoof. Then he went to lunch. The afternoons he spent in Brady's billiard saloon.

Reg Greer specialised in the clothing trade, which was the backbone of the newspapers. All the clothiers and drapers not only took a regular ration of advertising space every day, but at sale times bought whole pages and half pages to publish a full list of reduced prices of sale lines. The man who kept the clothiers happy was more necessary to the newspaper's survival than the journalists who wrote the news, although very few of the editorial staff ever realised the fact. *Newspaper News*, the organ of the advertising industry, remarked in an aside in the personality column in 1933, 'Some years ago an Editor met his chief space-seller in the office lift. The whole business was hushed up...'

In 1933 Wally Worboys went to Adelaide with his golf clubs, to take up his position as advertising representative for Colgate-Palmolive. He knew no one in Adelaide so he spent the first week with Reg Greer at the Victoria Hotel. 'It was a nice pub, full of young fellows. Reg's was a good big room, and the lads used to gather there to listen to the test matches on his radio.

'He was great mates with the Helpmanns then. The Helpmanns were in the meat business; Max was a playboy when he wasn't lugging sides of meat in his blue overall and cap. When asked if he was having any success he'd say, "I'm fucking 'em as fast as the Prince of Wales can pull 'em from under me."

'Performers appearing at the Palace Theatre used to stay at the

Victoria – the Russian Monte Carlo Ballet stayed there, Marian Winter, a very nice bloke, Teddy Harrisby . . .

'Reg Greer used to go backstage after the shows. He liked theatricals, got on well with them. . . . We used to go to Aussie Rules football, to cricket and the fights. . . .'

Wally would go with Reg and sit in the bleachers at the Amateur Sports Club in North Terrace. 'Reg would always get something going with someone two rows in front. "What do you know about it?" he'd say to someone who was expressing his opinion of the play somewhat forcefully. And when the row started he'd say, "I've got a boy here that'll take you on any time you like."' Reg Greer once played that joke with Jack Tosh, who did not get the point, possibly because in this case it ended in a punch-up of which Jack got rather the worst.

Wally remembered Reg on the beach at Glenelg, skinny in his woollen trunks. A bosomy dark girl walked past and all the lads hubba-hubba-ed like mad (Hubba-hubba, digga digga, woo-woo, what a figure!) till Reg said, 'I think I know her . . .' When Wally got to the Victoria Hotel that night, he caught sight of Reg just disappearing round the corner of the passage to his room, and blow Wally if he didn't have that gorgeous dame in there with him. . . . 'Never knew how he did it.'

'Harry Miles who worked for W. J. Bush the cosmetics people also lived in the Victoria Hotel. He was English, not unlike Reg actually. But Reg was a cheeky charlie, full of cracks, full of nonsense. Always having you on. We used to play table tennis in the hotel cellar, although there wasn't much room. Reg would arrange tournaments with the Lee boys.

'But he wasn't always ready to be in it. There was one night they all went to a nightclub, and Reg cried off. Didn't go. But Laurence Tibbett or John Charles Thomas, "You should have been there," he'd say. He loved that sort of thing.'

The Victoria Hotel belonged to Jack and Arthur ('Murt') Lee, who were very fond of their star boarder. Murt (now Sir Murt) remembered that 'he could always see the other fellow's point of view. He really put people at their ease. A new show'd come into town and the bar'd be full of strangers. Reg'd come in and soon they'd all be nattering away as if they'd known each other for years.'

From what Arthur Searcy and Wally Worboys both said, it seemed that Reg Greer had been in Adelaide for some time before either of them met him. He was secretary of the committee of the Adelaide Advertising Club Ball that year, and evidently did a very good job, for no fewer than twelve hundred people paid to dance the night away at the Adelaide Palais, and applaud the glamorous floor show which featured beautiful models stepping out of the unfolding pages of a huge magazine. Reg Greer probably took along his girl-friend, some say his fiancée, Iris Powell, the trim, dark daughter of the licensee of the Kalgoorlie Hotel, which was a little way down Hindley Street, on the other side from the Victoria.

Try as I might, I could not track Reg Greer further back than this point. He seemed to have evolved as the space-seller's job itself evolved, out of nowhere. It was the space-seller's job to persuade local merchants and manufacturers that they could not conduct their business in a satisfactory manner unless they kept their names and their products in the public eye by having their names printed, preferably in very large format, in the newspaper for which he worked. When Reg Greer was a boy the job of putting the newspaper together was seen as one only, whether it dealt with advertising copy or editorial. Juniors spent less time on collecting news than in reading, correcting, and shortening copy. Reg Greer's account of his career, going from 'reader to reporter to advertising representative', is possible, but not probable.

According to one story that he told my brother, who was not really interested, Daddy had a Chevrolet that he drove around the country shows, doing business for his newspaper or chain of newspapers. The point of the story was to impress my brother that he had had a car before any of the other employees of the paper, including the top brass. My brother did not ask which newspaper, or where or even when. Reg Greer may have begun as the kind of travelling adman who carried a selection of stereos in his suitcase to which the name of a local merchant had only to be added before it would be a made-up advertisement for the local paper. If he had been a newspaper proprietor's son with no particular gift for the literary side, he might well have been given the safe sinecure of a job in the advertising department, but if he was not, he must have worked his way into the glamour job by sheer flair and hard work.

In the case of the larger circulation newspapers, the old job of canvasser, which combined the functions of soliciting subscriptions, selling space and filling the space with advertising copy, gradually resolved into three separate avocations, circulation, space-selling and the designing of advertising campaigns. The last was eventually taken over by separate organisations, the advertising agencies. Many of the early agencies were set up by men who had originally worked for newspapers. The whole field was one in which personal contacts and patronage were of the greatest importance; as the industry expanded the old school network quickly became the principal source of personnel.

In the mid-thirties a concerted attempt was made to take the hucksterism out of advertising, and put it on a 'scientific' footing, with proper market research and assessment of effectiveness of campaigns as the basis for the setting of fees and tariffs. 'Scientific advertising,' its proponents argued, 'is the only force which can control the crowd and direct its spending.' As advertising became geared to exploitation of mass media and less to local visibility, the selling of advertising space became a more inert business, for advertisers had no choice but to take space in the mass circulation newspapers. Before a space-seller could take over a job in a mass circulation paper, he had to prove himself elsewhere – or be related to the proprietor.

Reg Greer was a space-seller of the old school 'who depended upon his personality, his capacity to make and hold business friendships, and his knowledge of advertising, which was always available to the client with whom he came into direct contact. There was no audit report of circulation to authenticate his statements. Were not his proprietors men of honour whose word could be relied on? Was not he a sincere and trustworthy man?'

The answer to the rhetorical questions is of course, no. The article appeared in *Newspaper News* as part of the polemic that preceded the setting up of an audit bureau of circulation in 1936. The purpose of this body, to which all newspapers were meant to be subscribers, was to give clients hard facts about the degree of penetration into the body politic of any given organ.

By 1933 Reg Greer was an established and respected member

of his profession. Somehow he had found a job and hung on to it while all around were losing theirs. In 1928 newspaper proprietors were demanding not only that staff work longer hours for less money, but also the return of lineage, the iniquitous system by which reporters were paid per line of print they supplied. (Keith Murdoch, Rupert's father, began as a penny-a-liner.) In 1928 or thereabouts (for his own statements vary) Reg Greer collapsed in the street in Melbourne and was taken to St Vincent's Hospital, suffering from pleurisy. He stayed there for six or seven weeks by one account and by another he was ill for five months. His lungs were aspirated six times and at one point he came out of a coma to find the priest anointing his feet with Extreme Unction. His indignation at this may have saved his life, for he was determined not to allow any such liberty to be taken again. I have always imagined that this episode represented the lowest point in his fortunes, for the seriousness of his illness seems to indicate that he was weakened by privation. Perhaps he decided then and there to go to Adelaide, where the dry air and longer hours of sunlight would heal his lungs.

At first he probably had to work hard, persuading old-fashioned businessmen that it paid to advertise. 'The space-sellers go about singly or in swarms, irrespective of weather conditions, and enter, forcibly or otherwise, any door whereon they see printed the words "manager" or "managing director". Once inside these space-sellers are almost impossible to get rid of....' By the time Arthur Searcy and Wally Worboys knew him, Reg Greer had built up a clientele and needed to do very little actual work to keep up his selling record, but in mid-1934 his career received a check.

Perce Messenger was to be moved sideways, and sent to represent *The News* in Sydney. As the senior (and star) space-seller, Reg Greer expected to replace him as advertising manager. Instead he was passed over, and his junior, Arthur Searcy, was promised the job. If the management thought that their idle cheeky charlie would not be bitterly disappointed by the snub they were wrong. Reg Greer demanded a move, and was sent to Perth, where he stayed for a year. When Arthur Searcy saw him again he was shocked to see that his shirt-cuffs were frayed. (My own suspicion is that Reg Greer eked out his salary by hustling

124

in the billiard saloons, which was a very much tougher pro-position in Perth than in the 'city of churches'.) Reg Greer told Arthur Searcy that he was on his way to Melbourne to take up a job selling advertising space for a new newspaper, the *Star*.

The *Star* came into being in Melbourne in October 1933, as a rival to Keith Murdoch's evening paper, the *Herald*. It was pub-lished by the *Argus*, the rival morning paper to Murdoch's *Sun*. Many of Murdoch's senior staff had defected to the new paper; Murdoch said to one, 'What will you do when I close the paper down?' and he replied, 'My boy'll be selling the *Herald* on street corners and I'll live off him.' Tradition holds that Murdoch put pressure on the newsagents, threatening to remove their fran-chise to sell his papers if they undertook to sell the new paper. It was also thought by some that Murdoch moles within the *Star* organisation were paid to sabotage it. In the first edition the weather map was printed upside down. On another memorable occasion the letter r inexplicably dropped out of the fourth word of a headline that should have read, 'General O'Duffy's Blue Shirts striking again.' The fourth word was left out altogether in the caption to a picture that showed one man carrying another piggy-back up a ship's companionway after a fire; the caption should have read 'The ship's cook *helping* up the unconscious ship's carpenter....'

The *Star* is remembered nowadays, by those who remember it at all, as the green newspaper. Unwisely the paper promised never to call any edition final that was not the last of the day, and to make the final edition unmistakeable it was printed on green paper. What that meant in practice is that the earlier editions remained unsold. The management insisted on absurd restric-tions: reporters were not allowed to smoke, were limited to one pencil a week, had to bring their own typewriters and had to queue up for copy paper. Circulation dropped to a low of 45,000 copies.

When Reg Greer met Peggy Lafrank he was working for the *Star*. He was too canny not to see that Murdoch was winning, by dint of such shifts as offering newsboys bicycles as bonuses for selling the *Herald*. He left the *Star* and took a one-off job organising the advertising campaign for a special book offer being marketed by the *Mail*. On New Year's Day 1936, *Newspaper News* announced, under a photograph of Reg Greer with his own teeth, that he was to be appointed Melbourne Representative of the *Daily News* Perth, a job which he apparently did not take up, for the name of the rep was given in May as R. J. McCartney. Instead he took another one-off job, selling space in the centenary edition of the *Advertiser*, for which he returned to the scene of his greatest successes, to Adelaide.

The centenary edition of the *Advertiser* was to be 'a hundred pages, printed on 36lb newsprint, nip finished with a specially designed cover in gravure'; eighty of those hundred pages were advertising. When every inch of that space was sold more than a month before the date of issue, a record was set that was not equalled for many years. A hundred thousand copies of the paper were sold, and 15,000 extra had to be printed. The total population of Adelaide at the time was only 330,000. Reg Greer came back to Melbourne and took Peggy Lafrank to Nathan's and bought her a large solitaire diamond.

There was no vacancy for an extra rep on the *Advertiser* once the centenary bonanza was over, but Advertiser Newspapers had a better plum to offer Reg Greer. W. E. Davey, the Melbourne representative of the *Advertiser*, had decided after many years in Australia and New Zealand to return to England. In November 1936, Reg Greer's appointment to the job was announced; this was the pinnacle of his career. The *Advertiser* was read in 85 per cent of households in metropolitan Adelaide. Advertising in a paper with this kind of penetration sold itself. The job was well paid, glamorous, easy and stable. On the strength of it, Reg Greer and Peggy Lafrank decided to marry as soon as Reg should have received religious instruction. Peggy left her job and never took paid work again.

In January 1939, twenty-two months after they were married, 'when fishes flew and forests walked', I was born.

Hush-Hush

Each false thing ends. The bouquet of summer
Turns blue and on its empty table
It is stale and the water is discoloured.
True autumn stands then in the doorway.
After the hero, the familiar
Man makes the hero artificial.
But was the summer false? The hero?
WALLACE STEVENS, 'EXAMINATION OF THE HERO IN A TIME OF WAR'

REG GREER did not volunteer until the war was two years old. His active service began on 17 January, 1942, and I was nearly three. I know that now; I tell myself over and over, but it means nothing. I tell myself, 'You knew him for three years, before he went away,' but as I can't remember anything about those three years, the information is useless to me. Why did I tell myself such a silly tale, that he was already in barracks when I was born? He wasn't. He was sitting in a flat in Docker Street, having a few beers and many cigarettes with a couple of friends while they waited for the call from the hospital.

Reg Greer was just an ordinary bloke. He didn't want to fight a war, didn't rush into it early but stayed out of it as long as he could. That wasn't good enough for me. I had to tart up his image, had to turn him into a committed warrior against fascism; I needed my father to be a hero, exposing himself to all that death and danger dare. I don't approve of heroism, and yet I demanded heroism of my father, imposed it on him. Across the dark gulf of years a sharp thought leaps like a spark; perhaps I was Reg Greer's problem. The very idea makes my touchy tummy boil up under my ribs until I feel nauseated, my father's nausea in my stomach. (Oh, Papa, forgive me.)

Australians were not quick to enlist in the European war; Australian men with families were more reluctant than most. Two years into the war they found they had no choice, especially if they sold advertising space. There were no ships free to carry newsprint to print the advertisements on and the clothing merchants had only the barest essentials to sell. Rationing was inevitable. The newspaper proprietors were only too happy to release men who wanted to volunteer. The men were happy to go, on the understanding that their jobs would be waiting for them at the war's end. The men who did not volunteer stood a pretty good chance of being given the sack.

The need for trained men, especially in the Air Force, grew faster than it could be supplied. In the closing months of 1941, a concerted attempt was made to recruit 50,000 men, most for the Empire Air Training Scheme. On 30 October, 1941 the Royal Australian Air Force announced that in addition an Officer Entry Interview Board would be held at No. 1 Recruiting Centre in Melbourne, otherwise the premises of an electrical company, on the corner of Queen Street and Little Collins Street. They asked 'what you knew, what you did'. Some time in November Reg Greer, advertising salesman, went along and satisfied the board that he was who he said he was, no older than he said he was, had done his cadet training and knew how to 'put on a bullshit parade' as Australians called the rituals of militarism.

He gave them the account of his life and education on which all my fruitless researches were based, secondary senior public school until the age of fifteen and a half, reader, reporter and representative on a newspaper or newspapers, sports cricket, rowing, football. The men interviewing him had the same background and they fell for it, hook, line and sinker. If I had only known it, this was Reg Greer's finest performance.

He was thirty-seven, too old for a combat pilot, but there were other jobs to do and a shortage of officer material to do them.

At his first medical examination, on 13 November, Reg Greer was found to be five feet ten and a half inches in height, and to weigh 147 pounds. His chest circumference was a mere 34½ inches. His mentality was alert. He had a firm appendical scar, a scar on the second, third and fourth fingers of the left hand which I don't remember seeing, and a scar under his chin, which I do. It was not the white crescent that results from a child tripping with a glass raised to its lips, but a flat bubble of shiny scar tissue where no beard would grow. The little toe on his left foot was a hammer toe. He also displayed a 'slight scoliosis', a lateral curvature of the spine. I never noticed that either. He had had a tonsillectomy in 1927, if his memory was accurate. The ear-wax in his left ear was excessive, and his Eustachian tubes were blocked. Both problems were treated on 24 November. The Eustachian tubes were politzerised until they were clear; a second ear, nose and throat examination revealed a healed perforation of the right ear. Daddy's age, his chronic rhinitis and catarrh, and the state of his ears, all meant that he would not be passed fit enough for a pilot.

There was no way that Daddy could influence the medicos' dispassionate assessment of his physical condition. Once his fine clothes were off they saw a thin, narrow-chested, taller than average man, with a fairly representative collection of past traumas. It is too easy to suspect hardship during childhood as a cause of his skinniness, to wonder if his perforated eardrum was caused by a vicious box on the ear, or his curved spine by being made regularly to carry something too heavy for a growing boy. After all we children were all made to wear our schoolbags on our backs, because mother was so anxious about curvature of the spine, having suffered excruciatingly herself. My brother is as thin as my father was, despite my mother's Oslo lunches and drinking hectolitres of milk, and may even have as narrow a chest. Still, as he stood there before D. B. F., MO and J. S. E., MO, Reg Greer cannot have been an impressive sight. Wing-Commander W. M. Lemmon passed him A4B.

At the end of December he would have got the telegram from the Air Board saying, 'You have been selected to undergo officers' training course commencing seventeenth January stop wire if available stop letter containing special new conditions governing persons attending school will follow.' And so on 17 January he moved out of our house and into the Royal Melbourne Showgrounds as Aircraftsman Grade 2, No. 254280. The volunteers were divided into five flights, with seventeen to twenty men in each. Into flights A and B went the men who had said that they were willing to serve overseas; Reg Greer was in flight A.

Flight A? Daddy, what on earth were you doing in Flight A, virtually asking to be sent overseas? Did you want to leave us? Did you think that overseas was the best way to get promotion and promotion was the best way ahead for your little family?

In my mailbag, I find among the daily ration of unsolicited advice the following: 'Now you should be the first to know the hand-maiden of anxiety is guilt. The anxiety of the family man in 1940 was of a different order from that of the nineteen-year-old. It was composed of two conflicting questions (a) what is the first duty of a husband and father? and (b) what is the clear duty of a citizen of a threatened state? ... it just wasn't ON to say, "I can't go. I have a family...." If you did you were seen to be ducking it. And you couldn't get away with it, because the instant reply was, "If you don't go, you won't have a family after the Japs take over...." Dad never had any way of expressing his anguish for his wife and kids. He had to march off bravely. Whether he had a safe berth in stores or faced horrors in the field, whether he became a hero or a miserable slave in a POW camp, he never had an opportunity to express his guilt at leaving his loved ones. ...'

Perhaps the guilt at abandoning one's wife and child in the threatened country is worse when the soldier chooses it than when it is forced on him. Did Reg Greer run away from a difficult marriage and a trying three-year-old via his officer-training course? Doubtless my correspondent, who had heard a phone-in radio programme on anxiety neurosis that I ran in Sydney, meant to help me to understand my father, but the result of his contribution was that I understood him less. No one forced Reg Greer to march away; he chose to leave us and go to the other side of the world. His anxiety state could conceivably have stemmed from that completely avoidable situation, in which case it and the long series of inadequacies it gave rise to would be harder, not easier, to forgive.

For more than a year the Australian Prime Minister, Robert Menzies, had been resisting the imperial insistence on training Australians to serve in Europe and the Middle East. Again and again he pointed out that his first duty as Prime Minister was to see that Australia had properly trained and equipped forces for home defence. As long as the Air Force, in particular, would have to rely on British matériel there was little or nothing that Menzies could do to enforce his demands. Without independent forces

Australia could not influence Allied strategy and was a mere pawn in the war game. Every Australian politician and most of the Australian top brass struggled to impress upon the British that the Australians were allies, volunteering in the spirit of commonwealth, not colonials dragooned like serfs into fighting their masters' wars. Their protestations fell on deaf ears.

The first volunteers were crazy to get into the action, which meant going overseas. Nobody wanted to submit to the tedium of training and drilling in Australia. Everybody wanted a crack at the Hun. The Australian government bowed to popular pressure and voted time and again to send its divisions overseas. Under the Empire Training Scheme, air crews began training in Australia, South Africa and Canada for service with the RAF, where they would have no chance of promotion to the command of large air formations. The greater the part they played in imperial defence, the less they could contribute to home defence. The British for their part promised to defend Singapore in the unlikely event of Japan's entry into the war.

At first the British denied that there was a threat from Japan; then they simply insisted that the Far East would have to wait until the European situation had been dealt with. The promised naval support for Singapore never arrived. Australian forces were being used overseas in actions of which the Australian government had no knowledge. Australians doubted the competence of some of the British generals and insisted on being treated as a separate force rather than being absorbed into British divisions. The only visible effect of their insistence was that Australians made themselves unpopular with the British 'Union of Generals' and British ranks closed against them. Blamey lost the struggle to keep his soldiers out of action until they were properly equipped and trained. The truth was never told to the Australian people; young men still lined up to serve as cannon-fodder in North Africa and Greece, all unaware of the bitter telegrams flying back and forth between Britain and Australia. Unaware of the totally unacceptable casualty rates in wrong-headed and mismanaged actions.

Most of the other Australians who entered the war at this relatively late stage did so because the imminence of the Japanese threat stirred in them the desire to be actively involved in the defence of their homeland and their loved ones. Not so my father. He volunteered to leave us.

We used to have a picture of me in my buttoned-up coat with a velvet collar, the kind we called a Prince Edward coat, standing on the hard sand at Elwood Beach, smiling up at someone much taller than me with my eyes all crinkled up. Mother laughed when she mentioned it, because Daddy had buttoned the coat up wrong, which I never noticed when the snapshot was still to be seen. Mother has jettisoned it now of course along with almost all my books, all the china and furniture we grew up with and all the letters Daddy ever wrote her. All I saw when I looked at that picture was the sharp delight on my baby face and the eyes shut against the glare of the sky. The person I was smiling up at, whose shadow falls across the sand wrinkles at the edge of Port Philip Bay almost to the round toes of my patent leather shoes, was Daddy. Daddy must have taken me for a walk by ourselves with the camera loaded and ready. Daddy knew he was going away, perhaps forever, but I did not.

No wonder I hate being photographed. Being photographed is the prelude to being deserted. You look up and beam all your love and trust into the shiny eye at the end of the pleated bellows, because Daddy tells you to. Watch the birdie. Say cheese. And I said cheese so hard up into the light that my eyes filled with tears. And then he was gone.

Was I in your wallet at least, Papa? Perhaps I did ride with you in your wallet. Next to pictures of Mother with her hennaed pompadour, in clinging crêpe and crisp sharkskin, or hanging on your arm in Collins Street with the tiny felt hat tipped over her eye. Perhaps you did show me when the other men showed their children, but then I forget. In your job there was no fraternising.

The A & SD course placed heavy emphasis on cyphers. The only other things learned by the new aircraftmen Grade Two were handling men on parade, how to move five hundred men, how to give a command. They did a little unarmed combat, at which Reg Greer was probably not much good, and some work with gas masks for three or four hours at a time, at which I fancy Reg Greer was even less good.

On 21 February, the volunteers were examined and appointed to the lowest officer rank of the RAAF, that of pilot officer, which they were to have for six months' probation. Reg Greer was appointed to the Administrative and Special Duties Branch of the Citizen Air Force, called up for the duration and twelve months thereafter. Then the men of the five flights were posted to various chores at various RAAF establishments around Melbourne, which they did for five shillings a day. Every week they would 'crack on their best salute, show their pay-book and be paid the money in their cap'. Daddy was then posted to No. 1 embarkation depot, at Ascot Vale. Normally the recruits slept in the barracks at the Showground. You knew you were on your way when you were given leave every night, stood down at five p. m. and back at seven in the morning for roll call. When you were given your Australia badge to sew on, you knew departure was imminent. You never knew where you were going.

Daddy took training course No. 17 along with Mr Admans who wrote me an ironical, slightly rebarbative letter. I don't think Mr Admans liked Reg Greer very much, but he remembered him vividly. I wondered if he had felt the sharp end of Daddy's tongue or if he thought he was a phony. Mr Admans loved talking about his war. He remembered very clearly how he was given leave at two in the afternoon and told he had to be back by five a. m. The men were given a slap-up breakfast of steak and potatoes and then driven through the back streets to Port Melbourne where the *Glen Artney*, 12,000 tons and too nippy to be given an escort, was waiting for them. They sailed at about 7.30, unassisted it seems by the wharfies who played cards throughout. At Altona the ship took on board 2,000 tons of dynamite. Mr Admans is still angry that the unionists demanded danger money for the loading, while the airmen made do with their officers' pay of seven shillings and sixpence a day.

On the way to Fremantle, the officers formed a gun crew to man the four or five guns on the rear deck and the .5 machine guns on the bridges. 'Just as well we didn't have to fire any of them,' says Mr Admans now. At first the officers had lived in style, double-bunking in the *Glen Artney*'s luxury cabins, but after they picked up 4,500 American troops everyone bunked in relays and fed in relays. The men were not told when their sister ship was 'knocked off by the Japs' but the Chinese crew knew all about it. The *Glen Artney* made a great detour, sailing so far south that the weather turned freezing. Then they crept up the African coast to Aden. That was Mr Admans's story and he told it with relish. I never heard Reg Greer tell his.

On 3 April Daddy was called to No. 4 embarkation depot in Adelaide and learned that he had been officially attached to the RAF. He embarked on the same day. He probably followed much the same route as Mr Admans, crossing the Indian Ocean out of range of Japanese submarines and hugging the African coast as far as Aden.

First landfall Aden, huh, Daddy? They really dropped you in it, didn't they? Stinking, hot, dry, filthy Aden, brutalised by generations of military occupants, a town of prostitutes and beggars, baksheesh, baksheesh, steal anything that wasn't nailed down. I don't imagine that you prowled the Casbah in search of the exotic. I reckon you would have dashed to the nearest officers' watering-hole for a cold beer and a collective shudder. What a hell hole. Who would go with such women? Who could abide the sight of such children, dirty, emaciated, desperate, tugging at your sleeve, the incessant refrain, baksheesh, baksheesh, steal the cigarettes – and the matches – out of your pocket. You wrote your enlistment number on your cigarette packet and your matchbox so when you grabbed the little thieves you had proof positive that it was your pocket they had stolen from. That was the world you were risking your life to save.

The expression 'culture shock' had yet to be coined. The merchant sea-men on Daddy's ship might have warned them of the squalor that lay ahead, but nothing can have prepared them for the pressure of the desperate humanity that descended on them as their lawful prey. They had to learn fast that giving to one filthy cripple displaying his running sores meant giving to all. Before they could get over their astonished pity and revulsion, they were laying about them, mercilessly. Cute children no older than the ones they had left behind rubbed up against them to slip a hand in a pocket or undo a watch strap. If the men lingered to talk to them, the children told theatrical lies, 'Fazzer caput, mozzer caput,' and opened their eyes wide or squeezed out a tear. 'Give me money.'

Reg Greer thought of himself as sophisticated but in Aden and Cairo and Alexandria he was a mere babe. He could not have known that such towns are clearing houses for all the human debris that falls out of a repressive and unforgiving system. He could not have known that the leprous brothel that surrounded the clean and fragrant foreigners in their 'brand-new uniforms was created by their very presence. Frightened and revolted, the Australians fled for the nearest watering-hole. 'Kem wiz me to ze Casbah,' Daddy used to say, in his Charles Boyer imitation. Poor Daddy. He was too frightened ever to go there.

After twenty-four hours in Aden, the Australians were moved up through the Suez Canal to Cairo, and there they were interviewed to find out in which field of Administration and Special Duties they felt best able to serve. After the war, Flying Officer Magnus, A. C., of the RAAF tried very hard to track down Australian officers serving with the RAF. He found out that the first request for thirty 'Australian gentlemen' for cypher duties was made in September 1940. 'Eventually 212 officers of RAAF Volunteer Reserve went to the Middle East as civilians, and were posted when they got there'; from 1 July, 1941, A & SD personnel were recruited from the RAAF. At the conclusion of a rather brief report, F/O Magnus could only write: 'there must be other files dealing with the subject but they are difficult to come upon.' Of the two hundred men of the RAAFVR and the two hundred of the RAAF attached to the RAF, all of them about forty years of age, we know only that many resisted the pressure to go into cyphers and chose other work, most enduring, according to F/O Magnus, 'arduous conditions of service'. Reg Greer stuck with cyphers and he found it arduous indeed.

Reg Greer arrived in Cairo at the beginning of the hottest month of the year; the mean daily temperature was 97.8. Like most newcomers he would have celebrated his arrival with an attack of gastro-enteritis. He would have been issued with salt tablets to fend off heat exhaustion. Ten thousand Egyptians died of louse-borne typhus that year; all ranks would have been warned against brushing up against Egyptians in the streets, so Reg Greer would have stayed in the officer ghetto, 'Grey Pillars' and the Kiwi Club and 'wallah higori'. The lice were a better deterrent than the risk of venereal infection which had lost its terrors after many millions of rubber sheaths had been captured with the Italians. Even if the Berka brothel in Cairo had not been closed down by the authorities, apparently after being identified as the source of a serious intelligence leak, I doubt Reg Greer would have been attracted to the poon tang.

(Now there's a thing. I must have overheard that expression and remembered it. When Mother once invested in a cut-price side of lamb which proved to be half rotten, I was commissioned to dig a hole in the vegetable garden and bury it. This was a job very much to my taste; I dug until the sides of the hole rose up over my head and then we children held a ceremonial funeral with singing and flowers for what we called the 'poo-tanger'.)

A discrepancy appears in the record at this point. The Air Force Office of the Australian Department of Defence says that Daddy was disembarked at the RAF Transit Centre at Almaza on the 7th of May, 1942. His service record as given by the department of Veterans' Affairs has him arriving at something called MECCS on the second of May and staying there for eight weeks. I assumed the initials stood for Middle East Codes and Cypher School, which would make sense. The problem is that officially no such institution ever existed.

By now every schoolboy knows that the Allies broke the German codes and exploited their knowledge through the operation called Ultra. Because through Polish ingenuity the Allies had been able to copy the German encoding machine, which they called Enigma, they were able to intercept enemy signals enciphered by the machine, read them and distribute the intelligence they contained to commanders in the field. The system could only work as long as the Axis powers did not suspect its existence. Information based on the decrypts was transmitted in code from Bletchley, and passed on to the intelligence staffs of Wavell, Auchinleck, Alexander and Montgomery, by Special Liaison Units. The SLUs were always a shoestring force, with a handful of low-ranking officers pottering around inconspicuous trucks parked on the periphery of the headquarters of the commanding officers they were supposed to brief. The trucks held their transceivers and their precious one-time pads or Type-X machines; one of the problems was to persuade other personnel in the event of an enemy advance that this unmarked truck was too important to leave behind. Not all the commanding officers were convinced of the value of Ultra, nor of the importance of keeping this source of information totally unsuspected. In a case like that of Air Marshal Coningham, who used to stuff his Ultra papers into the top of his flying boots, the SLUs were obliged to exert their authority without the benefit of rank. In the last resort they could radio Whitehall and Fred Winterbotham himself would intervene. In the Middle East all the SLUs wore RAF uniform.

Some of the encoded material received by the SLUs was decoded by using a one-time pad, printed under conditions of tight security in England and distributed personally to the units. They then delivered the decrypts personally to the commanding officers or the officers designated to receive them, who were to read them and give them back to the SLU officer who destroyed them at once. No Ultra signal was to be transmitted or repeated. Information derived from Ultra was sometimes ascribed to interrogation of POWs, or to aerial reconnaissance, or to no one in particular. 'It has been learned', 'we have come to know'. In the Middle East staff officers would refer to 'Uncle Henry' from Jerome K. Jerome's *Three Men in a Boat*, 'Always believe what your Uncle Henry tells you'. Sometimes it was called after Winterbotham, 'Fred'.

Liaising between Bletchley and higher command accounted for a relatively small proportion of the immense volume of Sigint activity in the Middle East; encyphered German wireless traffic was routinely intercepted, the meaningless material evaluated, re-encoded in a British cypher and transmitted to Bletchley for decrypting. RAF intercepts in Malta were passed on to RAF Sigint ME and then to operational commanders. Distinguishing between Bletchley material and material to be decrypted in the Middle East cannot always have been easy; there was moreover some chafing at the inevitable delay in receiving decrypts back from Bletchley and some rivalry between the services for better access to Sigint. It is possible that RAF commanders in the Middle East tried secretly to pre-empt Bletchley, but if this ever happened it has no place in the record.

There is another possibility that is even less likely to figure in the official record. Australian casualties in the Middle East and Mediterranean were unacceptably high. From Australia it seemed that the strategies were wrong, the leadership blimpish and feeble, and logistic support completely inadequate. Continuous pressure from Australian politicians and military commanders for greater participation in decision-making and independent deployment of Australian forces was producing no results whatever. In 1941 it would have seemed no more than the patriotic duty of an Australian officer seconded to the RAF to spy on the British, especially as Australian High Command was not fully in the picture about Ultra. Indirect enquiries at the Air Force Office of the Australian Department of Defence have secured information that they know more than they have any intention of telling me. (My own feeling is that whatever they are not telling me does not amount to much.)

It is now virtually impossible to sort out the intricate intelligence bureaucracy in the Middle East. The RAF set-up in Cairo was pioneered by P/O Hugh Waters in February 1941; that autumn it was beefed up by the arrival of W/Cdr. Rowley Scott-Farnie whose job was to co-ordinate and control all RAF intelligence operations in the Middle East. In December 1941, Aileen Clayton was flown out to set up a system for intercepting radio traffic, a job which in less remote stations was usually done by WAAFs. Clayton brought with her the drums for the Type-X machines and the one-time pads, in diplomatic bags. RAF intelligence was then to be found in an unfinished building on the Suez Road at Heliopolis, a vast dusty pile which had originally been intended for a museum. Clayton was under the command of S/L J. R. Jeudwine, but her job brought her into contact with all parts of the operation, including the Communications Bureau Middle East under Freddie Jacobs, which she called 'virtually a satellite of Bletchley'.

The Chief Signals Officer Air HQME, Air Commodore W. E. G. 'Pedro' Mann, told her that his greatest problem was training and organising a team to transmit the low-grade signals traffic that was being intercepted at Heliopolis in a secure code back to Bletchley for co-ordination and interpretation. She was 'put in the picture' about Ultra by Colonel Robert Gore-Brown, OC of all the SLUs in the Middle East. RAFHQ ME Command was housed then in a block of flats in the Garden City district of Cairo, a building known to the ranks as 'Grey Pillars'.

Reg Greer said that his job was called 'Secret and Confidential Publications Officer'. Given his penchant for upgrading himself whenever he could do so with impunity, he may well have worked for rather than as a Secret and Confidential Publications Officer. A publication which is secret has to be something like a one-time pad, which was both published, i. e. printed and distributed, and top, most, ultra secret. Once when I was in my Biggles phase I got interested in sending secret messages in codes. I wrote my code word, and then I made up the square with the other letters of a twenty-five-letter alphabet. Then I studied how to break a code like that by checking the frequencies with which certain letters appeared, and substituting for them the most-used letters in the language. Daddy was only mildly interested in what I was up to and I was only up to it because I thought it might bring us closer together. The way military intelligence works it must have driven us further apart. When Commander Edward Travis was awarded a knighthood for his work at Bletchley during the war, his wife could not imagine what it was for. If she had shown any real interest, he would have had to deceive her or avoid her.

By mid-1942 more than a thousand people were working for RAF intelligence in the Middle East. Throughout the protracted struggle in the desert the delay in receiving information back from Bletchley had been crucial, but any suggestion that the work of decryption should be delegated to local centres was resisted in the interests of protecting Ultra. The only solution was vastly to increase the volume of intelligence traffic back and forth between the Middle East and the intelligence establishment in England. The more signals intercepted, the greater amount of material in any code, the easier it was to break it. Dozens of people meticulously transcribed gibberish for hours on end, and retransmitted it re-encoded in another kind of gibberish. Many did not know what they were doing; others doubted its application, especially as those actually flying operations sneered at them. They were up to their armpits in bumf, while others were fighting and dying in blood and sand. It was their fate to rot well behind the lines in the Cheadle of the Middle East, working long hours in stifling heat, badly fed, worse housed, and never quite well, with little or no prospect of promotion or decoration.

In 1942, in preparation for Operation 'Torch' the intelligence operation at Combined HQ ME was strengthened by the appointment of high-ranking intelligence officers with close connections with Bletchley. The Director of Intelligence ME was Brigadier Terence Airey; his opposite number in the War Department was the Australian 'Bill' (Sir) Edgar Williams, later Montgomery's Intelligence Officer.

Intelligence operations became very much more sophisticated. Intercepted signals were re-transmitted, especially if they concerned disinformation already disseminated by the 'deception people'. One way of cracking the codes of the day was to transmit a readable British signal and wait for it to appear in code when it was re-broadcast for the information of German officers. Finding one's way through the maze of genuine and phony signals needed expert interpreters of signals traffic. We must assume, I think, a shortage of cypher officers especially in view of the role projected for intelligence in Operation 'Torch'. It would not be surprising if, for a time anyway, Air Intelligence Cairo ran their own indoctrination and training school specifically to train officers arriving from the Dominions; British intelligence officers must have been trained in conditions of tight security in England.

Daddy's friend, Mr Admans, was offered work in Sigint, which he refused, calling it 'a woman's job', but Daddy, who arrived at the same time, took it on. While he was at MECCS the Australian Casey visited the Middle East as a special envoy. Like Daddy he was appalled at the poverty of Egypt. He noted in his Diary that Egyptians were 90 per cent illiterate, and that a labourer was paid sevenpence ha'penny a day. He went forward into the Western Desert where 'our deception people showed me a German Order of Battle of the enemy (us), with details of our divisions that didn't exist, with names of unit and formation commanders and where each located. This revealing book was taken in the Western Desert. Our deception people told me it had taken many months of work to get the enemy convinced that these two Divisions existed, and they explained some of the means used in the process.'

While the deception people were seeding this kind of disinformation Rommel was getting accurate information about planned British counter-offensives from intercepted messages being transmitted to Washington by the American observer in Cairo, Colonel Fellers. Both Germans and Italians were reading his new top-secret code 'Black' thanks to a copy of the code-book, which was indeed bound in black, that had been stolen from the American embassy in Rome. Ultra meanwhile was providing information got from reading the traffic between Rommel and Kesselring and registered the German supply problems. The whole rigmarole would have seemed pretty far-fetched to the soldiers who were being driven pell-mell back across the desert to within sixty miles of Alexandria. Intelligence cannot win wars.

On 21 June Tobruk fell. Rommel raced for Cairo and Alexandria. Reg Greer went on studying his cyphers, but the tension must have been terrific. On Ash Wednesday GHQ in Cairo began burning documents in preparation for retreat. Regardless of present danger the intelligence network had to be built up if the Allies were to profit by their access to the German codes. The personnel being trained for intelligence work had to keep their heads down and concentrate on their frequency tables.

What did they do to you, Daddy, in those two months at MECCS? Did they make of you a 'deception person' or did they realise that you were a deception person already? Did they simply build on your natural secrecy, your non-committalness, your distaste for intimacy? Or did they secure your silence by more aggressive means? By emotional blackmail? By psychological pressure? Perhaps they made you take an oath.

Every member of the Secret Service catches the disease. They all live as if the right hand was not to be trusted to know what the left hand is doing. Once the initial breach has been made in the self, once a man has learned to live a double life, it is a simple matter to live a treble or a quadruple life. Did the boffins in Cairo discover that Daddy was a liar, a phony, fitted by temperament and experience to be a member of an SLU pretending to be something else? Mind you, compared to life with me, life in the RAF must have been easy. I won't take 'hush-hush' for an answer.

The signals officer's job was not without its dangers. The signals trucks were just at the right height to be hit by flak; under bombardment the officers had to wait until the last minute before jumping into the slit trench dug beside their vehicle. If a signal was being intercepted, it was the tradition not to take cover until it had been transcribed. Nevertheless, regardless of personal courage in sticking at their post, intelligence officers were not in line for promotion or decoration because they had to remain inconspicuous. The Sigint teams were not allowed to be daring. They were prevented from explaining what must have seemed to be cowardice and standoffishness. They were forbidden to fraternise or confide. They were true to their word; they held their peace. Most, including F/O Greer, died with their mouths still shut. It was a 'woman's job' after all.

Most of the intelligence teams had only the haziest idea of what their contribution actually was. Their daily reality was drudgery, and not merely mechanical drudgery, for they had to concentrate on accuracy. A mistaken letter or figure could cost lives. Hans Fischer, a German cryptanalyst, described his work to Bruce Norman, for his book *Secret Warfare, the Battle of Codes and Ciphers*, in harrowing terms: 'staring at something which is meaningless and doing that for hours and days and sometimes weeks on end can be extremely boring. You may well go to sleep doing it. On the other hand you have to be alert all the time. It's a tremendous strain, a psychological and nervous strain. You get into the attitude where you see figures and letters everywhere and try to read a meaning into them. Car numbers, telephone numbers. If they begin with 66 and end with 44 then you think that must have some significance. It's with you all the time. You can't escape it. It almost sends you mad.'

All the evidence points to a high level of stress from which there could be no relief, for intelligence officers were discouraged from fraternising. As an Australian Reg Greer had little in common with the English whether officers or men. His career as an intelligence officer seems to have been one of loneliness, tedium and tension. The big adventure quickly turned into a big ordeal.

P/O Greer emerged from MECCS on 1 July and hung around AHQ Egypt for five days, then got posted to something called 234 Wing which seems to have done anything but fly. On the fifteenth he went down to RAFHQ Western Desert, which if I'm not mistaken was at Burg el Arab. These were exciting times; things were definitely on the move. Montgomery had been appointed, and moved his establishment to Burg el Arab too. On 3 August Winston Churchill himself arrived in Cairo with his entourage, for a pow-wow with Smuts, Wavell, and the commanders of the three services in the Middle East, Auchinleck, Harwood and

Tedder, all of whom were subsequently replaced for Operation 'Torch'.

In 1942, 17,150 British officers and 268,000 British men, according to Lord Casey, were serving in the Middle East; 3,659 Indian officers, and 111,600 Indian men served with them, together with 3,260 South African officers and 61,750 men, 1,485 Australian officers and 30,500 men, and 1,970 officers and 29,700 men from New Zealand. Among the British, and their close relatives the New Zealanders, there was one officer to every fifteen men. Australians and South Africans had roughly the same leaven of officer material, about 5 per cent. Of the huge Indian force which numbered almost as many as all other Commonwealth troops, only one in thirty was considered worthy of officer status.

As an intelligence officer and an Australian in the RAF Reg Greer was doubly isolated. He was isolated first of all from the other services, then from the other ranks in his own service; he was a non-flying officer and therefore unable to enter the cameraderie of the air-crews, and he was involved in top-secret work, the nature of which could be never so much as hinted at. When Aileen Clayton went about her secret business in the desert, no one thought to challenge her usefulness, because she was a woman. An Australian unit sporting robust growths of beard in deference to the scarcity of water and the cruelty of the sun showed their appreciation of her civilising presence by appearing at lunch neatly shaven. They did not feel so kindly towards the male officers who were shining their bums in Heliopolis, while they struggled back and forth across the Western Desert, but called them the 'Short Range Desert Group' and the 'Gabardine swine'. The fliers felt equally bitter about the Army which was unable to take advantage of the air cover that they were offering at such cost. In a situation of unremitting tension tempers quickly frayed; a South African showing up at the Kiwi Club three weeks after the first battle of El Alamein was asked by an Australian if he had run the whole way. In the ensuing brawl no prisoners were taken.

After Japan's entry into the war, and after the cock-up in Crete, Australians became quite desperate to get out of the Middle East. Just how desperate can be judged from a sad episode in the official medical history of the RAF in World War II. 'Cases of macular degeneration largely restricted to the left eye occurred among personnel of a Commonwealth Air Force during 1941. Such cases also displayed symptoms of neurosis and loss of confidence, the condition corresponding to no known syndrome. The possibility of over-exposure to direct sun rays was considered but could not be substantiated. Cases of night blindness were uncommon and mainly hysterical in origin. Ocular muscle defects among trained pilots frequently showed disappointing and even harmful response to orthoptic treatment. Such cases proved on investigation to be allied to psychiatric disabilities requiring treatment and usually lowering of category.'

It is unbearable to contemplate the desperation that drives men to stare at the sun, holding their eyelids apart so that the direct sunrays would burn blind spots on to their corneas, but clearly the medical officers thought it the only way the lesions they observed could have been produced. Morale in the Western Desert was a serious problem for all fighting men, but particularly for those who thought their lives were being thrown away while their loved ones were left unprotected at home. It was Montgomery who would point out that men are capable of extraordinary feats of endurance and courage if they are convinced that they are highly valued. If their living conditions are unbearable, if they do not get sufficient food and rest, if they are not convinced that they will be taken care of if wounded or ill, their motivation suffers. If they are treated as a rabble by commanding officers who understand nothing of their background and make no attempt to put them in the picture they will be more prepared to kill him than to die for him.

Commonwealth troops in the Western Desert were unimpressed by the British leadership and the British system of promotions and rewards that by-passed the ranks for a hereditary military caste of no proven ability in modern warfare. Many knew that the German military were organised on more democratic lines, with promotion strictly tied to merit and ability. Everyone in the Western Desert knew that the enemy commander was called Rommel; many did not know who the commander of the Allied forces was and could not have pronounced his name if they did. The coming of Monty, the most skilful self-promoter the

British military have ever produced, on a par with the American virtuosi Patton and MacArthur, changed all that and with it the fortunes of the war. Montgomery stressed his Commonwealth links; on the strength of a period of his boyhood when his father was Bishop of Tasmania, he wore a sundowner hat for a while. The infantry loved it; not so my father.

Daddy's dislike of Montgomery, who 'arrived from England August 15 or 16, summed up the desert situation in a trice, issued quick ruthless orders, and behold! Victory!' was shared by other intelligence officers. Montgomery had Ultra and had been briefed in how to use it. Even though he was not free to acknowledge Ultra in his memoirs, the intelligence staff who briefed him every day were sickened by the avidity with which he sought personal credit for extraordinary clairvoyance and cunning in the field. He made life unnecessarily hard for his SLU, by positioning their quarters as far as possible from his own bivouac, on the grounds that their meagre signalling might attract unwanted enemy attention. All this meant in practice was that every time a top-secret signal came through for Montgomery, the liaison officer had to run half a mile in the blackout to deliver it, only to have Montgomery pretend that it was of no consequence.

One of the very few war-stories my father ever told me contains part of the justification for thinking that Daddy was involved in Ultra. He was supposed to be flying from somewhere to somewhere with a machine, a decoding machine, I understood. As he sat beside the airstrip in a jeep, waiting to board the aircraft, someone ran up with orders to hand the machine over to a superior officer who was to take Daddy's seat in the plane. Idly Flying Officer Greer watched the plane take off. Before it had climbed to its cruising altitude, a German fighter came in out of the sun and strafed it from end to end. The plane crashed in flames in sight of the airstrip.

Once upon a time we had letters from the desert, written in Daddy's rather formless upright scrawl, all about how cold it got at night, so that two blankets weren't enough, about Jerry coming over, and flares lighting up the landscape. There were photographs of men skinny-dipping off the North African coast. Nothing about what he was doing of course. In one of her ritual purgations Mother has destroyed these letters. They were

145

addressed to her after all, and, if of no interest to her, of interest to nobody.

Reg Greer must have done well in the Western Desert. On 21 August he was promoted to the rank of Flying Officer and transferred to No. 22 Personnel Transit Centre where he had to hang about for three weeks before setting out on his worst ordeal. (It was probably here that the episode related above took place.) He was on his way to Malta. Flying into Malta was not impossible; but it was dangerous. If the aircraft carrying the Type-X machine had ditched over the Mediterranean the Ultra secret could well have been blown right there. Reg Greer was stood down to wait for another means of transport, and probably another Type-X machine.

Cambridge,
September 1987

Là, tout n'est qu'ordre et beauté,
Luxe, calme et volupté.
CHARLES BAUDELAIRE, 'L'INVITATION AU VOYAGE'

FOR THE wine circle after dinner at St John's, the Master, Professor F. H. Hinsley, kindly invited me to sit on his left and grill him to my heart's content. On his right sat the famous American endocrinologist, Professor Rosenberg, who had that day given his lecture on 'Endocrinology and maternal behaviour'. The candlelight vied with the firelight to make the glasses sparkle, and the port, the malmsey and the burgundy glowed in their decanters. 'The port is only twelve years old,' said the Master. So I chose the burgundy, which was five years old, and the Master took it too. It was as smooth as cream. The fellows on my left were eagerly discussing hemlock, in particular its hollow stem with purple spots, and the curious fact that in America hemlock is a tree.

The college servants brought in the coffee. Snuff and cigars were handed. The long gallery filled with the delicious aromas of empire. The Master filled his pipe from a silver pot and held a taper to a candle. When he had sucked the flames into the bowl and laid the taper by, he turned to me.

'This young woman,' he said, 'has read my book.' He seemed surprised, not because a woman had read *British Intelligence in the Second World War: Its Influence on Strategy and Operations*, but that anyone had ploughed through the three volumes.

Professor Rosenberg expressed interest. 'So you wrote the official history of British intelligence in the Second World War. Is there an American equivalent?'

The question was more complex than it appeared, for the Americans made better use of British intelligence than the British did. The Master had avoided a mildly vexed problem by confining himself to the European theatre, so we sidestepped the question of Magic. It was plain that he loved his subject and was delighted to find anyone else who was interested in it. So I asked my first question.

'What do the initials MECCS mean to you?'

The Master was puzzled, 'Middle East ...?'

'Codes and Cypher School?'

Well he might look puzzled. None of the histories of intelligence including his mentions such a thing. And yet there it is on one version of Reg Greer's service record as plain as a pikestaff, and there it isn't on the résumé provided by the Australian defence department. Curious.

I wrote to Fred Winterbotham, who 'invented the Special Liaison Unit, recruited the men, trained them and distributed them to the various commands and visited them all from time to time to ensure absolute security'. He thought Reg Greer probably was part of an SLU or perhaps connected with MI6. The other intelligence bods I wrote to cautioned me against relying on Winterbotham, and thought that Reg Greer had nothing to do with Enigma. Winterbotham's mention of MI6 flashed a warning that we were on the threshhold of *Boys' Own* fantasy-land. Intelligence, more perhaps than any other branch of the services, relies upon the old school network, upon known backgrounds, family relationships, proven loyalty.

Ralph Bennett, who was involved in Cairo Ultra from October 1942 to March 1943, replied to my letter: 'if neither Harry Hinsley nor I have heard of MECCS (and I certainly have not) then I think it must have been either (1) a transient cover-name for something quite different – there were lots of cases like that, (2) a branch of Communications Bureau Middle East, or (3) a cover-name for part of SOE. The second is the more likely. CBME was the intercept station for Enigma and other enemy transmissions, and was located at Heliopolis.'

If MECCS was a branch of CBME what did it do? What did Reg Greer do in it? Certainly I thought it no more likely that he had been involved in the Special Operations Executive than that he was part of MI6. He was more hush-hush than cloak-and-dagger.

Sir Edgar Williams pointed out to me that the Special Liaison

Units did only one job, that of conveying Ultra information to commanders in the field; there were many times more people involved in interception and retransmission of Enigma traffic, and in reception and decryption of Bletchley traffic, than in this one specialised part of the operation.

The Right Honourable J. Enoch Powell chose an oddly imprecise form of words in order to dismiss my enquiry: 'I am sorry to have to say that my duties in Middle East Command 1941-43 and in North Africa Command 1943 afford no means of giving you any information that would be of interest to you in your quest.'

Sir David Hunt could remember only a few names from RAFHQWD of which my father's was not one, but thought that my deduction that F/O Greer was part of the Malta SLU was 'very sound'. The Middle East SLU had been set up by A. E. Dilkes; the Middle East was the first place that Ultra was exploited effectively. The Bletchley story had been told a dozen times, the Cairo story never. Winterbotham had blabbed, but not Dilkes.

'You know,' said the Master, 'there is a history of the SLU, a book. I know because I've seen it, but I don't know if it's got to the PRO yet.'

'So it's still in the Office of the Cabinet.'

'It may be,' said the Master, with a grin. If the primal elder has anything to do with it, I thought, it will be lost on the way to the Public Records Office.

'There are personnel files, in the Directorate of Signals. Your father should be mentioned there.'

'What does the description Secret and Confidential Publications Officer mean to you?' I asked him.

'I think it means your chap was responsible for the security of British cyphers,' he said.

'What would these things that while published were also secret and confidential be? One-time pads?'

'I suppose so.' The Master was mildly bemused. This sort of nut-and-boltery was not what his book was about, but it was obvious that the Ultra operation had been designed as a whole down to the precise methodology of interception and distribution in the field. There was nothing to indicate that Reg Greer had ever been involved in Top Secret U, nothing but my tendency to aggrandising fantasy, that I had inherited from him and have tried all my life to inhibit and control.

'Who would know?' I asked. 'Would Lewin know?'

'Lewin is dead,' said the Master. He could have added many more names to the list of those who died with their story untold.

'What I hate to think is that Daddy beavered away in that underground dungeon for eight months, painfully decoding and encoding without any idea of the importance or the relevance of what he was doing. I don't want to think that he was entrusted with only a meaningless fraction, just used as a secure conduit, unable to betray because he knew too little. I would hate to think the British used him that way.'

'No, no,' said the Master. 'He would have known what Ultra was; even if he was not himself in an SLU he would have had access to the Malta SLU.' He put his hand, sadly distorted by arthritis, on my wrist, knocking off the little pile of scented snuff that I was gradually working into my nostrils.

'What was the oath you took when you entered the Ultra programme?' I asked. 'Can you remember the exact words?'

'Something like I am engaged upon important secret operations for the government and I promise never to reveal their nature until released from this bond by my government.'

(Well, I thought, they can't have used that one with Reg Greer. It wasn't his government. Maybe they said, 'I am engaged on important secret operations for my king.' A bit of pomp goes a long way in the circumstances. Maybe the king sent a personal note, 'Reg Greer, we are relying on you. G. R.' Certainly the indoctrination was effective; you would think the oath would have required something more than a handshake, but Ralph Bennett couldn't remember taking any oath at all when he was recruited for Bletchley in 1941. 'No one thought of betraying secrets in those days,' he said.)

'Weren't you surprised,' I asked, 'when Winterbotham spilled the beans? He hadn't been released from his oath, had he?'

'No, he hadn't,' said the Master, 'and yes, we were. We weren't formally absolved from the duty of secrecy until 1976.' Reg Greer had only seven years to live; the Australian papers made nothing of it. Perhaps he never knew that the secret was no longer secret.

'Did it do any harm after all? We won't use the system again, will we?'

'No,' said the Master with glee. 'Nowadays we all have unbreakable cyphers. Computers, you see; each message we send can have its own completely arbitrary cypher. That's why spies have become so important. If you can read the other fellow's traffic you don't need spies.' He smiled hugely, as if Ultra had been a most satisfactory jape, the boffins' finest hour.

As I walked back through the cobbled courtyards, between old brick walls that glowed rose in the light reflected by the leaded panes of the pointed windows, I wondered what Reg Greer would have made of the sight of his daughter in her doctoral gown drinking deep of the burgundy in such distinguished company. I loved it; I loved the limed oak panelling, and the stylised stucco grape vines that rioted symmetrically above my head. I loved the scent of good coffee and fine tobacco and the bouquet of my burgundy so carefully decanted by the college servants. I liked the playfulness of perpetual students.

'Have you heard this one?' said a senior fellow. 'God made an application to the Science and Engineering Grants Committee. It was refused on three grounds. The work was done too long ago; the literature has no apparatus; and the experiment has never been successfully repeated.' We roared, but the senior fellow went on: 'Then there was a wrinkle in reality; the Science and Engineering Grants Committee did not simply cease to exist, it had never existed at all.' And he smiled so widely that his eyes closed up tight.

I loved that way the junior fellows rose to refill our glasses and get closer to conversations they suspected of being interesting. I loved the way the fellows used Latin to explain things to visitors whose English was halting, and how simply they expressed their ignorance of fields that were not theirs. Better still I loved the way that the fellows warmed to the exposition of their specialities, if given a chance. From hemlock we went on to water hemlock. And how a Scots family died when they used monkshood instead of horseradish as sauce to their beef. And how effective leopard's bane is, for never a leopard has been seen within miles of it.

Daddy would not have liked any of it. He would have found it high-falutin'. He would have wanted a beer and a cork-tip rather than wine and cigars. I don't know if he would have been proud of me for holding my own or even if he would have known whether I was holding my own or not. As far as I know he never read a word I wrote or saw or heard any programme I made.

When I got my Ph.D. I sent him a telegram – or did I just plan to send it? *You have a doctor in the family.* When my brother was expected my father tried out names, 'Dr Gideon Greer', 'Dr John Greer'. He never tried out 'Dr Germaine Greer'. When I went home to Melbourne to tell my family that I had won a Commonwealth Scholarship and was on my way to Cambridge, my father called me to him and pressed something into my hand. 'Don't tell your mother,' he said, making signs to be secret. I put whatever it was into my sleeve. When I was in the street walking to the train station, I pulled it out. It was a five-pound note.

When I came up to Cambridge my fellow-students were showing their parents around their rooms, the lecture theatres, the Backs, posing for pictures in the family album. The families beamed with pride and pleasure, shouted and ran about, gathering images of their successful children against the background of Erasmus' bridge and the Wren Library and the stone nougat of King's College. Nobody photographed me, not then, not when I knelt resplendent in medieval red and black with my hands joined in prayer within those of the Vice Chancellor, Germaine Greer Philosophiae Doctoris Cantabrigiensis. I collected my degree by myself. There was no victory supper, no champagne. I had worked all my life for love, done my best to please everybody, kept on going till I reached the top, looked about and found I was all alone. My parents were too ignorant even to appreciate what I had achieved. I thanked my lucky stars it was English poetry I studied, so that I had the charms and incantations to lay upon the wound in my soul. If I had chosen to study dentistry or computer science, I might never have won through to happiness.

Malta

'Malta is not only a fortress, but the home of the Maltese.'
LIEUTENANT-GENERAL SIR WILLIAM DOBBIE, JUNE 1942

ON THE twenty-first of August, 1942, Pilot-Officer Greer, having successfully weathered his six months' probation, got his promotion to the rank of Flying Officer. If he was, as I think, part of the 'Y' service, he could expect no further promotion. With the good news of the promotion came the bad news. He had been posted to Malta.

Since the first raid by the Regia Aeronautica, seven hours after Italy entered the war on 11 June, 1940, Malta had been taking punishment. The island, no bigger than the Isle of Wight, had a population of a third of a million. The Maltese had been told to prepare for attack by gas, rather than bombing. Despite the daily Italian broadcasts that promised that the Regia Aeronautica would reduce Valletta to rubble in a day, no underground shelters had been prepared. The island had been left, moreover, without air defence of any kind. Four squadrons of Hurricanes had been promised, but did not arrive. The harbour lacked the most elementary protection against air attack, having not so much as a single smudge pot to provide a smokescreen.

The Air Officer Commanding, F. H. M. Maynard, commandeered six Gloster Sea Gladiator bi-planes that had been left still crated on the wharf by HMS *Glorious* when she left hurriedly to join the Norwegian campaign, and took seven officers, none of whom had had combat experience, off desk duties to fly the three planes that were operational. This was the truth behind the legend of the defence of Malta by 'Faith', 'Hope' and 'Charity', as the three planes became known long after their serviceability was at an end.

More significant than 'Faith', 'Hope' and 'Charity' in the

defence of Malta were the anti-aircraft batteries, manned by the three Coastal Regiments, two Maltese and one British, but at the beginning of the Italian bombardment they had only thirty-four anti-aircraft guns and eight Bofors, besides an odd assortment of old guns salvaged from the dockyard. There were no fighters to provide cover for their exposed positions. In the very first raid five members of an anti-Parachute Squadron and a boy working as duty telephonist at the Harbour Fire Command Post were killed; by the end of the day eleven civilians were added to the number of the dead, all Maltese.

At that stage British thinking held that if France fell Malta was indefensible. However, though they had no plans to defend the island, the British had drawn up no contingency plan for surrender. The island's rulers, the Governor, and the naval and air commanders, were left to defy the enemy with the few men and totally inadequate equipment that they had. The Royal Navy decided Grand Harbour was too hot to hold them and moved out to Alexandria. If the Italians had invaded at any time in 1940 there would have been a short sharp massacre and Malta would have become an Italian island. Doubtless the Maltese would have learned to tolerate the Italians as they had tolerated most of the foreigners who had ruled the fortress. To this day Italian analysts do not know why Italian high command failed to prevent the garrisoning of Malta, why the island was then neutralised at maximum cost to the Regia Aeronautica, or why when Malta was quite incapable of mounting any resistance the island was not occupied, but allowed to re-garrison. The failure to take Malta cost the Axis Africa.

The island was a rock fortress and could shelter its own, but it could not feed them. The Maltese population had increased exponentially under British rule, and as a result the island's dependence on imported food and fuel and manufactured goods had also increased. The Italian bombardment eased off, and the Axis concentrated instead on starving the Maltese into hoisting the white flag. From June to September 1940, no supplies at all reached the island. From September 1940 to September 1941, convoys reached the island at intervals of not more than two months but between October 1941 and October 1942 the blockade of Malta was penetrated by only eleven merchant ships, of which two were sunk in the harbour before the bulk of their supplies could be unloaded.

Not having been told to capitulate, the islanders dug in and resisted, with all their native toughness and stoicism. The British press reported with astonishment and gross insensitivity, 'Malta can take it.' It made no sense that an island sixty miles from Sicily was remaining British against all the odds, but the fifty or so influential Maltese who might have said so had been interned.

In January 1941, Malta's war took on a new and terrible complexion. A convoy mounted to relieve Malta and Greece, escorted by the new British aircraft carrier *Illustrious*, was attacked by the Luftwaffe from bases in Sicily. The carrier was hit six times; 126 members of her crew were killed and 91 injured. People on Malta heard the furious sea battle and watched in awe as the crippled vessel dragged herself into Grand Harbour. For four days all was quiet. On the 16th all hell broke loose, as Malta took the first of many raids by the Luftwaffe. For the first time the people heard the ear-shattering roar of the box barrage put up to protect the dockyard, and the screaming sirens of the dive-bombing Stukas. In January there were 57 alerts, in February 107, in March 105, a total of 963 alerts for the year.

In January 1942, Fliegerkorps X in support of Rommel stepped up the aerial attack on Malta. In the first three weeks of January, there were 950 raiders sent against Malta, 150 sorties a week. In January there were 263 alerts, in February 236, in March 275. Bad weather often kept Malta's fighters grounded; there was nothing for it but to take the merciless bombardment, hour after hour, day after day, week after week. Men worked day and night to repair vessels and aircraft only to emerge from their slit trenches after yet another raid to discover that they had been 'spitchered' again. There was no way of protecting aircraft on the exposed airfields until the army was called in to build stone pens to protect them from all but a direct hit and to repair the runways.

History records the heroes of Malta who were fighter pilots; the fighter pilots thought that the ground crews who serviced their planes and the 'pongos' who filled craters day and night, with no relief from tension, no proper food and no sound rest, were the real heroes in the air battle of Malta.

When possible Malta-based bombers attacked Axis airfields, but losses were quickly replaced and the assault did not weaken. On 7 February there were sixteen alerts in twenty-four hours. One wag suggested that the BBC news report of raids against Malta would give a more accurate and concise account of what was going on by saying simply, 'Last month Malta had six all-clears, one of which lasted for twenty-five minutes.' Between the beginning of the year and 24 July the Maltese had known only one period of twenty-four hours in which there was no raid.

As the bombs fell day and night (14,000 tons of them) the Maltese people hid out in the 'catacombs', tunnels hollowed out in the rock. Above, flak rained down over Cottonera as the bombers came over the box barrage in wave after wave, doing their best to smash Grand Harbour and the air-fields at Luqa, Hal Far and Ta Qali. The civilians who remained near Grand Harbour lived in the galleries carved out of the rock by the Knights of Malta to accommodate their galley slaves or in the old railway tunnel, which by late 1941 had been equipped with tiers of bunks, electric light, radio, piped water and ablution blocks. Each tunnel had been given a street name and divided into numbered cubicles where postmen delivered the mail. People fell in love and married, babies were born and baptised inside the rock.

Some lucky people with houses on the perimeter of the bombarded areas dug themselves shelters below them, and equipped them with bedding and a few necessities. Here they could sleep all night in privacy, avoiding the terrifying scramble with sleeping children through the unlit cratered streets when the alarm sounded. Unfortunately, too many of these homemade shelters were too shallow to be safe, and more became sealed tombs when houses collapsed on top of them.

For the unlucky there were just the small neighbourhood shelters, low tunnels where the only air supply was from the doorway. During the raids the doorways were often jammed and the air supply became so fetid that the people's candles guttered and went out. The space allotment was two feet per person. They stood shoulder to shoulder in the dark, women holding moistened handkerchiefs over their babies' noses and mouths, as the limestone dust loosened by the bombing showered down on them, praying, praying hardest that their shelter would not become their tomb by collapsing on them or filling up with sewage or water from shattered pipes. The bomb-blasts sucked the air out of their lungs; many found they could not swallow. For some people the ordeal of the shelter was more terrifying than the prospect of death or maiming under the open sky. The British for their part maintained a foolish preference for 'coolly finishing their drinks' and defying the raids.

The Maltese noticed that no preparations were made to ready the underground shelters until after months of bombardment, that there was no money available for shelter improvement, for enlarging them or drilling ventilation shafts or providing facilities for disposal of sewage. They saw that there was no political will to improve their existence or to minimise the risks they ran. There was no pretence of keeping them informed, or consulting them. In 1941, conscription had been introduced to bring the Maltese regiments up to the same numerical strength as the British, 15,000 men; for some reason the Malts were paid less than the Tommies. The Maltese watched and learned and made their plans to unload the British once and for all when the agony was over. Through the fog of propaganda about Maltese loyalty the authorities sensed that the Maltese though stoical, cheerful and co-operative were disabused. Terse telegrams advised Whitehall that the Maltese were politically unsound. The only effect was an increase in bullshit parades, in pomp and panoply and martial music. When the remnants of the shattered convoys dragged themselves, or were dragged, into Grand Harbour, the watchers on the heights raised their massed voices and sang 'Roll out the Barrel', corny but it made them feel defiant and unbowed.

By 1942, thanks to Rommel, the British were totally committed to the defence of Malta but, despite their best attempts to relieve the garrison and beef up its fighting force, the situation continued desperate. The February convoy never got near Malta. Of the four ships of the March convoy only two made it to harbour. The Maltese dockers struggled to unload them in between raids in which both were badly holed and settled in the shallow water. A third ship was unloaded at a makeshift mooring on the south-east side of the island, despite the unremitting attempts of the Luftwaffe to sink it. The crews working day and night to refit damaged vessels could only watch helplessly as they were blasted at their berths in Grand Harbour, without even the protection of a smoke screen. When the all-clear sounded they would start patching up again.

Resistance had its usual reward; the old residential area of Floriana was flattened; the Inns of the Knights of Malta were destroyed, their Military Hospital was badly damaged. The opera house was burned out. The basilica of St Publius was reduced to rubble. In April, 10,000 Maltese buildings were destroyed or damaged; the shortage of housing was acute, even before preparations for Operation 'Torch' brought increased numbers of service personnel.

The British response was to devise a new tax on property owners with which to finance reconstruction, as well as continuing to collect estate taxes for destroyed property. People who inherited bombed property from owners who died in the bombardment were still expected to pay inheritance taxes. Compensation for personal injury was made at an insultingly low level. The British answer to accusations of niggardliness was simply that there was a war on. The Maltese could beef if they wanted to, the British were not listening.

A colonial officer might have been expected to sympathise with the Maltese, for he too was a nonentity in Churchill's army. RAF aircrews were one-third colonials, and later in the war the proportion of colonials to British increased to almost half, but the Air Ministry kept no separate record of the colonial contribution. It was galling enough that the colonials kept their own pay-books and were to be given better rations than the British where possible. As far as the record was concerned they would all be called British.

The April raids came from all directions, three a day each lasting about an hour, making a total of the time spent actually under bombardment twelve days, ten hours and twenty minutes. The most Malta could marshall in defence were six fighter aircraft for each raid, four to engage the enemy, and two for airfield defence, to be sent up at the last moment to save petrol. Sometimes – only the AOC knew quite when – they had no ammunition, and had to fake it. Newly captured prisoners of war turned cocky, saying they weren't afraid to fly over Malta any more, and would soon be rescued. The battle, they thought, was all but over. On the eleven days in April when there were no fighter planes operational, Malta's only defence was the anti-aircraft battery, which claimed 102 enemy aircraft destroyed in that dreadful month. The gunners were badly exposed as the enemy concentrated on the fringes of the airfields where the aircraft were held in their pens. Casualties were heavy. All services followed a policy of publishing only the enemy's losses. The Maltese disbelieved what they read in the *Times of Malta*, and what they heard from the local radio relay. They had no other source of information besides rumour.

Churchill was acutely aware that Malta could not be allowed to fall. He was also aware that both military and civilians were near collapse. On 15 April the people of Malta, who had lived through nearly two years of hardship, short of food, often without light or heat, and even without water when bombs hit the mains, were awarded the George Cross. Churchill persuaded Roosevelt to give him the use of the aircraft-carrier *Wasp* to bring Spitfire replacements; three days later, they were all unserviceable, 'spitchered' on the ground. The disappointment was bitter; Malta began to prepare for invasion. The lull in the air offensive at the end of April and the beginning of May was taken to be the calm before the storm.

In fact the Axis was in no hurry to occupy the island itself which would have been costly to take. Considering Malta neutralised they turned their attention to supporting Rommel's desert advance. If they had launched their invasion attempt then, the course of their war might have been very different. Appalled by the suffering of the Maltese, Governor Dobbie told Roger Strickland, head of the elected majority in the Council of Government, 'Strickland, I cannot ask them to suffer any more than they have.' The word reached London. Churchill sent Casey for a confidential first-hand report on the situation; Casey endorsed the recommended replacement of Dobbie by Viscount Gort, who arrived on 8 May. He was said to be more vigorous and enterprising; he was certainly afflicted with less ruth. The next day, sixty-four Spitfires were successfully delivered; this time they did not wait to be spitchered on the ground, but were immediately refuelled and armed and aloft ready to attack the raiders sent to disrupt the delivery. There were nine raids that day, some lasting more than an hour. For the whole day the air-crews stayed in the pens, flying the Spitfires in turns, while army and ground crews refuelled them from cans by hand, and re-loaded ammunition. At dawn the next day HMS *Welshman* docked with a cargo of ammunition, spare air-crews and spare engines. The battle of Malta was on again.

On 14 July, 1942, Air Vice-Marshal Hugh Lloyd welcomed his replacement, Air Vice-Marshal Keith Park, who had flown in from AHQ Egypt in a Sunderland which landed during an air-raid. According to Park, as they travelled in the car from Kalafrana to Sliema, Lloyd puffed out his chest and said, 'Now you will see how Malta can take it! Aren't we brave?' to which Park answered, 'I think you are dumb. Why don't you stop the bombing and get on with the war instead of sitting back and taking it.' In fact the turn-around was due as much to the fact that Malta now had sufficient planes to mount the offensive as it was to Park's 'Fighter Intervention Plan,' by which wave after wave of fighter planes was sent to attack raiders as soon as they took off from the airfields in southern Italy. Given the continuing shortage of everything, of fuel, planes, men and munitions, every raid had to produce a pay-off; good intelligence was an essential factor in the strategy. Park and Gort knew what Ultra could do. Ultra could both give them accurate information about enemy movements and supply phony information to the enemy about their own.

When on 25 July, 1941 (for example) 'it was learned' from Ultra that 'a surface force was approaching' the Vice-Admiral Malta chose Lieutenant Commander Carnes to decypher the Ultra information warning of the raid, telling him that 'this was in fact information from an enemy spy in Naples'. The Malta Special Liaison Unit was evidently not then in place. As a result of the Ultra information, the Vice-Admiral 'ordered all coastal gunners, including the Royal Malta Artillery, to stand-by, sleeping at their guns, ready at a moment's notice to repulse any possible raid on the Grand Harbour'. As Ultra had not been able to give further details, the whole coast was watched, and the troops guarding possible landing beaches were put on alert. So the human torpedoes of the Decima Flottiglia MAS found the Malta batteries ready and waiting for them. The operational instructions captured with the boats made no mention of what to do when encountering resistance, so completely had the planners of the raid relied upon surprise.

If the Germans were surprised at the number of times raids were intercepted and bombers sunk and fighters strafed from above or out of the eye of the sun, they did not guess what lay behind the uncanny accuracy of the attacks. They did not suspect how few planes Malta had to send after them, or how short of fuel and ammunition the island was. Official explanations stressed the expertness and daring of Malta's aerial intelligence gatherers and the excellence of their photographic reconnaissance. The truth behind the extraordinary losses that Malta's tiny Spitfire force inflicted on an enemy vastly superior in numbers and firepower was not however 'Malta's eyes' but Malta's ears. To say this is by no means to detract from the well-deserved glory of the PR squadrons, who flew accurate and dangerous missions and brought back the goods. In order to protect Ultra, all Ultra information had to be verified from another source before it could be acted upon. The most obvious way of doing this was to fly an aerial reconnaissance sortie within sight of the target before attacking it. At last Ultra was being properly used.

The Maltese housewife had no idea that superior intelligence was coming to her aid. She found clean water for her family to drink, somehow washed and mended their clothes, ran the gauntlet of the black market and the rationing, queued for everything, husbanded the meagre fuel ration, and the firewood that she and her children could scavenge from the bombed buildings, and remained cheerful and patient even when scabies and fleas and bedbugs and sandflies made their lives a misery. By the autumn of 1942 when her children began to die, the possibility that she would mutiny should have occurred to the island's leaders. One in three of the babies born in Malta in 1942 died before its first birthday. The death rate had leapt from 5,385 in 1939, to 8,603 in 1942. Pneumonia and other respiratory diseases acquired in the catacombs decimated a population that had been undernourished for months. In the autumn of 1942, as Reg Greer waited at Personnel Transit Centre No. 22, diphtheria swept through the shelters; 21 cases were recorded in the RAF itself. In July typhoid, caused by the seepage of sewage into the Ta Qali reservoir, which had been cracked by bombing, spread through from the Victory kitchens where food was prepared on a communal basis; the epidemic which raged until December afflicted 1,566 people of whom 202 died. Again, RAF personnel were afflicted in 23 cases. The most horrible epidemic, of polio-encephalitis, reached in to the heart of the officer corps of the RAF, crippling 28 men.

The most terrifying aspect of sickness in Malta was that the medical equipment that was in place before the war had worn out and not been replaced. Medical supplies were brought in by submarine but they were not adequate to cope with epidemic conditions. There was no penicillin until the end of 1942. A typhoid vaccination campaign was successful, but otherwise prognoses for the sick, even those suffering from relatively commonplace afflictions, were not good. One in eight of all the patients admitted to a Maltese hospital, civil or military, for any cause whatever in 1942 died. To the shortage of medicines and equipment was added the impossibility of maintaining hygiene given the chronic shortage of fuel and clean water. In 1942 the Maltese death rate jumped from 20 per thousand to 32 per thousand. If the extra 12 per thousand are thought of as war casualties, the number of Maltese war dead leaps from 1,500 to 4,500. Some authorities put the number of casualties much higher, in the region of 15,000, claiming that the Maltese did not always report deaths because they needed to draw the extra rations, especially given the niggardliness of the ration for larger families. One thing is certain, at the outbreak of the war the British did not know how many people lived on the islands of Malta and Gozo. Estimates of the population vary from 220,000 to 300,000.

The number of casualties civilian and military was played down all through the siege of Malta, nevertheless it was in actuality remarkably small given the scale of devastation. More people died as a result of disease and accident than as a direct result of enemy action. The only possible explanation for the fact that people were not killed during the rush to the shelters through the narrow entrance ways and down the uneven stairs in the dark is that the Maltese were aware of the feeble and young and the problems of women struggling with babies and toddlers and did not panic and trample the more slow-moving. It was a point of honour to walk to the shelter, not to run. It was in England, not in Malta, that, during a raid in March 1943, 178 people died of suffocation because a woman carrying a baby tripped and fell on her way into a shelter.

The Maltese themselves had another explanation for the low number of casualties. When on 9 April, 1942, a 500-kilo bomb fell through the roof of the crowded church in Mosta where three hundred people were waiting for the evening service of benediction, bounced off one wall, hit another, flipped down the sanctuary steps and slid the length of the floor before coming to rest by the west door, the people knew whom to thank for the fact that no one was hurt even by falling masonry. On the steps of the church lay another of the enormous bombs, it too unexploded. Two such coincidences equal a miracle. The Madonna herself, patroness of the church, had protected her devotees.

Reg Greer despised such mawkish superstition. He saw the priests moving among the people, consoling them, praying with them, calming them, and noticed only that they were sleek and well-fed compared to their hollow-eyed parishioners. He compared the wretched houses the faithful lived in with the sumptuous churches stuffed with tasteless gilding, and hated the priests whom he saw as the oppressors of the people, milking them of money they should have been using to feed, clothe, house and educate their children properly. Reg Greer was frightened of the people's Malteseness, their poverty and their piety, their lack of respect for the values of clubland.

While enemy losses mounted, anxious telegrams to Whitehall warned that the Maltese were 'now feeling the cumulative effect of shortage of food and domestic fuel'. Bread had been rationed from 6 May, at three-eighths of a *ratal* (ten and a half ounces) per head per day for all except men between the ages of sixteen and sixty who on working days could have half a *ratal*. The tenth submarine flotilla had been stood down for a much-needed rest and refit. Both the June convoys were attacked; one of them turned back to Egypt; of the other only two ships made it through from Gibraltar to Malta. Flour, fuel, ammunition were all in short supply. The situation was desperate, 'exhaustion date', as it was called in the secret telegrams sent to the Air Ministry, only weeks away.

In August Operation 'Pedestal' was mounted to cover the progress of a much bigger convoy, including the new Texaco oil-tanker *Ohio*. Despite the deployment of a dummy convoy and the support of all the Malta-based fighters and submarines, on 13 August only three of the thirteen merchant ships reached Grand Harbour; the cheering was heartfelt, but the truth was heart-breaking. The *Ohio* was not among them; she had been hit six times in all, and twice had to fall out of the convoy. The precious fuel, life-blood of Malta's resistance, had not arrived.

The next morning another merchant ship, her bows blown open by a torpedo, limped into the harbour. And on the next day, the feast of the Assumption, by another miracle of Santa Marija, came the *Ohio*, under tow, deck awash, steering gear out of action, held upright in the water by a RN destroyer on each side. The Ju88s had followed her every mile even when she came under cover of the Malta-based Spitfires; the wreckage of one of the German bombers was lying on her deck when, as her escorts nosed her into her berth, she settled on the bottom. This was the Malta convoy which ran the gauntlet of the seven hundred aircraft, three U-boats, eighteen submarines, six cruisers and ten destroyers, assisted by untold E-Boats and MTBs, that the Axis sent to intercept her. The 32,000 tons of cargo the convoy brought had cost nine merchant ships, one aircraft carrier, two cruisers and a destroyer, and many lives. At such cost Malta was able to play her part in the mounting of the second front.

In August two transport planes left by night for Cairo carrying some of the worst-affected mothers and children to a place where they could be nursed back to health. When they disembarked at Almaza, battle-hardened men wept to see them. I do not know if F/O Greer saw the pathetic procession of emaciated women and children covered with sores before it was scooped up and swept off. Even if he had, he was probably well enough 'in the picture' to know that the worst of Malta's agony was past.

Reg Greer in Malta

So stand by your glasses steady,
This world is a world of lies,
Here's a toast to the boys dead already,
And here's to the next one that dies.
ANON, 'THE AIR-GUNNERS' LAMENT'

REG GREER probably came to Malta on the 'Magic Carpet Service', provided by five of the mine-laying submarines of the First Flotilla based in Alexandria, *Porpoise, Parthian, Regent, Cachalot* and *Rorqual*. The submarines brought in petrol in their freshwater and main ballast tanks, and necessarily small supplies of kerosene, medicines, ammunition, mail and powdered milk, and passengers.

It was Mr Admans who told me that my father was taken into Malta by submarine. He found the idea of my father cooped in a submarine for an undersea journey of 820 miles hilarious. 'Reg Greer in a submarine! He must have had a stroke!' he chortled. I don't know why he thought being in a submarine would cause Reg Greer such stress; perhaps Mr Admans knew that Daddy suffered from claustrophobia. There is of course no official record of the use of submarines for the movement of Y personnel into Malta which was now effectively mined in. Daddy arrived on 13 September, the very day that the George Cross was formally presented to the people of Malta, now to be known as Malta G.C.

Reg Greer probably travelled on *Porpoise*, which was the principal carrier of the flotilla, and had lettered on her flag PCS for 'Porpoise carrying services'. The Germans were well aware of the importance of the submarines in running the blockade; in four days *Porpoise* attracted a record of 87 depth charges. Reg Greer was probably less affected by the consciousness of the risk that he was running than he was by the no-smoking rule that prevails on submarines even when the cargo is not so inflammable.

If he walked up from the docks in the luminous morning of a Mediterranean autumn he would have seen a small crowd gathered round the ruined Palace Square to witness the George Cross presentation ceremony – a bullshit parade if ever there was one. The backdrop was the ruin of the Grand Palace, open to the sky, flanked by the Casino Maltese with its cornice blown off and the roof collapsed at one corner. On the other side stood the Palace of Verdelin, abandoned now by the Civil Service Sports Club. The corps of photographers climbed on to a pile of rubble and stood together on a massive door panel blown out of one of the portals of the Magistral Palace. All the forces were represented, the Royal Navy, the RAF, the Army, the Police, the Special Constabulary, the ARP, the nurses; practically everyone was in uniform of one kind or another. Only a few of the older women wore *faldettas*, shiny, black veils held over their faces by a stiffened brim. Colour was supplied by the clergy who swept by glorious in magenta taffeta, against which the tassels of their hats burned like green flames. Viscount Gort, representing the King, solemnly presented the George Cross, the highest civilian decoration for gallantry, to Sir George Borg, the Chief Justice, resplendent in his black and gold robes, representing every man, woman and child in Malta. The crowd then dispersed quickly. The siege was not yet lifted.

As the new 'wingless wonder' fresh from the fleshpots of Egypt walked up the steps through narrow streets lined with roofless yellow stone houses piled high with rubble, he would have seen the starving dogs and cats that the householders had been unable to take with them when they moved with their families to the interior, foraging in the mess, eating paper or rag if they could find it. He would not have seen the English ladies distributing the dog biscuits that had been sent by the RSPCA from England, each one embossed with a V for victory, for the people had got to them first. He would have seen the rats liberated from the broken sewers, now running out of control inaccessibly inside the rubble, feasting on human and animal remains. He would not have known that the last outbreak of bubonic plague in Malta was only six years before. He would have seen the hollow-eyed children, infested with scabies, scavenging, trading bomb fragments. He might have seen the long lines of tins left waiting on the street corner for the arrival of the kerosene cart, and the housewives waiting patiently for their daily ration of bread or in the queue outside the Victory Kitchen. He must have seen civilians and military sifting through the bombed-out wreckage gathering every sliver of wood for cooking fires. He would have noticed the absence of cars, the uncanny silence interrupted only by the fanfares from the square. He would have marvelled at the number and the size of the churches, one in every tiny street, and shuddered at so much superstition. The damp wind called the scirocco might have been blowing, as it does most days in September.

Reg Greer may not have bothered to take a look at the presentation ceremony. He was never one for martial music and gold braid, for bacon-and-eggs and gongs. I had thought there was no other entertainment in Malta, but I reckoned without the ingenuity of the officer class. Fliers returning without drop-tanks used gin for ballast; though the Cisk brewery at Ham Run had closed down and there was no beer for the Maltese, and the Gut was no longer thronged with sailors and prostitutes but mostly dark and choked with rubble, something could always be found for 'the bloody boys in blue'.

When Fred Chappell, an Intelligence Officer with the RAF in the Western Desert, visited Malta in November 1942 he managed to have quite a pleasant time:

'More rain today and no ops because of weather ... got to know more of the local Intelligence people who are a very nice crowd. With the Wing Commander and Squadron Leader I went back to the billets and then to an evening out at the flicks, *These Glamour Girls*. The film was not bad, and two "glamour girls" tried to attract us afterwards, who were quite young girls, only fifteen to eighteen years of age.

'We went to the "Chocolate Box" and "Charlie's Bar" and had more drinks than ever before in my life – owing to the CO's "another one for the road" repeated about seven or eight times. We talked to two English girls married to civilians on the island and learned the truth of the situation. They get one tin of bully and one tin of sardines per fortnight and live mainly on bread. This explains the nasty blotches on many legs and arms of civilians. We walked back to the mess with them and gave them

167

a tin of bully, a tin of sardines and a tin of the Squadron Leader's cigarettes and so to a late meal and bed.'

Many soldiers would have envied Reg Greer his officer status and the fact that he was forbidden to place himself in any personal danger. To any member of the PBI (the Poor Bloody Infantry) Reg Greer's war would have seemed positively cushy. There was never the remotest possibility that he would have to come under fire, or kill or maim another human being. And he would have all the glamour of the RAF, a tidy uniform, a good billet in a Sliema hotel, an officers' mess where 'neat-handed Maltese girls' served and 'one reads the newspaper at breakfast', as Chappell, used to the rigours of the desert campaign, noted with astonishment. As an officer Greer would not have been expected to sleep in the poorhouse near Luqa where 890 airmen were obliged to put up. The building, which was badly damaged by bombs even before the RAF moved in, adjoined a leper colony, whose inmates were allowed to roam the district at will. This is just as it ought to be, but the airmen did not appreciate the fact. They were obliged for lack of space to sleep in three-tiered bunks, where sandfly nets could not be used; sandflies were the only species profiting by the bombing which provided ideal breeding grounds. In the RAF alone there were 322 cases of sandfly fever in 1941.

F/O Greer would have had an open invitation to all the officers-only dances, the dances that the pretty girls went to, with genuine drinks, when he was not doing his stint as a Secret and Confidential Publications Officer. The bars stayed open even during alerts; when the red flag went up the bar-tenders would dash down to the shelters, leaving the till drawer open to collect the money for the drinks that the servicemen went on drinking. Officers frequented the Union Clubs in Sliema and Valletta, or Captain Caruana's or Marich's Smoking Divan or the Monico Bar. There was plenty of live entertainment; at the Command Fair, set up in the damaged ward of the Knights' Hospital, the PBI Parade did its stuff together with the RAF entertainment officers, who called themselves the Raffians or the Fly Gang. A professional troupe marooned on Malta by the blockade called itself the Whizz Bangs and put on shows at the old police barracks in Port St Elmo. Every night one or other of the regimental bands struck up for a dance somewhere or another, or for a concert of classical music at the British Institute. There were eleven cinemas, three of them in Sliema, that showed fairly recent English and American releases, as well as the most recent propaganda movies. There were boxing tournaments at the Command Fair, and the military played soccer, rugby and Australian rules football but on 2,100 calories a day they were not playing conspicuously well.

Reg Greer probably celebrated his arrival with an attack of Malta dog, the local form of gastro-enteritis which was virulent enough to send a steady proportion of cases to hospital. It would have joined up with the gyppy tummy he had never quite got rid of, and never did get rid of, come to that. It was understood that all personnel would have stomach upsets at each change of location. The best available treatment was probably gin and lime. Rest, good food and relief from tension were in short supply. Many years later the repatriation medical services identified the chronic amoebic infestation which was the root cause of the recurrent gastric problems of returned servicemen. Until then they were all classed as idiopathic.

However he spent his time off, F/O Greer had to do his stint in the underground offices in the Lascaris Bastion. Nowadays tourists are shown tall, whitewashed chambers, where the air is kept sweet by the air-conditioning installed when they were used by NATO. These rooms were excavated at the end of 1942, to serve as ops rooms for the allied commanders during Operation 'Husky'. The rooms used by Ultra personnel lie beneath them; other signals personnel worked on the other side of the entrance tunnel. Malta limestone is easy to tunnel, for it is soft; it hardens on exposure to the air, but the surface remains friable and constantly generates dust. Worse, the stone is porous; during the rainy season water leached through the rock on its way to the underground aquifers which ensure Malta an adequate year-round supply of pure, cold water. The tunnels attracted the water like sumps; navy cypher personnel were given sea-boots as regulation issue. When Reg Greer was working under the bastion there was no ventilation in the tunnels except the natural openings in the rock face; the air was thick and damp. Mould grew on everything; within hours, clothes, shoes, papers were covered with it.

The strain of the communications work would have been terrible without the ordeal of being trapped within the airless rock. The Sigint personnel not only had to listen intently to their headphones, sorting out their signal from the general cacophony on the airwaves, but they had also to absorb bad news, and keep it to themselves. They heard the preparations for the massive raids on Grand Harbour and knew the scale of the attacks. They knew better than anyone how close the island was to exhaustion, and how close it remained even after the blockade eased, for the supplies that began to arrive were barely enough to meet present needs. They also knew the full scale of casualties and losses; guilt at not sharing the danger began to erode the efficiency of the most level-headed. The tension of intelligence work in these conditions, without the relief of action, or even of kicking up a fuss, 'getting it off your chest', took its toll, especially as tours of duty lengthened into months and even years without leave, but it did not and does not figure in accounts of war casualties.

The only other Secret and Confidential Publications Officer I know besides my father is the man who co-ordinated, in conditions of utter secrecy, the printing of one-time pads for use in the Ultra programme as it was deployed by the Allies in the Pacific. He too took an A & SD course, but he worked in the Directorate of Signals in the RAAF. His work was supposed to be meteorological; the stuff he was sending all over the Pacific theatre was supposed to be weather reports. Somehow after the war he never got quite straight; he was successful in business, he made money, but something was wrong. So seriously wrong that he had to be given colchicine. He seemed to be in pain all the time. He gave up his business. In 1961 he asked if his difficulties could be ascribed to his war service. He blamed the 'intense and incessant mental strain'; 'the nature and extent of my secret duties during World War II imposed on me, of necessity, constant very heavy mental and nervous strain with my ever-widening responsibility. It is to this that I attribute my post-war deterioration in health to its present state of complete incapacity.' Before the Repatriation Commission could decide if this man, who contributed more perhaps to the Allied victory in the Pacific than any other individual, was entitled to a pension, he was dead.

It must be a terrible business, being stuffed full of secrets, keeping a guard on your tongue day and night. 'Any way for heaven sake, So I were out of your whispering!'

Margaux Hemingway is quoted in my daily newspaper saying: 'It's the secrets you keep that make you sick.'

As I sat in the Public Record Office, reading smudgily typed top-secret telegrams, I wrote in the margin of my notebook, 'A good man cannot live with secrets. A good man cannot watch over himself even in sleep to be sure that he does not give away the secret locked around his heart which dares not murmur in its systole and diastole. The only hope is to neutralise the secret by forgetting it, but you can't do that either. Never forget, 254280, you are the custodian of a secret. You can never tell, you can never explain, you must let everybody down, you can never justify yourself. You must accept misunderstanding. You must push away the people who love you most for they are most dangerous to you. You must forget them and cleave only to your secret. Your damnable secret.'

The words are wobbly and smeared, because my hands were sweating and I felt giddy. I laid my pencil by and went out for some air. I kept on walking till I got to Kew Gardens. There was something that I was failing to see. It was right in front of me, looming over me, and I was unable to look up and recognise it. I walked away from the path, over the thin grass until I found a grove of great rustling beeches. The trippers were left behind. I sat on a mossy root and drew up my knees until I was curled against the bole of my tree with my cheek against the bark and stayed there until my heart had stopped pounding. The suspicion that Daddy had a secret gradually ebbed; the world righted itself again.

That night a terrible roaring woke me from my first sleep. The house was shuddering as the wind tried to suck it out of the ground. I did not hear the crash of the laburnum that fell against the back door or the groaning and snapping as the sycamore was torn with its roots bodily out of the ground, nor the terrible howl of the wind as the mother-goddess wielded her flail. That night my beeches and half the other trees in Kew Gardens were destroyed.

Some people are proud of secretiveness. Ronald Lewin begins his book, *Ultra Goes to War*, with a chilling story: 'A quarter of a century after she had been in charge of the Intelligence War Room in Field Marshal Alexander's Headquarters at the Royal Palace of Caserta in Italy, Judy Hutchinson began to suffer from

171

a brain haemorrhage. Her condition was critical. As she was rushed from her country home to the Oxford hospital where a long operation saved her life she was in great pain and confusion of mind. Yet when she looked back she remembered how the only fear she had felt was not about herself: it was the terror, over-riding all other concerns, that in delirium she might give away the secret of Ultra. There could hardly be more poignant evidence of the dedicated attitude that throughout the Second World War – and for three decades afterwards – guarded the most com-prehensive and effective system for penetrating an enemy's mind that has ever been evolved.'

Some people like secrets; they love knowing things that other people don't know. They specially like knowing things that other people need to know and not telling them. They like to lead people on in their ignorance, sniggering at them inside. There are men and women who only really enjoy sex if it is a guilty secret. There are others who love to hear the betrayed spouse defending a treacherous partner. There are people who cannot answer the telephone without lying; 'Just a minute. I'll see if she's in,' they say, looking 'her' right in the eye. There are people who mime in the presence of the blind. Our whole lives are lived in a tangle of telling, not telling, misleading, allowing to know, concealing, eavesdropping and collusion. When Washington said he could not tell a lie, his father must have answered, 'You had better learn.'

As Reg Greer struggled to explain his pitiable condition at Heidelberg Hospital, the Medical Officer wrote on his file: 'When posted to Malta patient found he was more affected by the food situation and working conditions than by enemy raids. The food was very poor and consisted mainly of bread with limited fats.'

When Reg Greer arrived the *Times of Malta* was running a convoy fund for the support of the families of the three hundred and fifty seamen who had lost their lives trying to relieve the island, reminding the people by such means that, however relent-less their hardship, they were at least relatively safe. Every day the *Times of Malta* carried news of the heroic resistance of Stalin-grad, and the people willingly tightened their belts still further. They were not tempted to make the invalid comparison between Malta and Stalingrad that outsiders made, because every day they were reminded of the huge loss of life among the Soviet troops and civilians. Their architecture was gone, their sewers and gas mains and electric light cables were gone, but the Maltese were alive and could rebuild it all. They gave more than £7,000 for the seamen of the convoy, and then they opened a fund for the families of RAF casualties (292 RAF personnel are buried on Malta).

The military ration in 1942 allowed for eleven ounces of bread a day, an ounce each of biscuits, flour, M and V (Meat and Veg), tinned steak-and-kidney, chocolate, tinned potatoes, processed peas, fresh fruit and margarine, and four ounces of tinned meat, and two ounces each of tinned vegetables, and fresh vegetables, and a smidgin of jam, salt, tea, and too much sugar. F/O Greer was also entitled to forty cigarettes a week, two ounces of tobacco, and one box of matches. This provision is markedly more varied than what was available to civilians, yet Reg Greer described his diet as if he had been given civilian rations.

'Meat consisted of goat and horse.'

At no time were horses slaughtered to feed the Maltese population. The only time they were lucky enough to get horse-meat to eat was when a horse had been killed by enemy action. Fuel supplies were desperately short; even Lord Gort rode around on a bicycle. For all journeys too long to be made on foot or bicycle people had to use the horse-drawn *karrozins*. At one stage an antique horse-drawn bus was serving Valletta. The owners of horses had ration cards for them; horsemeat was never on the menu at the Victory Kitchens or anywhere else. Horsemeat is especially rich in iron and can still be bought from equine butchers in the Mediterranean at a higher price than other meat.

The goats did not enjoy the favoured treatment meted to the horse. The Maltese had been told that they could not continue to keep their goats, because the little fodder available had to be reserved for the horse population. No significant improvement in fodder supplies was to be expected, as it took up far too much room in the ships on which they depended. The decision to kill the goats was probably mistaken; goats supply not only milk and cheese, but kid which is palatable, whereas goat is not. Goats can survive in desert conditions. They are by no means as fastidious about their diet as horses, and can grow fat on the thin cover of scrubby aromatic shrubs on Malta's coralline plateaux. Before the war the goatherds used to bring their goats into the cities each morning and milk them on the doorsteps, but concern about the organism that causes undulant fever which was found in their milk, led to the banning of the practice and the setting up of a pasteurisation programme. The people were strongly attached to their fresh goats' milk and persisted in buying unpasteurised milk, despite the risk of fever, long after bottled milk was available. Cheeses both fresh and aged are eaten at almost every Maltese meal, including breakfast and elevenses, but instead of goats' milk and cheese the authorities thought they would be better off with milk powder and goats' meat.

The unfortunate goatherds, who were supposed to be given thirty shillings per carcase, were cheated by middlemen who bought up their flocks for a song. The people did not normally eat goat, and nobody knew how to make it palatable, but the military authorities were convinced that feeding the poor beasts to the hungry people was the only course of action to follow. On 3 September, A. V. M. contributed a humorous poem, called 'Farewell to the Goat' to the *Times of Malta*.

> *Gone are those halcyon days when door to door*
> *(Consuming the odd newsheet on the floor)*
> *You never failed in your deliveries*
> *Of pints and pints replete with calories.*
> *Ravages of war now wrench you from us.*
> *Speed on your way to Capricornus.*

Another by an RAF poet wished the goats a happy journey 'per abattoir ad astra'. If the military authorities realised that horses will not make do with what goats are prepared to eat, or that goats milked on the doorstep are less efficient vectors of disease than powdered milk made up with water from broken mains, they never said so. They were wedded to their 'slaughter policy', probably because, being northerners, they overestimated the importance of meat in the Maltese diet. Besides, since 1905, members of the armed forces in Malta had been forbidden to consume goats' milk. On 7 October, 1942, secret telegram OZ1458 advised the Air Ministry in Whitehall that the slaughter of all animals other than draught animals would yield a thousand tons of carcase meat and postpone the exhaustion date of the Maltese population one week. For most of the year 'Harvest Day' or 'Target Date', as the exhaustion date was known for communications purposes, had never been more than a week or two away.

'Patient found he could not eat goat due to distaste for odour.'

The Maltese agreed with the patient. Goat is no more revolting than any other meat if it is properly prepared. The housewives of Malta could probably have made something of the carcase meat if they had had the fuel to cook it. Unfortunately in May it had been decided to set up Victory Kitchens for the communal preparation of food to be dished out ready-cooked into vessels brought by the people. Food can be prepared more efficiently and economically in bulk, but the results of the communal feeding programme in Malta made a bad situation very much worse. Hungry people were given food that they simply could not stomach. Deep-frozen liver was not allowed to thaw properly before being cooked at the wrong heat and speed; the result was jaw-breaking and nauseatingly bitter. The people who had paid for it threw it away. If the goats' meat had been properly hung or marinaded in a smidgin of garlic and oil or in sour goats' milk or yoghurt, or rubbed with pepper, it would not have smelled so disgusting that only the starving dogs and cats would eat it. If the meat had been minced and used as the basis for the *salsa* it would have gone further as a condiment for the hard bread ration, in one of the myriad versions of the Maltese *hobzbzeit*.

Every day the *Times of Malta* published anguished correspondence about the Victory Kitchens. People were given unequal portions, too much or too little, were told that food had run out after queueing for hours, produced evidence of waste and pilfering. People who brought an extra dish for the goats' meat (so they could give it to a starving pet or somebody who liked it) were told that everything had to be put in the same dish, slop, slop, slop in traditional army (and prison) style. *Bulguljiata* (the Maltese version of the Arab *eggeh*) made with egg-powder and beans was curdled and inedible, the beans fermented or under-cooked. The authorities answered that the cooks were all professional restaurant cooks, or navy or NAAFI cooks, which to this latter-day observer explained everything. If housewives had run the Victory Kitchens they would have known how to improvise. A committee of inspectors recommended on 22 October that the Victory Kitchens be disbanded and the food rations distributed to the people. The Governor refused, on the rather good grounds that the poor of Malta would have had no vegetables at all if what was grown on the island were sold in the open market. Even if undercooked, overcooked, half-rotten or fermented, vegetables were served to all comers by the Victory Kitchens.

'Main vegetable – carrots.'

Most of the available vegetables were not grown by the peasants who went to work their exposed fields and lay down in the shelter of their low stone walls to escape the flak when Jerry came over, but dehydrated stuff brought by the convoys. Most people found dehydrated carrots harder to tolerate than bombardment, but few can have taken repulsion to the lengths that F/O Greer did. After he left Malta he never, never allowed a carrot, no matter how succulent, to pass his lips. He would hunt out the smallest slice of carrot that had hidden under his pot-roast or insinuated itself into his Irish stew and, holding it on the tip of his fork, with his face averted, tip it onto somebody else's plate. Carrots were Daddy's Room 101.

Was it a way of forgetting, Daddy, or a ritual of remembering? Were you really reminding us, through the carrot carry-on, that you were a survivor of the Malta Siege? Or was it really unbearable for you? Did the sweet smell of carotin make your gorge rise and your bowels quake as it used to when you were anorexic in Malta? For it wasn't that you didn't have enough to eat, was it, Daddy? You had the teenage girls' affliction, didn't you? Poor Daddy, I am the last one to despise you for that. But I'm not so sure about Mr Admans.

'Patient was working 80 ft. underground in a very damp section and also very dusty. There was no air-conditioning and ventilation was poor – humidity high and also hot. Wet all day due to perspiration. Also working long hours 8-9 hours per day.'

Reg Greer never worked an afternoon in his life, except for eight months as a Secret and Confidential Publications Officer in a cavern eighty feet underground beneath the Lascaris Bastion. Some might say he just wasn't used to hard work, couldn't knuckle under, a play-boy, a spiv. But I couldn't work in the underground cavern either, although I can and usually do work many more hours than eight or nine in a day. Flight Lieutenant Morrissey who was assessing Reg Greer for his medical board in Melbourne thought he was an ordinary anxiety neurosis case, so he asked him about the strain of living through the bombardment. Daddy could have made much of that; most people thought he had been worn out and shaken to pieces by the Malta blitz. He could so easily have lied, but instead he said, 'Never had a raid nearer than half a mile at any time.' He was 'never unduly distressed by air-raids', and although he 'slept above ground' he 'might have lost six nights sleep the whole time he was there.' I only know one other person who would rather sleep above ground among the falling buildings and the flak than safe in the catacombs, who would defy the ban on placing oneself in personal danger and reject the offer of eighty feet of solid rock between oneself and the bombs. That person is I. Like Daddy I'm claustrophobic. Seriously claustrophobic. In a room without a window I can become dizzy, pass out or throw up. I wouldn't have lasted in the catacombs eight hours, let alone eight months. Claustrophobia is hereditary.

On 11 October the Luftwaffe began a last concerted attempt to contain Malta. Six hundred aircraft, bombers with fighter escort, came over in waves. The Maltese Spitfires went out to meet them, following AOC Park's policy of 'forward interception'. Between 11 and 19 October there were 250 daylight raids on Malta. Enemy losses were so heavy that German fliers developed a state of anxiety known as Malta Sickness, for despite the daily bombardment of the airfields every night the RAF continued its attacks on enemy shipping. Rommel's supply-line remained cut. On 23 October, the Eighth Army took El Alamein.

Top-secret telegrams to the Air Ministry in Whitehall began to deal with other things beside the constant begging for more Spitfires. The Director of communal feeding, Rowntree, flew to London to beg supplies of vitamins. The order went out for flour, dried meat and dried vegetables.

During the night of 7-8 November, Allied forces landed in French North Africa, covered by the Wellingtons from Luqa bombing Sicilian and Tunisian airfields. On 16 November, a convoy reached Grand Harbour intact, watched and cheered by the people standing on the rooftops of the houses still standing in Valletta and the Three Cities. The tide had turned. It was time to look to the starving, exhausted, and ill of Malta.

On 14 December, F/O Greer complained to F/L K. M. Parry of a pain in his chest. He was thin, coughing slightly, unable to concentrate, and nauseated. The MO examined his chest and sent him to Mtarfa Hospital, where he was admitted. He told them that in the last twelve weeks he had lost one and a half stone and that in the eight months since he had left Australia he had lost two and a half stone. If he had lost so much weight he would have been no more underweight than the average Maltese, but in fact he had not. On entering the service he had weighed 147 pounds; if he had lost as much weight as he claimed he would now weigh eight stone, which for a man of his height would have meant emaciation. When he was weighed in April his weight was nine stone five pounds, and again he said that he was two stone four pounds below his normal weight, which he was not. Well might Major Tunbridge, 'medical specialist', remark that the loss of weight was 'excessive for this period'. He did not say that he did not believe the patient, who in truth looked piteously thin, but he did see that the problem was not in Daddy's lungs: 'There is a serious psychological background in that this Officer finds it difficult to acclimatise himself to service conditions. His insight into this is excellent. The loss of weight is not impossible for this cause.... There is a history of diarrhoea in Egypt for a short period – but there is nothing clinically to suggest amoebiasis. If there is no complaint about this Officer regarding his work, I do consider that the effect of change of environment and possibly a change of work might be tried.'

Secret and Confidential Publications Officers cannot change their work. Captain Donivan discharged him to duty, 'Medical category unchanged'. Sigint was losing valuable personnel who became real cases of tuberculosis; a phony case of nervous cough was not going to make it. He may have been skinny, grey-faced, drawn and wrinkled, with a nervous cough and difficulty in swallowing, but nobody in Malta was actually looking well. If Reg Greer was not fit for work, then nobody was. There was a war on, after all.

The grimness of conditions for civilian support workers is illustrated by an industrial accident that befell at this time, when 'an unusual series of cases of poisoning due to petroleum vapour occurred. At this period petrol supplies were vital and it was necessary to conserve all aviation fuel; in the interests of safety, therefore, a consignment of RAF petrol tins containing 100 octane aviation fuel were being moved into a disused railway tunnel, the task being undertaken by Maltese labourers working under contract to the civil government. The men had been working for some four weeks in 12-hour shifts, with an hour's break for a meal and two other half-hour breaks during each shift. Many of the tins had, unfortunately, become damaged in transit ... and leaked slightly at the seams.... Those employed on carrying the petrol tins along the tunnel (a journey taking about 10 minutes) and then returning to the open air ... were less severely affected than those responsible for stacking the tins at the end of the tunnel.... In all some 70 persons were affected and of this number four died.... Most of the reported cases were said to have had a prodromal period of anorexia, insomnia, headache, increasing salivation followed by general fatigue, tremors and pins and needles in the limbs. This was followed in the more serious cases by mental confusion and delirium, incontinence, rapid loss of weight, in the fatal cases, a progressive mania leading to coma with convulsive athetoid movements. The milder cases complained of headache, sore throat, dyspnoea and coughing, while many fell unconscious but recovered after being in the open air for about half an hour.... It was agreed that the cause of the poisoning was excessive hours of work in an atmosphere heavily loaded with fumes from 100-octane petrol combined with a lack of proper ventilation.'

Things were rough all over, but much less rough for an officer, a newcomer, a bum-shiner and a colonial than for any one else.

Nobody mentioned claustrophobia; nobody would have thought it a real ailment if they had. As long as F/O Greer did not have TB or any other communicable disease, he was fit. The word had come down from the Air Officer Commanding that 'moral fibre' cases were to be dealt with expeditiously and with the utmost severity. Reg Greer's bid for escape from the tunnels might have worked if there had been another trained cyphers officer to take his place, but in the event he worked on for four more months.

In my notebook I wrote: 'No matter how I try, no matter how loyal I feel, I cannot make this man a hero. He was the one who lost his head when all around were keeping theirs. He tried to chicken out; he exaggerated his symptoms to the investigating officers and they believed him. He tried to impose on them; they believed him and treated him courteously, but he failed, because conditions were too grim for his malaise to be significant. Other people were working on, trying to conceal the fact that their chests were filling up with muck, and here is No. 254380 trying to get invalided out with a chest that despite his heavy smoking rings clear as a bell. They ask for sputum to examine and he can produce none. Perhaps I am having to face the fact that Daddy was a bounder. I think of Mr Adman's satiric smile and my heart fails. I remember the fear and shame in Daddy's eyes. I wonder if he could not love me any more because he had let me down.'

Why am I applying these standards to him? Why do I demand that he be gallant and brave? I don't demand that my mother be gallant and brave, do I? But yes, I do. I want both of them to be tough, dinky-di, reliable, stalwart, straight. Both of them, in fact, in their different ways, are bounders. I am a bounders' child. The blood of bounders runs in my veins.

What if, what if it was not Reg Greer who took himself off to the MO but the CO who noticed this pale and anxious man and recommended that he go for a check-up? 'Can't afford to lose you, you know.' I don't know that Reg Greer initiated all this medical brouhaha after all. Certainly he didn't come back to the MO the way most malingerers do. He went back to work and he stayed there in the sodden tunnels.

On 9 January, 1943, all places of public entertainment were closed because of the polio-encephalitis epidemic. The Merry Lads Swingers, the Gypsy Feather Orchestra, the Alaska Trio, the Rhythm Swing Orchestra, the War-Time Gang and the King's Own Orchestra had nowhere to play. The Command Fair went dark. Pilot Officer Wilkinson RAF decided, with Sergeant Don Nithsdale, producer of the PBI Parade, to entertain the troops confined to barracks with a play-reading of *Richard II* on the Information Office Radio Network. The cast was announced in the *Times of Malta* on Monday, 18 January. Besides Wilkinson and Nithsdale, it was to feature F/O Druce, Corporal Goble, Captain James, and – F/O Greer.

It was a measure of how fast I was losing faith in my father that I could only sit at my green baize covered table in the State Library of Valletta and worry that Reg Greer might have let P/O Wilkinson down. My hands shook, not only from the chill in the vast marble-paved room, lined with its carved bookshelves of chestnut wood, in which the shelving still follows the original order, and the books still wear their original calf and vellum. I went downstairs to the Café Premier, that still serves cheese pies and *ravjul* as it did before the War and during the Blitz, and ordered a cup of coffee to warm my hands, as my father might have done in the wet January of 1943. When I came up the great stone stairs again, the librarian had turned on a small blow-heater angled towards my chair. For some reason this act of simple kindness made my eyes fill with tears. Why had my father never a good word to say for these people?

The Maltese are special people. As I criss-crossed the island on the apple-green and sky-blue buses that roar and grind down pitted cart tracks thinly crusted with tarmac, I had to notice how good-humoured the people were, how courteous and considerate and respectful of the privacy of others. If the bus was crowded, people took each other's children and shopping bags on their laps. Once when there was room for only one more, I saw the people waiting at the stop consult to see who was in the biggest hurry. When they pushed her on the bus she was loaded with the shopping of the women left behind so that the food would be in time to be cooked for lunch. To be sure the Maltese are short and squat, and by no means the best-looking people in the Mediterranean – especially as respectable Maltese women now think that frizzed dyed hair and garish make-up and extremely short, tight skirts are all the go – and the fields smell of night soil, but what of it? As I roamed all over Malta and Gozo, photo-graphing wild flowers and trying to sort out my feelings about Reg Greer, I encountered a thousand examples of kindly concern without interference, of courtesy without ceremony or undue shyness. There is about Maltese people something nuggety, solid and unassuming, straight and deep, a kind of poise that comes

181

from their own certainty of who they are, the people of the rock.

Richard II was reviewed in the *Times of Malta* on 26 January. I learned to my surprise that Lieutenant R. Dickinson RNVR had played Bolingbroke to Wilkinson's Richard, and the adaptation had skipped John of Gaunt's famous 'sceptred isle' speech (which would hardly have appealed to the large numbers of Commonwealth personnel serving on Malta). The supporting cast was described as 'admirably balanced' which I take to mean that they were all pretty terrible.

Anxiety

I'm on a lorry, with a lot of other PNs ('psychoneurotics')....
I was to be reception clerk, that is, I sat in a tent at the
entrance of the Camp, with a lot of Army forms. As the PNs
came in I took down their details and put them in a file. All
day long the battle-weary soldiers filed in; I was asked the same
question, 'What are they going to do with me?' And there was
a hollow fear in each voice, some cried. God made gentle people
as well as strong ones.
SPIKE MILLIGAN, *MUSSOLINI: HIS PART IN MY DOWNFALL*

PSYCHOLOGICAL disturbances accounted for more manpower
wastage in the RAF than any other cause. Of all medical
discharges, 31 per cent were on psychiatric grounds. At first it
was thought that if the initial medical examination had been
more searching, this costly wastage of trained men could have
been avoided. The British rejected only 2 per cent of would-be
recruits on grounds of instability or unsuitable temperament,
while the Americans who used psychological testing rejected
one in seven as 'mentally or emotionally incapable of serving
effectively in a war'. Unfortunately for the argument from
inherent defect, 45 per cent of American medical discharges were
on psychiatric grounds.

It did not occur to the MOs that men capable of serving effectively in war might have been a natural minority, or that in
conditions other than those of total war they may have been a
liability. The creation of a military caste is an intensive business,
involving indoctrination and discipline over generations. All
kinds of rituals, of dress, of initiation, and a system of reinforce-
ments and rewards are needed to keep up the *esprit de corps* and
instil unreflecting loyalty. Why professional soldiers, themselves
heirs of this elaborate and self-serving system, should have
imagined that they could hew good soldiers out of conscripts in
a few weeks has never been explained. Most of the officers in fact

did not try to, but treated their infantry as an unthinking rabble, encouraged in this belief by the fact that so many of them were uneducated, provincial, working class, colonial and black.

Medical officers are not usually so well educated that they are aware of the limitations of their field of expertise. Most of them feel no reverence when confronted by vast regions of human affairs of which they know nothing. Most do not know the difference between a diagnosis and a moral judgment. They examined the men who had lost confidence, who did not sleep, who could not eat, and certainly could not attack the enemy with any gusto, and found that 58 per cent of them had 'some defect of personality'. Such a decision was way beyond their brief, which was simply, after all, to decide if these men could be useful to the Services at that time or foreseeably thereafter. The men they judged on such imperfect criteria had no way of doubting, let alone rejecting, the stigma they so blithely conferred.

In fact the sick men were suffering from what in an earlier war had been called 'shell shock' or 'battle fatigue'. The medical services of World War II found that such expressions were unpsychological and old-fashioned; what was more, they implied that falling apart was a forgivable reaction, perhaps inevitable, and opened the way for thousands of defections when things got rough. The term 'anxiety neurosis' was coined in order to throw the onus back on the soldier himself. Anxiety neurosis was not something that could afflict anyone; it afflicted people who were already a screw loose, not all there, or lacking in a mystical entity known as 'moral fibre'.

From the medicos' point of view the logic was blindingly simple and totally ineluctable. The men who fell ill were not the ones who flew most sorties, faced most danger, or even the ones closest to the blasts or the ones on the longest tours of duty. The heroes carried on; the anxiety neurosis cases were the ones who let those fellows down, by skimping their routine jobs, by insubordination, by reporting sick every other day, by not concentrating. Many of them were in safe, tedious jobs, ground crews or bumshiners, with nothing worse to worry about than bad food, interrupted sleep, loneliness combined with lack of privacy, anxiety about what was happening at home, humiliation at the hands of their superior officers and the mockery or antagonism of their peers.

Almost none of them had the satisfaction of getting a crack at the enemy; they felt that they had ruined their lives for nothing, for a stupid, pointless, drudging job in a disease-ridden hell hole on the dark side of the world. Some lost their identity behind a number and a uniform, were overwhelmed, terrified of rejection, unable to join in the verbal rough and tumble, disgusted by their comrades' ways of speaking and thinking and banding together. The medicos learned to hobnob, crawled the bars and the brothels with the men, and shared their collective contempt for the misfits.

The medical officers did not accept that a man might look on the worst that man can do to man and sicken to the soul. There was no diagnosis for a broken heart. There was no gland that secreted faith and hope, and therefore they did not see their significance. If on Malta an airman, who saw poor and ignorant people living in the lee of other men's war, surviving by shifts, by fraud and theft and capitulation to the enemy they knew, while their children sickened around them and their priests grew sleek and fat, lost his belief in the innate goodness and grandeur of human life, this was likely to be because of some mole of nature in him. The medicos' belief in an innate defect which predisposed to anxiety neurosis was not shaken by any reflection that to be an inherent defect this invisible inadequacy ought to have been evident in peacetime as well.

Nowhere in the literature do the medical services who diagnosed anxiety neurosis describe the syndrome. They talk vaguely of mental backwardness, by which they mean presumably that the men appeared not to understand what was being said to them. This may have been passive aggression, especially if what they were failing to understand were orders. Delinquency is mentioned, or 'military crime', by which they seem to mean insubordination, failure to salute, or to turn out on parade or to action stations, or going AWOL.

Flying Officer Greer did none of those things. Neither did he get drunk and fight his fellows, as many did. He simply stopped eating. In a place where nobody had enough to eat, he did not eat what there was. He was not the only one. Lord Gort himself was skin and bone after three months of Malta. Reg Greer lasted from September to December, before his condition gave cause for concern. And, after they registered the fact that he was starving himself to death, he worked another four months. When the MO had asked that he be given a change of work, he had added a rider, 'If there is no complaint about this officer's work.' Most people as ill as Reg Greer were not working efficiently and were thus putting others in jeopardy. The MO cannot have known what Reg Greer was doing; he was not given his time off but there seems to have been no complaint about his work either.

Montgomery had said that the morale of the soldier is the single most important factor in war. He placed great stress on officers making men feel wanted and valued, consulting them wherever possible, handling touchy issues with sensitivity. When soldiers mutinied Montgomery blamed their leaders; he would not blame the men on principle. His position was far from democratic, for it underemphasised the soldiers' autonomy, but against a fascist enemy it worked. Most important, Montgomery thought, was keeping the fighting man in touch with family and friends.

The medical officers agreed. When they examined men exhibiting signs of serious disturbance they almost invariably found the root cause in pre-war experiences, mostly 'domestic'. This strengthened them in their belief that the sick men were not first-grade material. Some had even had breakdowns in civil life; others, astonishingly, were *homosexual*. There was no way such bounders were going to be evacuated while better men faced the music. In Malta no psychiatric case was ever evacuated.

As an Australian intelligence officer in a British air force my father can have had few friends. There was probably not much badinage and bonhomie underground where everyone was either straining to unscramble the cacophony in their headphones or nutting out codes. Crammed into their damp airless shelter they were all spiritually alone. Many felt closer to the German wireless operators than they did to the people sitting next to them. They learned their idiosyncrasies, recognised their styles and voices. Some of the German fighter pilots joked with the invisible listeners to fighter traffic and some of the listeners wept when they heard them screaming in the cockpits of their burning planes. If Reg Greer made a single friend in Malta, he never mentioned him. To all intents and purposes this un-Australian Australian with the super-hush-hush job was completely alone.

I do not remember if we at home did our part to support him.

Perhaps we did write, and perhaps he got our letters when he was in Egypt, but it was generally understood that mail was low on the list of priorities. I do not know that any of the letters Daddy wrote to my mother ever mentioned receiving one from her.

Letters from Australia had to cross the Indian Ocean, and then to be redistributed through rather unsteady lines of communication to the forward bases. If the Japs didn't get them it seemed the Egyptians did. None of the food parcels we sent ever arrived. During the blockade post rarely got through to Malta, but when the merchantmen began to arrive in November and December of 1942 some letters from Britain should have got through. It is not so hard to have no letters when nobody else has them, but when other men are opening theirs and you have none, then the heart may pound and the throat seize up and the nervous cough start its scratching. I know we tried to send a parcel of food. I remember its being sewn up in calico and the name, rank and serial number being lettered on it in India ink. And I know Daddy didn't get it.

The military proposition, that it is not war that makes men sick, but sick men that cannot fight wars, is clearly wrong, but most of the military medical corps believed it.

The experiences that make real men also reveal many who are not real men at all. Real men are a minority even among heroes. Even the flying aces occasionally flew cautious; the more sorties they had done the more cautious they flew. They began to realise that they had more in common with the men who fell past them to crash in flames than with the brass who had ordered them to stalk and kill them. As long as they could tell themselves that it was Jerry, a something not quite human, they could hunt efficiently; once they felt glad when an enemy pilot succeeded in bailing out, the end of their ruthlessness was in sight. It was as good a time to die as any.

Military mythology has to pretend that real men are in the majority; cowards can never be allowed to feel that they might be the normal ones and the heroes the insane.

The principal cause of anxiety neurosis, according to the military, is fear, not stress. Because they insisted on associating anxiety neurosis with fear, they consistently failed to identify the most likely sufferers, who were not those exposed to most danger.

Real danger provokes a real response; the human organism goes into overdrive. Noradrenaline floods the heart, giving the frightened one a cocaine high, making him feel cool, detached, superhuman. And so the aces pulled off those legendary stunts; a Spitfire pilot coming in over Grand Harbour on a wing and a prayer, already shot up, one engine aflame, apparently unaware of serious injury, saw a floating bomb on course for a village on the periphery and, coming up under it, tipped it with his undamaged wing and sent it out to sea again. Cool was what the groundlings called this kind of thing. The pilots lost their cool when they were forced to climb down to the pace of ordinary life. Then they shuddered and wept in noradrenaline withdrawal. The MOs scratched their heads. These were brave men, no mistake, so why were they grey-faced and sweating, screaming in their dreams like the worst of the shirkers and the yellow-bellies?

Sometimes the medicos took a risk and sent the men back to flying operations. Most times it paid off. The men flew and flew effectively. Many of them were killed in the clouds, still high. The most dangerous part of any flight, especially on Malta, was landing. Not too many of the aces survived to the end of the war, and those who did had a terrible time. When the excitement ebbed, soul-deep exhaustion took its place, and then they remembered the screams of their victims, the friends they had lost, the stupid mistakes, and with all the reflection that they had had no time to do came guilt, guilt that they were still alive when so many were dead. Even Monty in the last years of his life was haunted by the thought that he had led so many to their death. When he died he said that he was going to join 'the men he killed' in North Africa.

RAF medical history is mostly concerned with the special health problems of the fliers; actually fliers were a small élite, served by a squad of earthbound individuals who outnumbered them five to one, not counting bods like non-flying Flying Officer Reg Greer. The fliers were the heroes of the squadrons, lionised, petted, praised. The fliers and the ack-ack gunners were the only ones who had the satisfaction of getting a crack at Jerry; everybody else had to sit tight and take it. The first bombardment caused shock and terror; when that subsided and people adapted to life under the bombardment, the health consequences were more insidious. The constant stress of irregular alerts, of months of interrupted sleep, and of appalling noise levels, sometimes for many hours at a stretch, gradually wore down men and women, military and civilians, the young and the old, all at differing rates and to different degrees. If men building aircraft dispersal pens or unloading ships in the harbour, or women plotting the box barrage or fighter control, became inattentive or began to doubt their efficiency and demand constant reassurance, the cause was not fear, after all, but the fact that, on a poor diet, in crowded conditions and with little sleep, they had run out of resilience and endurance. The authorities compounded their distress by accusing them of fear. They were actually too tired and too dispirited to feel fear.

Whoever wrote the Malta section of the official history of the Army Medical Services in World War II had deep reservations about the official attitude to anxiety neurosis.

'The official attitude in Malta during the period of the siege seems to have been based on the view that, when there is no escape from danger, there are no psychiatric casualties, or at least very few.... The medical specialist who had been appointed to act as the command psychiatrist suggested that an adequate survey should be made in an attempt to assess the health of the troops and that a rest centre should be established where the overstrained might rest and recuperate. These suggestions were not accepted. Later he reported that as the strain of the siege increased, mental backwardness came to be more in evidence among the out-patients who were seeking escape from the intolerable in sickness and in military crime. Indeed, he came to recognise that approximately 50 per cent of all these outpatients showed evidence of some major psychiatric disorder. In his opinion at least 25 per cent of the garrison displayed a response to aerial attack in March 1942 that bordered on the pathological. By the end of April the proportion, in his considered opinion, had increased....

'There was at this time in Malta, as elsewhere, a difference of opinion concerning the best methods of dealing with the progressive demoralisation that comes to an individual taxed beyond his endurance ... the "tough" school holds that the expression of fear in any form is a display of cowardice and should be treated as such....'

In March 1942 a sign was put up in every gun position in Malta. It said:

Fear is the weapon which the enemy employs to sabotage morale.
Anxiety neurosis is the term used by the medical profession to commercialise fear.
Anxiety neurosis is a misnomer which makes 'cold feet' appear respectable.
To give way to fear is to surrender to the enemy attack on your morale.
To admit an anxiety neurosis is to admit a state of fear which is either unreasonable or has no origin in your conception of your duty as a soldier.
If you are a man you will not permit your self-respect to admit an anxiety neurosis or to show fear.
Do not confuse fear with prudence or impulsive action with bravery. Safety first is the worst of principles.
In civil life 'anxiety neurosis' will put you 'on the club'. In battle it brings you a bayonet in the bottom and a billet in a prisoner-of-war camp.

In Malta anxiety neurosis remained a dirty expression. The MO at SSQAHQ Malta who sent Reg Greer over to Imtarfa Hospital thought he might have a serious lung infection, '*NYD chest C/O pain in the left side of chest anteriorly – 1/52 – more marked after exercise. Increasing dyspnoea past 6/12. Morning cough with expectoration and anorexia past 3/12. Loss of weight - 1 and a half in 3/13 and general malaise.*' This time Reg Greer's bout of pleurisy had moved up from 1927-8 to 'nine years ago', or 1933.

In April, Reg Greer came before the RAF medical officers at AHQ Malta; their diagnosis was that he was suffering from bronchial catarrh, not contracted in service, and 'a well-developed anxiety neurosis', which was; the date and place of origin of the second was given as Malta, December 1942. The anxiety neurosis was moreover 'aggravated by service in Malta under siege conditions and by unsatisfactory accommodation in which he was required to work'. This time the pleurisy had retreated to seventeen years before, 1926, but the treatment had taken five months in hospital. Again they noted that he had arrived in Malta during the siege and that he had lost two stone and four pounds, his weight being nine stone and five pounds. (His enlisting weight was in fact ten stone and seven pounds.) For eight months he had been working underground. His temperature and pulse were normal. He could produce no sputum for examination. He could produce very few symptoms at all. Wing-Commander Knight and Flight-Lieutenant Dowd decided that 'this Officer should be invalided from Malta and returned to Australia'.

It was a month before F/O Greer got as far on his way home as Cairo. Mr Admans came across him in the Kiwi Club. 'You look terrible,' he said. Reg Greer tore him off a strip.

'Been in Malta, jumping out of the signals truck into the slitty every time the bombers came over,' said Mr Admans, which was odd, because it was quite wrong. Mr Admans felt quite sorry for Reg Greer, as everybody felt sorry for anyone who had endured the siege of Malta, which they mostly confused with the blitz. If civilians thought that he had endured the worst that the Luftwaffe could unleash, he let them think it.

How F/O Greer got from Cairo to Bombay and then to Devlali, I cannot say. In the crowded tent city of Devlali Reg Greer probably had to endure more uncomfortable conditions than he had encountered in Malta; inadequate sanitary arrangements were made worse by the mixing of men from all theatres of the war. Disease was rife, and boredom is no relief from stress. On 22 July he was admitted to No. 1 New Zealand Hospital Ship at Bombay, 'in debilitated condition and showing signs of general exhaustion'. After sixteen days he had 'improved greatly in appearance and his general nervous stability' was 'much better'. The NZ Medical Corps Officer noted further that 'his improvement during the last two weeks is such that the prognosis appears good and with an adequate spell should be suitable for duties in Australia in accordance with his training and ability'.

At Fremantle they took another look at him and, finding him unusually fit in that he had been subjected neither to malaria nor bilharziasis nor amoebiasis, they granted him three weeks' leave and packed him off to Melbourne.

And there we met him on Spencer Street Station. My aunt

asked me, 'Do you know where you spent the night before you went to meet your father?'

'No,' I answered, a little puzzled as to why she should ask.

'With me,' she said, and waited for it to sink in.

'All night?'

'Your mother picked you up in the morning.'

'I see.'

When F/O Greer's three weeks were up, he was admitted to No. 6 RAAF Hospital at Heidelberg, and he stayed there for more than three weeks. There he was interviewed by Squadron-Leader Forgan, to whom he told the story of his life, in more detail than his wife and children had ever been given. Sick though he may have been Reg Greer remembered himself well enough to distort the truth, as I could see from his description of his newspaper career, which culminated in the impressive word 'manager'. Reg Greer was not a manager, but a rep. He continued the exaggeration of his weight loss, adding seven pounds to his enlistment weight and claiming that when he was evacuated his weight had fallen to 125 pounds. And he still allowed people to think that he had lived on Malta through the blitz.

These small lies might all be construed as permissible ploys in a bid for compassionate leave. Besides, Reg Greer was being loyal to his wife: 'He had a lot of dreams last night, dreamt someone had tried to sell his wife frocks without coupons and when he got home he was very annoyed about it. His wife has always been very dependant on him and devoted to him. Suggest relationship between dream contest and actual return from overseas with slightly modified home relationship.' Squadron-Leader Forgan was doing well but not well enough. When Reg Greer enlisted his wife was a sheltered twenty-four; she had grown up a lot in three years and had come to some of her own conclusions about life, helped by the flattery of her dancing partners. Reg Greer's home-life was not slightly modified but completely transformed. If his marriage was to survive he was going to have to work on it. Now I know that in his description of his childhood and education there was not one word of truth, now I know that his wife and child were the only kin Reg Greer could ever call his own, I know that he was lying for me.

Lies are vile things, with a horrible life of their own. They contaminate the truth that surrounds them. Looking at the record of my father's desperate lying to Squadron-Leader Forgan, I am troubled by a nagging suspicion that the anxiety neurosis was a calculated performance. Reg Greer was not just a salesman, but a crack salesman. A salesman's chief asset is his trustability. He had learnt to use the techniques of manipulation in the desperate struggle for survival during the depression; S/L Forgan was putty in his hands. 'Patient very keen to remain in RAAF,' he noted. Actually the patient was very good at conveying the impression that he was keen to remain in the RAAF at the same time that he marshalled symptoms to ensure his discharge. At Heidelberg Hospital the professionals examined his urine, his faeces, his sputum, auscultated his heart, lungs and abdomen, much the way that I have ferreted away in the archives for verification of his autobiography. ND. Nothing detected. No acid-fast facts to be found. Except that after three weeks of my mother's loving care and attention Reg Greer was losing the weight he had gained on the hospital ship.

On 11 October, 1943, the Central Medical Board agreed that F/O Greer should return to work, the kind of work that would allow him to live at home and sleep at nights in his own bed, but nine days later the patient was complaining that he could not carry on. 'He has been at work for only three days and all his anxiety symptoms have returned,' wrote S/L Forgan. 'He feels that he cannot take the responsibility or stand the long hours of work. I now consider that he is unlikely to be able to carry on in the service, and recommend his discharge on medical grounds.'

Reg Greer's war had lasted not quite two years. He joined the Returned Services League so that he could wear the badge and not be asked embarrassing questions about what he was doing in civvy street while Australians were dying in the Pacific. Everybody knew he had been on Malta during the siege, and that no more could be asked of any man. His marriage survived. On 5 February, 1945, my little sister was born. Seven months later the Japanese surrendered.

I do not know why a certain little girl mis-remembered that her father went to war early and stayed late, when he went late and left early. I do not know why the time he was gone seemed to me so long, when in fact it was so short, except that I must have missed him very much. There is a sliver of memory that snags my mind every so often: I am wheeling my little sister in her pram and the war is still on. I am aware of it, afraid of it, just there beyond the housetops. I remember that, you see, but I do not remember that when my sister was born my father was home to look after us. There were fireworks over Port Philip Bay to celebrate the armistice; I remember being allowed to stay up and watch through the long window of the 'lounge'. When the explosions began and light fell from the sky like tracer, I began to scream, certain that the invasion had begun. There were shadowy people in the dark room with me, one of whom must have been my father. But I did not recognise him.

That is the truth of it, you see. I did not recognise him.

The Overcoat

> Now Israel loved Joseph more than all his children, because he
> was the son of his old age; and he made him a coat of many
> colours.
>
> GENESIS XXXVII. 3

WHEN ONE is in the business of snatching at straws, an
overcoat is a sizeable clue. When I went up to Melbourne
University and out of the school uniform which was all the clothes
I had had, I acquired a gabardine raincoat. This was the current
version of academic subfusc, dignified, drab and clerkly. As sales-
persons say about their drearier lines, the gabardine coat went
with everything. It was rainproof. It was necessary, especially if
you had no other overcoat.

The second or third time I wore it, the coat was pinched off the
hook behind my chair in the university cafeteria while I was
table-hopping. It had cost me more than twenty pounds, and on
eight pounds a week there was no way that I was going to replace
it. The Melbourne winter was just getting underway. It is a season
of deep, intractable seaside cold, that cannot be held at bay by
walking briskly or running. The damp winds blow so cold that
the skin on your legs on the windward side goes quite numb. I
had no car, nor any prospect of one. Even if Barry Watshorn gave
me a lift in his P-type MG, and it didn't break down in Swanston
Street, the lack of a hood for it meant that the cold progressed
through my shoulderblades and into the narrow lungs I inherited
from Daddy. Still it was better than sitting in the unheated train
as it crawled the sixteen stations from Flinders Street to Mentone.
The bronchitis bacilli had a good year that year. My mother
occasionally asked me to eat in the kitchen because my breathing
was so noisy and my breath smelt so of phlegm that I was putting
the others off their food.

Then I discovered hanging in the back of Daddy's wardrobe a coat he never wore. It was hand-woven Harris tweed, pepper and salt, flecked with tiny speckles of every shade of red, and yellow, even green, that you couldn't see unless you came up and looked really close. Then the warp and weft became a sort of Highland landscape, of fells and pebble-strewn runs, of bracken and ash and rowan. Pre-war quality, it hung on me like a sack, for the weave had sagged here and there, from being sat in in a hot car, instead of striding over the moors in the mist. The coat became my uniform, too ratty for Daddy's taste, too idiosyncratic to be pinchable.

When I went walking on the cliff top in a gale one day, staggering under a load of adolescent despair, wondering if my life would ever begin, the Harris tweed coat saved my life. The cliffs had been weakened by recent rains, and hand-lettered signs from the council warned walkers to keep off. I stepped under the temporary fence and deliberately walked where the red sand-stone drooped like a stalactite over the void. I stood on the shakiest piece, asking God in my teenage arrogance to save my life if it was worth saving. There was no noise as the spur came down. I shot down the cliff face with no sound but the scratching of the low scrubby bushes that were all there was to break my fall. Suddenly the bushes stopped flashing past me, as the Harris tweed coat caught on some stump or another. I hung there by my sleeves with the coat spread out behind me. Then the spur gave and I fell again, but more slowly this time, sliding and rolling down the shallower pedestal of the cliff.

As I sat in the deep coarse sand of the beach, getting my breath back, a stone I had dislodged came bouncing down behind me and cracked me a painful blow on the head. This seemed an apt comment on the foolishness of the proceeding. Though I went through a period of reading the Sonnets in graveyards and getting *Hamlet* by heart, I did not try to gamble with my life again. And, if I should so forget myself in misery as to think again of ending it all, there was a three-cornered tear in my beloved coat to remind me.

One of my father's boon companions has sent me a letter about him. The high point of his story describes an incident in the Grosvenor, when Bill Lynch came in wearing a new coat, 'saying,

"Reg, what do you think of my new overcoat?" The reply came quickly, "It's (expletive omitted). (shithouse? ed.) Drop everything and I'll get you something much more suitable." They both then left and returned half an hour later with (certainly) a much better - and definitely dearer – outfit. That was the way Reg was. He was most fastidious, forthright (and usually right at that) but with a charm which allowed him to get his way – certainly with men. He took great pains with his own appearance – always attired "for the occasion" – whether this be striding along Collins Street or as manager of the St Kilda cricket team on Saturdays.'

So Daddy took Bill Lynch to Flinders Lane, did he and bought him a good coat at cost from the Jewish *shmatte* merchants he hated so? If only he had done as much for me. I might have had a gabardine coat as good as the one Anne Kornan carried over her arm or slung over her shoulder when her daddy dropped her off at the caf door in the Jag and every man and boy in the room rushed to hang it up for her. When I lost it, I might have been able to afford another. He let me pay full price for rubbish, and found good stuff at cost for his friends. And, when I lost my cheap and nasty coat, he did not notice that I had no coat at all. Funny.

My correspondent continues: 'I recall him saying that he was "critical" (to put it mildly) about the type of youth you were bringing to the family hearth during your University days. Anything savouring of scruffiness was alien to Reg and his own efforts to describe his feelings probably account for the brilliant essays of our wonderfully descriptive language in his daughter.' Unable to speak to me, Daddy seems to have waxed eloquent about me.

Of course all my friends 'savoured of scruffiness'; we were university students, not salesmen. Most of us had only what our parents could spare after paying for our tuition. My tuition was paid for by my scholarship. Everything else had to come out of the allowance I got as the holder of a Teachers' College Scholarship, eight pounds a week, from which my loving mother exacted a nominal rent, meaningless to her, crippling for me. To this my father added nothing, not even a trip to his mates on Flinders Lane, yet I am told he made great fun of me in my sagging tweed coat and my sloppy joes. It wasn't that he didn't notice how poorly dressed I was; he noticed and laughed at me for it. I made my own skirts and knitted my own cardigans, because once I had paid for my fares and my stockings and underwear, and my books and writing materials, there was no money left. Sometimes I bought my shoes in sales. Some of us would go into the store in worn-out shoes and leave them by the sale table, walking out in a new pair. It took a long time before the authorities worked out that they should only put out one shoe of a pair. We would tell each other when there was a cosmetic promotion and carefully husband the tiny vials of Je Reviens that were given away as samples.

What can Daddy have expected me to bring home but young men as shabby as myself? We lived so far away in the outer reaches of suburbia I was doing well to bring home any boys at all. The only dapper men of our age were spivs and lounge lizards, who would have seen nothing in me to interest them. Was Reg Greer so naive that he thought that embryo doctors and lawyers were already dressed in the three-piece chalk stripes that would be their uniform after they qualified? If Daddy was so good a judge of quality in cloth, why was he not a better judge of quality in people?

In fact Daddy met very few of the men I knew. Most of them had no car; if they took me home on the train at night, they had to walk home. I was what was known as GI, geographically impossible. There was never any suggestion, nor did it cross my mind, that I could have used my mother's car. Who would pay for driving lessons?

Bringing boys home was a high risk business. Unless I was really sure of a young man's loyalty, I could not allow him to glimpse the bizarreness of my domestic reality. As like as not we would be assailed at the door by mother wearing an old pair of underpants on her head, to protect her hair, and very little else, except the suntan for which so much was sacrificed. My best mates knew what to expect, because the satiric wit that Daddy expended on me I expended on my mother. Nevertheless she could still take their breath away. About six months after I lost my gabardine coat, Tony Archer (who said he quite enjoyed walking home the fourteen miles to St Kilda Road) and I were confronted by mother clutching a bundle of gabardine, sprouting black and white mould and smelling to high heaven.

'I know what you did with your gabardine,' she said. 'You

stuffed it in the attic.' The attic was just the sloping eave of our
Cape Cod house.

'Why would I do that, Mother?' I took the bundle and shook
it out. The coat was quite different from mine, rather better
quality in fact. 'Mine had a brown and green check flannel lining.
This has red silk. This has been up there for years.' We had
bought the house only a year before.

'Don't lie,' said Mother unabashed. She turned to Tony. 'She's
such a liar,' she said conspiratorially. 'A foul-mouthed liar.' Tony
did not doubt the foul-mouthed, but he had painful reason to
disbelieve that I was a liar. He held my hand under the table and
squeezed it so hard that my eyes smarted. Dear Tony. *In pace
requiescat.*

Queensland,
December 1987

What shall I do here, blind and fatherless?
Everyone else can see, and has a father.
                    MARINA TSVETAYEVA, *THE POET, 3*

THERE WAS still one stone left unturned. When I asked my
mother about the legend of my father's jackerooing, she came
up with two incantations. 'Googie Bassingthwaighte,' she said,
'Thargomindah and Jackson.' Thargomindah is a town in south-
western Queensland and the Bassing-thwaightes are sheep-
farmers in the Darling Downs. My mother didn't know why she
remembered these names or what they could refer to, so I went
to Australia again to find out.

Googie Bassingthwaighte, or Muir as he was christened, known
to all as Googie for reasons that no one can remember, got to
dreaming of being a cattle baron in the early twenties, and decided
that he'd like to try for a big cattle lease up in the Warrego.
'You'd better find out what it's all about,' said his dad and packed
him off from the family sheep farm at Jinghi Jinghi, where the
native grasses grow feathery and tall, to the red dust country up
near Longreach. Goog was small, 'born in a drought,' he says,
'never had much condition on me', but he was wiry and strong.
He rode in the picnic races at nine stone seven and won more
than his fair share of them. If you ask him what his best day was
he has trouble remembering whether it was the day he rode six
winners or the day he won three races on the same horse.

Nowadays he keeps no horses and he doesn't raise cattle in the
west of Queensland, for he bought a farm near his father and his
brothers when he got married and he called it after a long-
submerged memory of the Bassingthwaightes in England,

200

'Marnhull'. The Bassingthwaightes are unlike the Greers. They are calm and steady and continuous. Googie looks through the long windows of his weatherboard house out under the galvanised iron verandah to where his nephew's sheep graze on his land because his nephew's pasture has gone dry, and his grandson's utility truck roars past on his way down to the gate. His nieces and granddaughters drop in to leave treats in his refrigerator. But since Googie's wife died the grape-vines are slowly withering in the garden on the north side of the house and the flower beds have disappeared. Googie keeps no horses now. His brother is the secretary of the Racing Board and regularly tours all the country race tracks, but since drugs and big money took over Australian racing Googie has no interest. He keeps no dog, which might seem odd, but people who have worked with dogs, and loved the dogs they worked with, don't like lapdogs.

If you pet a drover's dog you'll get the rough side of his tongue. Petting will ruin a good dog, they say. An Australian kelpie, called after the first breeding bitch of the strain, will work until it drops, and it won't drop, they say, until both the drover and the mob have been dead a week. Drovers and musterers are attached to their dogs, I think, but they never pull their ears or pat them, or give them treats. Showing affection to a good dog ruins it, turns it into a flatterer and a fawner, a slobberer and a groveller, which is what most of the dogs you meet have become. A dog will rule you if you let it. If you die, of course, it's just as likely to stay by your corpse until it starves to death, when if it had any sense it would eat you and move on. Man and dog are supposed to have a wordless attachment. Perhaps my father thought of me as his kelpie. Maybe he believed a rough caress or a word of praise would have ruined me. I think it's no truer of a dog than a woman, actually.

The dogs got their revenge. They went bush and bred and now they run in packs throughout central Australia. The graziers who abandoned sheep-farming 'when the dogs got bad' blame the blacks who made no attempt to keep down their numbers on the central Australian reservations. They forgot the truth of the adage, 'Every dog will have its day.'

Nowadays Googie's a cat man. 'There's always a couple round

the house,' he said and grinned. 'I shoot the kittens when there's too many.' I looked shocked. 'Just put the saucer of milk down, kitten puts his head in, I put the barrel up against his head. Never knows what hit him.' I thought of the terrified cats I had taken to the vet to be put down, that clung to my sweater as the vet tried to pull them off and take them behind the scenes. I've begged the vets to kill them at home in my lap but either the vets won't come or when they come they prove to be clumsy with the lethal injection. If only I had the courage and the steady hand and the gun, to pour a saucer of milk and steady the barrel against an unsuspecting head. I liked Googie very much. He took himself totally unseriously, but he was game, funny, strong, uncomplaining and unexpectedly tender. He complimented me ironically on my bushcraft, when I didn't get lost driving through the fenceless properties on the Darling Downs. We both smiled bitterly at the joke, for bushcraft is now map references and sign reading.

I didn't ask him if he missed the horses, because I knew the answer. Every Australian who lives outside a city, not that there are many of them, misses the horses. The horse has gone from the Australian bush. There's not an old-timer that doesn't regret it bitterly. They'll buttonhole you in the bar and tell you, 'Two things ruined this country, the road train and the trail bike.'

The road trains are built for the wide highways and vast distances of the United States. European road trains are dinky-toys by comparison. These have enormous tractor engines with huge staring eyes and vast wheels broader in circumference than my car was high. On the narrow metalled roads of rural Australia they blast along spewing empty stubbies out of their windows. Even when I drew as far over on to the soft shoulder as I could get, the side draught lifted my Holden off the road as if it had been made of paper. These enormous gleaming missiles mow down confused kangaroos, wallaroos, wallabies, emus, sheep, and occasionally the feral pigs that feed on the corpses of all of them, even buffaloes, without knocking the ash off the driver's cigarette.

From Roma to Cunnamulla I drove through an honour guard of dead animals, mostly kangaroos that lay like sleeping schoolgirls with their elegant heads pillowed on the edge of the tarmac and their small hands tucked under their chins. Others had been knocked head first into the ground and pushed along at high speed so that their heads had completely disappeared. Around them lay huge shiny stains like varnish where the blood had dried when the sun came up. There were some that were no more than jigsaws of whitening bones, others that were parchment, some that were blue and gleaming and wore a coronet of flies, others that had been slit open by the tusks of feral pigs, others that had been spread along the road like a carpet of fur. The distance from Roma to Cunnamulla is nearly six hundred kilometres and I reckon there was a dead kangaroo for every kilometre. Sometimes the stink crept into the car and once a sated blowfly came popping out of the air-conditioning duct.

The graziers from Darby were not ruing the slaughter of marsupials and emus, by any means. As they said bitterly, 'Americans always ask us if it's true that the kangaroo is becoming extinct. It's the damn grazier that's a theatened species!' Presumably, if Darwin is right, the kangaroos that are fond of investigating the strange lights and noises on Australia's roads at night will be selected out and the species will become road shy. It is my habit to hit the road just before dawn and drive slowly to see the creatures on their way to bed. None of them seemed to realise how dangerous I was. The male kangaroos would pause and turn and come towards me as if to ask my business. Major Mitchell cockatoos, corellas, budgerigars, would stop feeding and wait politely till I had passed, raising their crests like incroyables flirting their fans. Lizards would stop crossing the road, and lift their heads to see me pull up beside them, then they would puff up or display their frills or push their tails up like spikes, imagining that their fierce display would make me vail my crest and vacate their territory. They could not understand that I was a human bullet rocketing through their ecosphere. An Australian bustard showed me why he was almost extinct, for he refused to run let alone fly, and stood by the road, a tall bird on short legs, examining me haughtily and shaking his swept-back head locks in disbelief. I pressed the button and my window slid down. 'Can't you understand how destructive I am?' I asked him softly. Again he shook his head. I discovered that if I talked softly to the animals they would pause and listen with their faces towards me. All except the emus that is. The emus would always whirl in a fantastic frou-frou of plumes and dash off, running full tilt through fence wires that parted with a noise like snapping fiddle-strings.

The road train ruined the cattle country because the road train replaced droving. The stock routes now are empty. Instead the cattle are moved east for fattening on truck beds, standing in two tiers, jammed together so they cannot fall, faint with fear and thirst. Petrol is cheap and manpower is expensive. Mostly the animals are on their way to be sold, either to a slaughtering company or to a farmer who has grass or feed lots to fatten them on. They say that when the feed is good you will still find men droving cattle down the old routes, but the people who say that have never seen it. They are the kinds of people who think one article in a Sunday supplement describes reality. 'Don't know how to do it any more,' the locals said to me at Thargo-mindah. 'Only a handful of dark boys still work with horses.' The aboriginal stockman is dying out along with his beloved horses.

The drover might be an extinct species but the jackeroo is not. These days he dashes round in a cloud of dust in a Japanese four-wheel-drive pick-up truck, usually yellow, with his Japanese trail-bike stashed on the back. The pick-up is yellow so that it can be more easily seen from the air, for the annual muster these days is made by helicopter. The jackeroo rides his fences and checks his waterholes on his trail bike and he gets his orders by radio. That now you could imagine Reg Greer doing more or less, but the notion of Reg Greer on a horse, or a bike for that matter, is laughable. Still, Reg Greer at thirty-five could well have been a different animal from Reg Greer at eighteen or twenty. Perhaps he tried the jackerooing and perhaps he failed. And perhaps the country people would remember a dark-haired skinny boy with a weak chest who kept coming off his horse. There was one thing that bore out his story, such as it was.

When he was describing his dreams to the forces' psychiatrist in 1943, Reg Greer told him that he had a recurrent nightmare about cattle running him down, 'the idea of cattle running him down,' the doctor said, and then quoted him with mildly satiric intent, 'Fierce-looking things, you know.' When I told them this at Jimbour, the assembled country-folk shouted at once, 'He's been jackerooing! He's been in a rush!'

I had simply thought it funny that a man who was frightened of cattle had been sent jackerooing. 'No,' they said, 'everybody's frightened of cattle.'

'You can be travelling with a mob, and for no reason they'll panic and wheel and rush right over you.'

Then I understood. 'Oh, a stampede,' I said stupidly.

'Yes,' they said but they would not use the fancy word. 'You can be sleeping out on the track and they'll rush right over your campsite. There's no precautions you can take, because it's completely unpredictable. The cattle can get spooked by a shadow or the weather. Or anything. And then they rush. No. Your Dad had been jackerooing all right. It was the doctor who didn't know his arse from a hole in the ground.' As usual.

'There was a drover called Jackson,' said Googie thoughtfully. 'And he used to work Cooper's Creek way and the channel country. Worked round there for years. He was one of the best. Your father'd remember if he jackerooed with him.' I reckon he would have and I reckon he'd have told us yarns about it, if he had ridden with Jackson.

Most Tasmanians who came up to central and western Queensland were not young toffs coming for the experience – according to legend one grazier used to charge jackeroos £500 a year – but shearers making the long trek up the wool track, for money. Thousands of Tasmanians crossed to the mainland and travelled north every year. The town of Longford supplied so many men (who stayed on the mainland for nine months out of the twelve) that it was known as the shearers' widow. The three Greig boys from Longford started travelling the wool track before the turn of the century, and their sons joined them when they left school. There was a Bill and a Bob in that first generation. Young Bill said, 'You could have as soon stopped me breathing as stopped me going shearing.' He was off with his father and his uncles when he was fourteen. There were six Greig boy shearers in that generation; perhaps there was a Reg among them. Shearers often worked under assumed names; some were 'wife-starvers', others were on the run from the law for one reason or another, others were avoiding creditors. The tradition of changing names came easily to the shearers, especially if they had been involved in industrial disputes and their name was out on the bush telegraph as that of a troublemaker.

It's not illegal to change your name in Australia. You can be known by any name you like and you are not obliged to register the change. You may marry, vote, take out credit cards, open bank accounts as Mickey Mouse or Albert Einstein, and thereby commit no offence, provided you are not marrying or voting for the second time. Some of the shearing confraternity used so many different names that they had difficulty remembering what name they gave the woolgrower. The publicans cashed their cheques without fuss for most of the money came back into their tills anyway; to their mates the men were known as Lofty if they were short, or Bluey if they had red hair, or Curly if their hair was straight. Those were the names that counted; when the police came looking for a name the men on the track could honestly say that they'd never heard of him, and at the same time send a message on the bush telegraph that only the wanted man would understand.

I was doing something pretty un-Australian riding down my father's mysterious past. No names, no pack-drill is the Australian way. The 'Labor' government of Bob Hawke tried to introduce the 'Australia Card', so-called in a crass attempt to deny the fact that it was that most un-Australian thing, an identity card. In a most Australian way Hawke gave the dirty work of presenting this unpopular idea to the voting public to the only woman in his cabinet. It failed and her political career ended abruptly. The information is still stored on government computers, and the cards sit in the government store in Deakin, waiting for the tide of reaction to release them on the world. Meanwhile the real rulers of the country, the media oligarchs, keep up the pressure for the destruction of the last liberty, the freedom to go bush, by reporting every case of working-class fraud, known to Australians as 'dole bludging'. I sat in my Holden, encumbered with credit cards, driving licence, car-hire agreement, passport, enough identification to satisfy the Kremlin. What if all of it was in a shonky name?

The Tasmanians, completely ID free, went by train to Adelaide and then caught the 'Ghan' to the end of the line. With them travelled their Cressy bicycles (made in Longford). Unbelievable

206

as it sounds they rode to the sheep stations on their bikes, first up to Cordilla Downs and then south through some of the most inhospitable country in the world. The distances were huge. One man travelled three thousand miles on his bike in the year. And when they got home they won all the cycle races, as William Martin Greer did at the Caledonian Games in Launceston in 1910. When the tyres wore out or the tubes finally gave way after repeated punctures from the thousand million iron-hard burrs they rode across, they bound the wheel rims with greenhide. The Tasmanians were famous for their funny men. Tall stories are a tradition on the track; Ray Watley from Tasmania told Patsy Adam Smith that 'riding a bike from Bourke my tyre wore out so I killed a tiger snake and wrapped it round the rim, shoved its tail in his mouth and off I pedalled!' The only marking of the route were the pads left by the camel trains by which the Pathans brought essential supplies to the isolated stations. If there was a dust storm or a wind the pads blew away. If the shearers got lost, they died of thirst. The dust and the glare played merry hell with their eyes.

Nowadays Australians going bush travel in four-wheel-drive leisure vehicles, with winches and cables and spotlights, with water tanks and refrigerators, with dinghies tied to the roof and trail bikes lashed on the back. The outback is tourism now. I can remember laughing when some Americans took me for a trip down a bayou in Louisiana, and winched their aluminium boat into the water and unloaded portable refrigerators and air cushions and god knows what else besides. When I was growing up you didn't spend a couple of thousand dollars before taking off for the bush; you just shot through. When town life turned too hard, men went walking the track, with nothing but a swag, a blanket, flour, sugar, tea, tobacco and a water-bottle. The swagman is extinct, I think. I've driven thousands of miles on the unsealed tracks back of Bourke and Cobar and I've never seen a single man walking the track. Nowadays if you saw a man in a bowler hat riding a bike across the spinifex you'd know you were hallucinating.

When the shearers got cars they took off in them with the hoods down, sitting on the backs of the seats like young bloods going on a works picnic. I guess that's why I took my fancy

Holden sedan with no bush extras down roads where leisure vehicles with four-wheel-drive and steel-belted radials fear to go. I didn't even have any boots with me. Perhaps I am the grand-daughter of one of those hard-arsed cyclists of long ago. I'd have been embarrassed to do a trip like that in a land-cruiser with spare wheels and water-cans on the roof. The old Tasmanian shearers would have thought I took myself too seriously by half if I had.

And here's a funny thing. The mainlanders say you can always tell a Tasmanian because he 'loses his H's at Hamilton and picks them up at Ararat'. Daddy used to do that. 'I've hearned more money than you're hever likely to,' he used to say.

Googie's niece Mary Grant and her husband Jim made me welcome as only country people can. Mary thought the best way to spread the word that we were looking for a jackeroo from the twenties called Reg Greer was to activate the bush telegraph by having a party. People came from far and wide, bringing dishes for supper, along with good humour and kindly interest. They were good talkers, as the generation that grew up before mass media always is. The result was one of the best parties I've ever been to. Mary's daughter came home from the Dalby hospital, where she was nursing, to be in the fun, but really to visit the two horses that looked on from under the trees. She was wearing a thin dress of white lawn, but she made no move to change or even to put boots on before going out to the horses. When she appeared on the white horse's back in the doorway of the house she had not bothered to saddle him either. I understood then why there was a ramp up to the back door of the kitchen; the horses were in the habit of walking through the house to say hello. A half-grown golden pullet dozed on the window sill by the kitchen sink, opening one eye and cheeping if we splashed her when we were rinsing the glasses. Nothing more different than the cruel world of the road trains could be imagined. When the beautiful girl rode her horse up to the door and looked in to greet the guests, the visitors crowded to speak to this human-animal hybrid. The horse nibbled their palms with his soft lips.

I remembered one of the few interchanges I ever had with my father that had the grammar of conversation. I had come back from staying at the Hickeys' farm in Berrigan, in the Riverina, where for the first time I had seen the Australian country-woman in her element. Mrs Hickey was usually up in the morning at five, stoked up the firestove, put the men's boots in the oven to warm, stirred the oatmeal and left it to cook, brought in the cow and milked her, fed the fowls, collected the eggs, put the heavy iron skillet on the stove and fried the bacon and put the bacon in the oven to keep hot, and broke a dozen eggs into the skillet and by then the men were down and ate and went and it was six thirty. I remember the routine because I tried it myself one morning. Mrs Hickey and the girls went along with my idea and let me get on with it, sink or swim. The men noticed nothing in particular, but when they sat down at the breakfast table that morning I was prouder than I have ever been in my life. The only problem had been the cow. I was an inexperienced milker and she didn't like my hands on her teats so first she wouldn't come to me when I called her and then I had to ask one of the girls to strip her for me. I liked milking with my head against the cow's warm flank, and the sweet Jersey smell of her and the swish of the hot milk onto the steaming bucket and the warm smooth udder in my cold morning hands, but I could not say that I was good at it. It takes practice and muscles that don't develop until you've milked a month or two.

When I came home I told Dad that these country-women were real people. If we lived in the country I reckoned Mother's energy would be absorbed, and not frittered away in flightiness. 'I didn't know women could be like that,' I said. 'Like what?' 'Resourceful, straightforward, capable, funny, proud, independent, you know.' I might have said, 'Not vain, capricious, manipulative, unreliable, girlish, affected, infantile. . . .' I might have, but I didn't. *The Female Eunuch* was not yet to be written. I was only fifteen. Daddy didn't answer that if Mother had been like that he wouldn't have fancied her. He probably didn't want me telling him he had a depraved taste in womanflesh. Nevertheless I thought it.

When the Grants' party broke up I had more invitations to stay than I could count and I'd given out even more pictures of Reg Greer with details of my quest on the back. None of these people seemed to find my quest odd or incomprehensible. Blood lines were their business. 'Follow a family likeness,' said Mary. 'Flesh and bone can't lie.' She might have been thinking of the light chestnut out under the pepper trees, a racehorse who still carried the narrow muzzle of an Arab sire a hundred generations ago. Mary herself had the wide-set blue Bassingthwaighte eyes and cheekbones; when she sat with Googie and her mother, their obvious likeness made light of the fact that all three had different surnames. Which suggests of course that I should be making this search through my father's dam rather than his sire.

Googie did not remember Reg Greer; the round blue Bassingthwaighte eyes were sad but there was no shadow of doubt in them. But the hunt was up. Between them the guests at Mary's party had connections in every part of the state and beyond. The question remained of why Reg Greer dropped Googie's name to impress the child bride, but Googie had been quite famous in the twenties and thirties when he and his horses were known on every country race track. Googie Bassingthwaighte is not a name to forget after all. Which left the second of mother's incantations to investigate.

There were fewer dead kangaroos on the road from Cunnamulla to Thargomindah, because there is little traffic going that way nowadays. On the outskirts of Cunnamulla, on the football pitch in fact, I saw my first live kangaroo of the trip. She stood astonished, wringing her tiny paws, her large ears craned towards me like radar screens. I hoped it meant that my luck was turning. As the animals and birds watched me drive quietly by in the empty blue morning, I felt my spirits rise. I would discover that Daddy was the son of the owner of the Thargomindah *Herald* maybe, I would find him riding in the picnic races in 1922, or winning a prize in a fancy dress ball or singing 'Danny-Boy' in a benefit concert. I imagined Thargomindah as a nucleus of late-Victorian buildings, a town hall, a church, a cemetery, a pub with deep verandahs. I passed wide blue lakes where brolgas and herons stalked, and groves of emerald grass where emus grazed head down like sheep, their feather skirts cut off straight at the exact level of the grass. From the distance they looked like black rocks jutting up. I saw no cattle. No vehicle passed me coming one way or the other. The first vehicle I saw belonged to the Thargomindah shire council. It was parked at the side of a floodway with the door open. A good-looking Aborigine dressed only in cotton shorts was lolling in the driver's seat with his feet on the dashboard. A younger Aborigine was washing his dog in a waterhole by the side of the causeway. They looked up and stared when they saw a middle-aged woman at the wheel of a flash town car with no 'roo bars. I stared when I saw that though Thargomindah was little more than a grid of strips of metalled road in seas of red gravel it had a by-pass. I took the by-pass because I wanted breakfast and the usual offices. Scrubbie's, which offered toilets and showers, was on the by-pass.

As I pushed open the door, a surprisingly sweet and low voice bade me good morning. It belonged to a blond woman in a leopard-spotted nylon negligée who was drinking coffee, smoking and reading the paper at a table just inside the door. She had very clear eyes of an unusual shade of grey-blue.

Her husband came up behind her and offered to cook my breakfast. Keeping her back turned to him she widened her eyes in surprise. I didn't need the strange deadness of her face and body to tell me that something was terribly wrong. As she sat down at my table for a yarn, she sighed. Then she explained in a slightly flurried way, 'I need my vitamins. I'm out. I've lost four and a half stone in six months and I took six Vitamin E a day. I think that's why I didn't go scraggy.' She pushed up the sleeve of the negligée, and indeed she hadn't gone scraggy. 'How old are you?' I asked. 'Forty-seven,' she said. 'I'm forty-nine,' said I. 'They were good years, weren't they?' she said, and laughed. The laugh erupted in a noise like a rockfall. She glanced at the dour man standing at the skillet and grimaced, as she swallowed the commotion in her chest. When the rattling and grating had subsided, she lit another cigarette. The only other person in the place was her father.

I told her my story. 'Thargomindah and Jackson,' she said. 'Well, there's a Jackson's Creek here,' she said and pointed west. 'That's where they found the oil.'

'Whose station would that have been?'

'Bill Carr's the man you want.' She got up and went straight to the telephone. 'He's there. They're not supposed to open till nine, but he's usually there by seven or so.'

I'd noticed the shire hall on my reconnaissance of the town. It wasn't hard to remember it, as the only other building of any size was the school. Up on the by-pass there was nothing but the heat ripple to impede the view, because the two service stations, of which Scrubbie's was one, stood in huge red gravel parking lots where road trains could be turned out to graze while their drivers got the nosebags on. 'Beer,' the signs said, 'Ice.' There were no road trains standing with their loads of cattle in the sun which was a mercy. Scrubbie showed me her bird book, because I was a bit puzzled about some of the jewelled oddities that had greeted me along the road. Then I went to see Mr Carr.

He showed me on his wall map that Kihee station would have been the one that could have been called 'Thargomindah and Jackson's Creek' but actually everyone knew it as Carwardine's. I asked if he had a file of the Thargomindah *Herald*. Well, not a file exactly. He had a few numbers. Three to be exact. They were preserved for posterity in a cardboard carton in the drawing office. The fine red Mulga dust that sifts in under doors and around windows, even when you don't have the kind of dust-storm that means you have to eat your dinner under a table covered with a wet sheet, had rubbed into holes the corners where the papers had been folded. 'I had some photographs,' said Mr Carr, 'but someone who thought they had a better right to them took them away.' I could not say that I was sorry that the Thargomindah archive was not still at the mercy of the Bulloo River that occasionally boils over and laps against the door sills of the Thargomindah houses or the fierce drying winds that suck the red dust up in eddies that reach tens of miles into the sky as they bowl from ridge to ridge.

Nevertheless Mr Carr's feelings were not hard to understand.

In 1876 when the town was first surveyed, divided into a hundred lots in ten blocks along five streets running up from 'Adria Esplanade' overlooking the Bulloo River, mud-brick buildings of handsome proportions were built at the intersections. The main thoroughfare was called after the founder of Thargomindah station, Dowling Street. In 1872, Vincent Dowling was speared by blacks from a community called Bitharra while mustering cattle out near what is now Wongetta. In revenge the whole community of three hundred people was massacred by state troopers. Nowadays I was told blacks avoid the place; certainly few if any black faces have ever appeared in the annual photographs taken at Thargomindah state school. It is too late now to rename the main street of Thargomindah, Bitharra Street, for nowadays nobody walks in the streets. While they were drilling for oil at Jackson's Creek things livened up a bit, but once the well is capped only a pumping station will be left out among the purple ridges to the west, an iron bird dipping its sightless bill into the underground stream.

In the 1880s it seemed that Thargomindah would have to grow, for all the cattle to the west came here to the first green pasture for thousands of miles. The *Thargomindah Herald and Cooper's Creek Advertiser* began printing in 1884. The school had 42 pupils in 1884. In 1915 someone visited the bush metropolis by Cobb and Co coach and remained impressed:

'Thargomindah has a population of about 100, a newspaper! and a good one.... A post and telegraphic office, a hospital, a State School ... a branch of the Commercial Bank of Sydney, three stores ... racing, cricket and tennis clubs, and two hotels, the Thargomindah and the Club. The town is reticulated from the artesian bore, which also drives the electric light plant which lights the town. It was curious to drive along the main street of this far western town and see lamps a-glimmer with electric light, and the stores and hotels illuminated by the light the power for generating which came from the lower regions several thousand feet below.'

The anonymous correspondent would have been even more surprised to return to this go-ahead far-western town in 1991 and find no hotel, no aerated water maker, no bookseller, no butcher, no carpenter, no chemist, no draper, no hairdresser, no newspaper (for the *Herald* folded in 1936), no watchmaker or jeweller, in fact no shops at all, when all of those things were in place in 1891. The Royal Hotel, where the Queensland governor Lord Lamington was lavishly entertained with imported wines and fresh fruit on a richly dressed table, burned down in 1906. Speedy's department store burned down in 1914, was rebuilt and burned down again in 1933, and was not rebuilt again. Two shed-like churches, Protestant and Catholic, have appeared in its place. McColl's department store simply disappeared. The Club Hotel burnt down in 1914, in 1947 and in 1972. Each time it was rebuilt more cheaply and on a reduced scale. Now it is the Club Hotel-Motel with accommodation for a handful of truck-drivers and tourists on the trail of Burke and Wills.

Nowadays Thargomindah is on a life-support machine. 'There's nobody on the land any more,' said Scrubbie's husband. 'At Nockatunga Station in the thirties there were three hundred men employed fulltime just in trapping rabbits, so that'll give you some idea.' Everyone went on the land when the Australian economy collapsed in the nineties and again in the thirties. The only memory we have of the rabbit-ohs is that sometimes at bush fairs there's a rabbit-skinning contest. I forget what the record is, less than two minutes.

Reading of the succession of new starts and false recoveries that are the history of Thargomindah, I couldn't avoid the recurring suspicion that there was more to the story than the tyranny of distance and intemperate climate. Bad diet kept the children small and ill and stupid, and dust gave them trachoma; bitter hardship explained the burial of whole families at a time in the Thargomindah graveyard. Most of them lie in unmarked graves for there was no one to mourn them and no money for a monument. But no one was left to perform the obsequies for the Bitharra people either.

As I stood on one of the blue ridges above Jackson's Creek, looking west over an endless succession of shimmering ridges, I felt a strange cold fear. This is the country that killed Burke and Wills and Hume.... Becker, Stone and Purcell died at Koorliatto waterhole. This is not just hard country, it is angry and alien.

Before I left I went to Scrubbie's for petrol. 'As soon as I can sell this place,' she said in the privacy of the blinding sun on the dusty forecourt, 'I'm getting out.' I knew what was coming. 'He's a brilliant bloke, but he's having a love affair with a Four X bottle and I won't stand for it. He's bashed me once and once is enough.'

I knew from the way he stole around the café that he was contrite, but it was a drunkard's contrition, morning contrition. I felt sorry for him, but I felt sorrier for her with her brave blond hair and her petrel-blue eyes.

'As soon as I can unload this, I'm going to my kids. I've got good kids,' she said and smiled, but the smile did not touch her eyes. She was one of my proud, independent country-women and she had been beaten. She was generous, and lively, and loving, and hard-working, and she had been beaten like a jade. Australian dogs and Australian women will work for you for years with never a kind word, but don't try beating either of them.

'Do you reckon I can take this car over the Hungerford Crossing?' I asked her.

'Have you got water?' she asked. She brought a two-litre plastic bottle full of water and off I went, through coolibah and gidyea, mulga and lignum, the car juddering over corrugations or flouncing through the kind of deep silky dust that turns to bottomless jelly in the wet. The dirt road was deeply rutted in places but by straddling the ruts I managed to keep all my wheels on the ground most of the time. Scrubbie had given me four hours to Hungerford but I made it in two. I kept an anxious eye on the sky because my attendant storm was snickering somewhere on the horizon to the south-east.

The Hungerford pub has the kind of cavernous bar that feels empty with anything less than a couple of hundred men in broad-brimmed hats and elastic-sided boots jostling for a drink. A young woman in a sleeveless pink dress pulled me a beer and put a meat pie in the microwave. The only other people there were her two boys, home from school in Cunnamulla, who were watching television rather restlessly on the other side of the vast horseshoe-shaped counter, behind which a dozen sweating barmen were meant to have been pulling beer as fast as the dry-throated drovers could swill it down in the only pub in two hundred and fifty miles. As I ate my pie, two jackeroos came in, full of excitement about the dead file snake on the road. It was big to start with, but the sun was turning it into a boa constrictor, as its wide belly swelled up with gas.

As far as I could tell, the primal elder was placated for the nonce. For several days there had been no small disasters. The bar was wood and I was leaning on it, so I felt I could make this calculation with reasonable impunity. Just to be on the safe side I thought I should top up with unleaded petrol. The hotel-keeper looked a little uneasy. I'd have to drive round the back of the pub and into his backyard where the petrol was kept in drums. 'Three weeks ago I asked for an overhead counter,' he said in disgust, as he prized the cap off a new drum. The metal tore and gashed his palm. The blood welled and began to drip. He shook it off and it dripped again. The pump did not want to fit into the hole in the top of the drum. By the time he had begun to jerk the handle back and forth, the drum, the pump, the grass around us and the tree that shaded the drums were all splattered with gore.

'It pulls a litre at a stroke,' he said. When we heard the petrol swish into the tank we began counting. I was relieved when we passed the ten-litre mark, because I hardly liked to put him to so much trouble for so little, but I knew that the tank was only a quarter down. We passed the twenty-litre mark, and then the thirty. At thirty-eight dollars' worth we stopped. I paid and turned on the ignition. The tank was exactly as it had been when I pulled up at the drums. Not a drop had gone in, despite all the swishing and splashing. It was more than I could do to go back into the pub where the hotel-keeper was at last having his hand seen to and tell him that it was all to do again. Cravenly I drove up to the twelve-foot white gate in the vermin-proof fence and let myself into New South Wales. Let the elder have his laugh, I thought. But the elder had much better up his sleeve.

There is not much to be said for driving along a red dirt track a hundred miles back of Bourke at two on a December afternoon. The sun stands directly overhead, so the light is white and hard while the shadows under the scraggy trees are black and impenetrable. The heat shudder dims the distant prospect. My only intention was to make Bourke before nightfall, for unfenced cattle country is not good to travel by night.

I had gone about sixty kilometres when ahead of me on the track between borders of low scrub I saw what looked like a white curtain. At first I thought it was dust raised by passing cattle, then that it might be smoke from a grass fire. Then I was in it and it was neither. It was ice. Sheets of ice being blown sideways across the road. The hailstones, of all sizes, rang on the metal coachwork like shot. The Holden rocked and bucketed in the wind which dragged whole bushes across the road ahead of me. On either side I could see bright orange rivers coursing the same way that I was going. Which meant I was going downhill. Into a floodway, perhaps. If I hit a confluence of stormwater racing into a depression, the car would be thrown up and over and over like a cork until it lodged in a tree fork or against a rock. I checked my seat belt.

I was thinking too hard to be frightened. I could stop; that would mean that I would not actually drive into a floodway, but as I couldn't see I didn't know whether I was in one already, in which case sitting there would mean that I would eventually be overtaken, perhaps in a matter of minutes. Besides, if the ground underneath me got waterlogged, I would not be able to drive out. There was a remote possibility that something was on the road ahead of me. I turned on the headlights and kept rolling, so that the car did not settle. As long as the corrugations were clanking underneath me I was in good shape. At least the shallow sloping shoulder of the roadway was still taking most of the run-off. I dismissed the idea of turning around; the storm, my own personal storm, had come up to meet me from the south-east. To turn back in a north-westerly direction would be to travel with it and prolong the ordeal. I concentrated on keeping the car steady on the crown of the road. The wind kept lifting up her tail, urging her to slide off into the racing vermilion mud of the storm drains. Leaves, twigs, and even branches clanged off the doors and fenders. I hoped the windscreen would hold. On and on I drove, blind and deafened in that howling, clanging frenzy, hoping the storm-system was not more than a few miles across.

Suddenly it was daylight and black-opal-blue sky above me. The harsh sunlight flashed off tinkling droplets and sheets of bright water reflected the sky's burning blue. The air was loud with birdsong. I put down the window. Behind me I could still hear the muffled roar of the storm. Every kind of animal and bird was frolicking in the water but I had to hurry if I didn't want night to overtake me on the track. Navigating on these broad stock routes is easy enough by day, but by night you can be side-tracked, literally, and drive many miles in the wrong direction and find yourself at a bore-hole in the middle of nowhere with insufficient petrol to get you on the road again. I drove as fast as I could and hoped I would not collide with any of the bandicoots and kangaroo rats and goodness-knows-whats that were leaping and skipping and dashing about in all directions. All went well until I came up to where two kangaroos were washing their faces in a puddle, an unusual sight at three-thirty in the afternoon. The female looked, turned to part the fence-wires with her little hands and hopped through. The male kangaroo pricked his ears aggressively and then jumped the wrong way, right across my road. I stood on the brake and pulled the wheel around, hoping I wouldn't broadside him.

Kangaroos are in general impossible to avoid under these circumstances, because if you swerve to avoid the leading end you usually hit some part of the tail, which whips the creature around and slams it into the car. Any broken bone and the kangaroo is doomed. Generally it's better to hit the leading end and kill the animal outright than condemn it to a slow death, fly-blown and gangrenous and savaged by pigs. The worst thing to do is to risk your own life by braking and swerving and kill yourself and the kangaroo as well. But I did it just the same. I didn't have much choice, after all. If I'd hit the 'roo without 'roo bars, I'd probably have smashed the radiator, even if I didn't end up with the 'roo through the windscreen and in my lap.

The Holden did not hold the road well at any time. On loose sand and gravel it was usually sliding without the benefit of locked wheels. This time it whipped itself round and danced back up the road in an imitation of the prince's solo in *Swan Lake*. I have never liked ballet, and I didn't enjoy this performance, except for the part where I saw the kangaroo's astonished face flash past me as he bounded over the wire fence and off through the scrub. The Holden finally came to rest half-way up an embankment. I looked out of my window at the red gravel a foot away and hoped the car would not crown her gymnastic performance by tipping all the way over. I had to think for a moment to work out which way I was facing. I was going south-south-east, therefore I had been driving away from the sun. At first the car wouldn't start, and I thought I'd knocked out the transmission. Then I remembered to put her in park. She slid down the embankment, agreed to turn round in the road after some argument, and we were off again to Bourke.

I had done it. I had broken the primal elder's curse. I hadn't hit the kangaroo. Nor did I hit anything else until the Holden climbed up on to a tarmac road just north of Bourke and I increased my speed. A flock of galahs feeding beside the road rose and flew directly towards me. One hit the windscreen right between my eyes and bounced off dead as a doornail in a storm of pink and grey feathers. I had a chip out of the windscreen to remind me that it was back to square one. It was just like the witches in *Macbeth*, I thought. Though my bark could not be lost, yet it could be tempest-tossed. The old boy's trying his best to put me off, but he won't let me come to any real harm. And so he didn't, but by the time I reached the sea at Lake Tyers I had accounted for three wagtails, seven galahs, a yellow finch-like thing, three peewees and a large black dog. I think the large black dog must have been an apparition, because it shot out of a suburban garden to bark at my wheels, but its brakes failed and I hit it fair and square with my off-side fender. It rolled and bounced over and over, wriggling in mid-air. I was sure I had broken its back. Then it got to its feet and ran off. I reversed back up the road but there was no sign of it. No sign of it at all.

As I sat staring into the gateway the black dog had shot out of, I remembered a strange thing Daddy did once. A dog had run out of a gateway to bark at our car, and Daddy had jerked the wheel so the back of the car swung round and clipped the dog on the muzzle. 'Teach that dog a lesson he'll never forget,' said our father as we children sat horrified and silent, never to forget the soft scrabbling thump and the dog's screaming. We never had a dog when I lived at home, and I have never been at ease with dogs. My brother had a dog, but then my brother had everything. My brother got into Daddy's bed every morning of his life until he was at least twelve years old. Daddy mightn't have been able to hug me, but he had no difficulty doting on my brother. Perhaps my brother was a lapdog, and I was the kelpie.

Sidetrack

My soul saith: I have sought
  For a home that is not gained,
I have spent yet nothing bought,
  Have laboured but not attained;
My pride strove to mount and grow,
  And hath but dwindled down;
My love sought love, and lo!
  Hath not attained its crown.
CHRISTINA ROSSETTI, 'I WILL LIFT UP MINE EYES UNTO THE HILLS'

THERE WAS of course no sign of Reg Greer in Queensland, even though I had stopped asking after him by name and begun using a photograph. 'Do you know this man?' I wrote on the back of a picture of him taken not long after the war, in a Prince of Wales tweed suit, holding a cigarette with the burning end cupped in his palm. I read somewhere that men who have been in prison smoke in this furtive way. People suggested that I send the picture to the Stockmen's Hall of Fame, where it would come to the attention of all and any who had handled cattle or sheep in the Australian outback, but I spared myself this embarrassment. Instead I wandered off on a strange pilgrimage to Greer territories, in southern Queensland, in far inland New South Wales, dropping down through the wine growing district to Rutherglen and across to the coast at Eden.

The Eden Greers were part of a network that had spread out from Bombala in the Kosciusko High Plains. I went from the Southern Ocean up over the Great Dividing Range through fifty miles of state forest, where the bees worked loudly in the gum-blossom. Gum-blossom is not like other blossom. For one thing it has no petals, but only a froth of stamens like a star-burst from the rim of the calyx. Those stamens can be any shade from the milkiest cream to arterial or even venous red, and always the green of the leaves is the perfect complement, black green to foil

220

mother-of-pearl pink, blue-grey green for the corals and mahogany green for the brightest reds. You may see eucalypts growing all over the world, but you will not see these flowering mountain gums anywhere but in their own land.

Eucalypts cover most of northern Portugal and carpet the hills of Minas Gerais in Brazil, where they provide charcoal for the smelters; eucalypts provide all the firewood that is left in northern Ethiopia; eucalypts are grown in reafforestation schemes all over India; eucalypts shade the swimming pools in Beverly Hills. Cheap, fast-growing and inedible, eucalypts are exacting Australia's revenge for the despoliation and corruption of her territory. As fast as the human inhabitants can chop them down, the single species favoured for government forestry schemes coppice and creep on until miles and miles are covered with nothing but them. They drive out all native species and establish a dreary monoculture of one grey green in which the native creatures can find nothing to like.

The fact that Ethiopia has a fixed capital is directly due to *Eucalyptus globulus*. The Emperors had been in the habit of moving on when their huge entourage had exhausted local supplies of firewood. A Frenchman, Mondon Vidaye, suggested to Emperor Menilek that he could establish a permanent court at Addis Ababa if he planted *Eucalyptus globulus*, the Blue Gum, which would coppice faster than his entourage could use it up. He did not explain that in order to grow so fast *Eucalyptus globulus* uses up all the moisture in the fragile topsoil. It has now lost its place as tree of choice for reafforestation schemes, too late to save the landscape. For many miles in all directions radiating from Addis Ababa the hills are dressed in uniform drab military green. The gums are easy to propagate; people in desperate need of firewood are increasing the area under eucalypts, despite government policy. The native forest has been driven out forever; in place of hundreds of species there is now one, that every year eats up more hectares, dries out more topsoil and accelerates the disintegration of the Ethiopian ecology.

In the Kosciusko High Plains a single eucalypt species does not march like a cloned army over the slopes. The species that grow on a western slope are quite different from those that face them on an eastern slope; the species that grow at the bottom of the ravine are quite different to the ones that defy the winds on the ridges. The species that grow in sand are different from those growing on rock or in mud. There are tall gums, squat gums, straight gums, contorted gums, gums with smooth silver trunks, gums with cragged coats of iron grey, paper barks, and gums with boles redder than blood. Beneath the trees the papery Helichrysums glisten like blobs of fresh chrome-yellow paint.

I passed a wombat, who had foolishly desired something on the other side of the good metalled road, which is a short cut to the white beaches that stretch for two hundred miles along the Gippsland coast. Occasionally a battered old gas guzzler, crammed with naked boys and piled high with surfboards, barrelled past me, bouncing from side to side as it hit the capricious camber which is a feature of Australian road building. The wombat, who travels at half a mile an hour, never had a chance.

For more than an hour I tooled along the switchback road, eating nectarines and gaping into the scribbles and scrolls of bush. Over-arching branches broke the glare of the white summer sky to a soft dappled gloom that hummed and buzzed and rustled with activity. Then the car climbed the last slope and shot out on to the plateau. I stood on the brakes, blinded by sun-dazzle.

The tangled coat of vegetation was gone, torn off, wrenched out, burnt off, grubbed out. The blunt peaks of the ancient hills of the Great Dividing Range were nude; the dimples and groins between them were open to the sky, as obscene as shaven crotches. The curves of the exposed earth were criss-crossed with linear scarifications where some giant machine had gashed the ground into long cicatrices pimpled with green. The raised dots in this obscene tattoo were hundreds of thousands of shiny infant trees. I knew their parents well; they were millions of descendants of the *Pinus radiata* that can be seen in vast tracts of dead black-green at Cape Otway, battening on the rains that blow year in year out from Antarctica.

At Myrtleford during the Depression gangs of men were employed in a beneficent public works project to rip out the native hardwoods that clothe the Australian alps and replace them with commercially valuable timber. Into the exposed earth they stuck *Pinus radiata*. The creatures that fed on the eucalypt and its berries withdrew before the rage of the loggers. They did not venture into the plantations where the sun blazed down and the winds tore and the rain dug. The pines grew, tall and very close together. Under their sparse black branches the fallen needles accumulated but nothing grew in the dry darkness. Even the spiders moved on, for where there is no nectar and no pollen no bugs fly.

This field of blood, one of many scattered around south-eastern Australia, is called Rockton. Between the scarified squares, yellow roads had been gashed out. There are no weeds, no birds, just wheel tracks and the huge indifferent sky, which stretched down below eye level on every side. Beside the naked hectares stood hectares clothed in six feet of bottle green, and hectares clothed in twelve feet of greenish black. As the Holden scuttled down the creases of the hills, the sky line would show pinked like a saw blade against the white sky. They say that before the graziers tore off the natural vegetation so that Australia could live on the sheep's back, there was no frost in these parts. Orchids lived safe in the forest and bees worked all the year round.

Stupefied I asked myself why no native timber had been found for commercial use. Perhaps if we grew some natives in places like Rockton the environment would not die so utterly, Perhaps then there would be flowers in the forest and honey. Stupid of me. Of course the native trees would be accompanied by creepers and undergrowth and the creatures who dwell in forests. Loggers do not want triple canopy. They want uniform, upright, Teutonic trees that grow fast and straight and do as they are told. Native trees like native people do not understand or care for the profit motive. They are not clean and tidy. They drop their bark and bleed rich gums and harbour bees and termites and small furry things that sleep all day and carouse all night. Loggers want tall, fast-growing straight-grained trees that will neither blunt their axes, nor split. As I crept out of this sad place with its blind regiments of foreign trees growing desperately towards the light so that in their finest hour they could be chipped, I wondered why the Aborigines did not bring their firesticks and burn the lot.

The primary purpose of these dreary plantations of Monterey pines is to provide the newsprint for the worst newspapers in the world. My father's old boss, Sir Keith Murdoch, pioneered their development. The woodchip industry does not demand Monterey pine evidently, for the Japanese firm of Harris Daishowa would be perfectly happy to clear fell three million hectares of Australian forest, wildflowers, wombats and all. So happy are they at the prospect they gave $10,000 donations to the electoral campaigns of both sides at the last election. When the Labor government decided to declare the forest a World Heritage area, the Japanese asked for their money back, which was embarrassing because the ALP president had forgotten to declare the gift, as required by law.

I found my Greer, the founder of a dynasty of boat-builders, fishermen and poor farmers, resting in Bombala graveyard under a sober white marble stone. I did not find a stone that said 'Emma Rachel, beloved wife of Robert Greer' or any other Greer memorial. I did find bright pink oxalis, and pinker bell-bine. I found *Lychnis coronaria* in both kinds, the white-flowered and the magenta. I found the orange pimpernel and Soft Urospermum that made a clock as big as a grapefruit. There were two kinds of verbena, the kind called Paterson's Curse which has ruined great tracts of grazing lands, and the creeping kind that makes purple mile after mile of central and western New South Wales and southern Queensland. Only a handful of native plants grew in that upland meadow. Their clear china blue seemed almost grey among the bright stars of the European flowers, hot yellow, magenta and purple as they were. My Greer had left no descendants in Bombala, but the escapees from his wife's flower garden had made the entire district their own for ever more.

In the Australian alps I found dells filled with lupins, bearing huge panicles loaded with perfect flowers that would win prizes at Chelsea, just as European girls naturalised in Australia have won the Miss World Competition. In other dells I found Martagon lilies. These were welcome immigrants, perhaps, but the sweet-briars, blackberries, gorse and teasel that came with them have ruined thousands of miles of parkland.

In all the cemeteries I visited in this demented pilgrimage I saw the initial invasion re-enacted as the flowers planted on the graves escaped through the railings and took off. In Maldon cemetery, where two separate Greer strains are buried, some of the bereaved had planted spindly little cypresses inside the ornamental railings of their family plots. The people who planted them are long gone and buried otherwheres, but the cypresses have grown to giant proportions, until they have burst the railings, and shattered the head-stones. The dead lie crushed under vast grey roots each bigger than a full-grown man, bearing up an enormous column of grey wood twenty-five feet in girth. In other plots the head-stones and the railings have disappeared under a mountain of brambles, on which the dog rose blooms for a day or two in spring. Oleanders twenty feet across feed on the rare organic material furnished by human hair and bone. Scented geraniums, grown hard and odourless, have seeded themselves for miles. I have found their descendants growing behind the ocean dunes at Sydenham inlet.

Along the road to Cooma grow spires of vivid blue Viper's Bugloss, more spectacular here than ever it is in Europe, where it is only found in wild places clutching the scree. Most Australians think it is a native, but they should know from the very density with which it grows, crowding out all competing vegetation, that it is an invader. In Australia, Viper's Bugloss grows more compact, and brighter green, with many more florets on the stem. The flowers are always blue with red stamens, instead of budding pink and turning blue, as they do in Europe. Alongside the tracts of *Echium vulgare*, you can see tall spires of *Verbascum phoenicium*, and *Verbascum thapsiformis*, both the same unnatural height, with new spathes appearing among the ruins of old ones, because they never die down properly and lose their old vegetation. In that same upland pasture country you can find sea-holly, and thistles, miles and miles of thistles, which graziers are obliged by law to eradicate, but the struggle is unequal. The pastoral industry staggers from crisis to crisis, unable to concern itself with minor details like the loss of thousands of cleared hectares to bulrushes and noxious weeds.

The story is an old one. 'To clear this land,' wrote a Quaker settler in Tasmania in 1887, 'that is, to ring the large trees, fell the small ones and burn off the scrub and sow it with grass seed, cost altogether about three pounds per acre, but if the burn off is successful, sufficient is realised from the first crop of grass seed, when cut and threshed, to pay the expenses of the clearing. But it is many years before the ground is anything like clear as the large trees will stand when rung thirty or forty years and in fact

225

the settlers do not want to see them fall, as they take up so much room when lying on the ground and they will not burn until they are rotten and the labour of splitting them up is too great unless there is a market for the wood close at hand and means of getting the wood to it.'

The more energetic settlers destroyed the stumps of felled trees with gunpowder. 'A hole is bored with a two inch auger about four feet into the stump and into this about two pounds of powder are poured and this in exploding rends the stumps to pieces.' The others simply ring-barked them and left them standing till they fell, and then burnt them more or less. The results of these techniques can be seen all over Australia, where tree trunks and jagged stumps litter the degraded grasslands, long since given over to brambles and bulrushes.

The process was well advanced when our Quaker observer (who married a Greer from Ulster) was building his home in Tasmania in the 1870s. 'The sweet briar is a great trouble here. W. S. says it costs him a hundred pounds a year rooting it up. The cattle eat the hips and drop the seeds all over the field and they spring up everywhere. They generally wait until they are well-grown and then pass a chain around the bush and put a yoke of oxen to it and drag it bodily out of the ground.' In the prime pasture land of the Derwent Valley, farmers are now using herbicides and 245T to get rid of the weeds. All along the road-sides writhe scorched hawthorns and dog-roses, interspersed with clumps of fennel, swollen into gross yellow crozier shapes by the action of the poison.

The settlers soon realised that in inadvertently bringing with them thistles and ragwort they had made a serious mistake. As mile after mile of the land they had toiled to clear was taken over by thistles, the government brought in the Eradication of Thistles Act. A few years later, ragwort, *Senecio jacobea*, was declared a thistle in the meaning of the act. Then brambles were added to the list of noxious weeds, then prickly pear, which spread over 60,000 acres of arable land in Queensland alone. If the settlers had been in search of *Lebensraum*, the opportunist plants had far more capacity for exploiting it. In Europe, intensive farming can keep any weed from disrupting the ecological balance, but in Australia farms in order to be profitable have to be many times bigger than the average European smallholding. The weeds fought back. Most of the families who took up selections on Australia eventually abandoned them. If they were not defeated by noxious weeds, indigenous insects, and animal diseases, they were finally unable to mechanise or to tool up to modern hygiene and quality-control requirements.

No nation of independent farmers ever existed in Australia, despite policies of giving farming leases to virtually all who asked for them, returned soldiers, free settlers, new migrants. My Danish, Swiss-Italian and Irish ancestors were driven like most of the settlers by land hunger, but none of them remained on the land for more than a generation. Where they farmed abandoned fences hang in disrepair. Old sheep pens sag under tons of brambles. Felled trees lie higgledy-piggledy and tree stumps stand like tombstones. Between them grow acres of thistles and ragwort. Old fruit trees have turned to thickets of sterile branches choked with dead wood. The roses have escaped from the flower garden and turned to dog-roses growing in murderous thorn-bursts up and down the abandoned pastures.

More St John's Wort grows in the mountains near Beechworth than in all of England. The light shade of the eucalyptus woods and the frost protection they provide constitute an ideal environment. In Europe it grows in clumps in abandoned farmland and as an occasional in woods, but in Victoria it grows as a carpet, miles and miles of rusty yellow under the trees. By Christmas its flowering period is already over, but no natives overwhelm its spent flower heads, for all the nutrient in the fragile soil has gone to produce their brief blaze. There is no point in walking in these woods, for here there is nothing but St John's Wort to see. In Europe St John's Wort (*Hypericum perforatum*) is a welcome thing, a useful medicinal for man and beast. In Italy cows used to be given a nosegay of St John's Wort and garlic to eat at the feast of St John to clear their blood. Perhaps the early settlers brought it with them as a useful herb, not knowing that the aborigine pharmacopeia was at least as sophisticated as their own. When it became dominant their medicinal became poisonous.

Some of the farmers say that the opportunists do well for the first few years, but they overload the ecology and quickly exhaust the soil. As suddenly as they appear, they disappear. They might of course say the same about themselves. Australia used to live on the sheep's back, but sheep ate out the grasslands, whether produced by clearing scrub and forest, or natural. They nibbled away the groundcover and their hard pointed feet compacted the earth. The wind and the rain did the rest. Even today, sheep farmers run too many sheep to the acre, but costs of manpower, equipment and transport are high. The Australian shearer is the fastest and cuts the closest in the world, but his price, a mere $110 per hundred, is too high. The wool-growers are experimenting with a protein which administered in the right amount will make the sheep's fleeces fall off.

Nobody cares, least of all the grazier, if the shearer becomes extinct. There is no way of life to defend; the shearer himself was an itinerant worker who lived in a town when he was not on the wool-track. The most important consideration in Australia is to keep the profit margin wide enough to support the grazier's lifestyle. The shearer's job demands massive strength, endurance and skill, but the combination cannot earn him what the lessee of the land, who may spend less time on his estate than the shearer does, considers to be his just reward. Even if he manages to make the shearer redundant, it is unlikely that the grazier can continue to live in the old way off his wool cheque, educating his children in private schools and travelling abroad whenever he wishes. The Minister for Commerce, Industry and Development says that the independent graziers are a luxury. Like it or not, they will eventually have to sell out to big business. Corporate farming will manage far vaster tracts of land and will be able to move the sheep population in a more rational manner so that no area is degraded or eaten out. This could mean that the white man is learning the wisdom of the aborigine use of the land, but he will be able to make only limited use of his new understanding. Even if he were to acquire a taste for goanna meat and witchetty grubs, or anything else that Australia produces naturally (besides seafood) the white man could not live off them, because, like the Viper's Bugloss and the St John's Wort, he is too prolific and too greedy. When the corporate farmers seed their pasture, they will seed it with European and American trefoils, and they will not herd emus but sheep.

One of the assumptions underlying the celebration of the two hundredth anniversary of the First Fleet as a 'Bi-centennial' or Australia's birthday is that it was fortunate for the island continent that British people attended to its exploitation. 'If we hadn't settled,' the revellers snarl, 'someone else would have. Whaddyareckon would have happened to this country if the Chinese or the Indians had taken it over?' It is a curious fact that the 'Afghans' who ran the camel trains that kept the outback settlers alive, who were mostly Pathans, survived in the deserts where well-equipped explorers died, because they lived as equals with Aborigines and learned from them. They developed a cuisine which used native plants, and adapted aborigine technology in the finding and preparation of food. And they endured the same obloquy as the Aborigines. If their descendants had flourished, multiplied and become dominant, Australia might have developed a completely distinct ecology and economy, producing new foodstuffs for the vast Asian market, instead of the beef, and wool, and uranium that have been extracted at such cost.

Nemesis

But the Absolute Truth is so large, and human opinion so
small, that the latter cannot get away altogether, however
eccentric its course may be; indeed the more elongated the
orbit of Error, the greater chance of its being swallowed up by
the scorching Truth, on its return trip.
                                    'TOM COLLINS', *SUCH IS LIFE*

YOU MIGHT be excused for thinking that with all this wandering around gazing at wildflowers and trees and rumi-
nating – I'd say meditating but the word has been debased – I
was getting nowhere. I think now that I was paying my last
respects to my father's lie. The five-thousand-mile funeral procession from Brisbane to Melbourne to Alice Springs, to Perth
and back to Sydney, was extremely costly. When I fetched up in
the spare room in Margaret's house, with the usual mug of
gardenias and forget-me-nots and Cecil Brunner roses on the
night table, and my godson's drawings and photographs on the
walls, I knew that if Reg Greer had been a Greer I would have
found him. I thought that was all I knew, even though my god-
daughter liked to tease me by calling me Greeney. I had kept an
eye on the Greeneys; I knew exactly where to find them in the
record, but I refused to look. It was time for the women whose
eyes are terrible to take a hand.

The letter from my father's old secretary came out of the blue.
Seeing as Joyce had worked for my father before I was born, I
was surprised to recognise her name. The primal elder intervened;
her letter disappeared. (I put it down to the primal elder's mischief
that as I roamed the outback I had lost two rolls of film, three
pairs of glasses, all my photographs of my father, and my copy
of my parents' wedding certificate, and that the copies of documents that I mailed back to England took five months to arrive.)
I found Joyce in the telephone directory.

Since my arrival in Sydney the weather had been boisterous and unpredictable. As I set off for Elizabeth Bay Road the sky lay on my head like an army blanket. The air smelt used and spent. The car's air-conditioning blew cold on my arms and legs, filmed with uneasy sweat. I turned it off and opened the window. Still the sweat ran into my eyes.

I figured that I knew Joyce's name from my parents' conversations, probably because she had scaled the highest pinnacle of female aspiration and become an international air-hostess. She is still a pretty lady, dressed for her visitor that day in a black sleeveless top and a pleated white skirt printed with spidery black scribbles. Although she has not quite got used to her new hip, she wore high heels and a long necklace of huge blood-red beads. She had the wine ready chilled, although it was tea-time. I'd been playing Scrabble with Ruthy and Margaret and Hannah, and drinking the champagne left over from my birthday party. The last thing I fancied was more wine, but I could see that she was looking forward to it, so I took some too. Besides, she was a little bit nervous, and I didn't want to play Torquemada.

Joyce wanted me to get the feeling of the way it was in Daddy's office in Newspaper House, with its art deco woodwork. The secretary sat inside a sort of balustrade with a swing door. Inside were the small office where Gerry Bednall sat doing his crosswords, and trying to ignore the horseplay outside, and Daddy's larger office, with the books of art nudes in the desk drawer, and what seemed to me as a little girl an enormous expanse of green carpet.

'No, I don't think he had a car,' said Joyce. 'He lived so close you see, just there in Hotham Street. The man who had the job before him was English. I suppose I thought your father was English too. The reps were a bunch of characters; they'd all troop off to coffee in the morning, all except Gerry. He was a nice man but he wasn't part of the coffee clatters. All the reps'd go off for coffee together at eleven, and they'd make jokes about whatever story was in the news. Then your father'd come back into the office and he'd have made up a whole series of Confucius say jokes. They were all the rage then, Confucius say, you know?

'Your father loved to talk, always teasing, and joking and playing silly pranks. They'd egg each other on. Blue Langley, Jim

Shave from the *Courier Mail* ... Alec Mackay. You could see Alec Mackay meant to get ahead. Dudley Ward, now he was a delightful man. His family was posh; his mother lived at Cliveden, which was a private hotel at the top of Collins Street. He worked for the *Bulletin*, younger than the other reps. He got on very well with Reg. Alec Mackay used to have a go at your father. "You'd know all about that, Reg, wouldn't you?" he'd say. Oh, Reg didn't like that at all. He'd throw his head back and give you that haughty look. He looked like Basil Rathbone, but that's before your time. They'd go out to lunch, and then tea in the afternoon and at five o'clock they'd all go over the road for drinks at the Australia.'

'One of his old yoke-fellows told me once that Reg Greer never worked an afternoon in his life.'

'I don't think that's quite fair,' said Joyce. 'Your father had to chase the agencies up, you know, and send the block of the ad or the matrix off to Spencer Street. And he had to compile a monthly report. He always came back into the office of an afternoon because he was scared there'd have been a call from Adelaide.'

'I thought that job was mostly romancing clients.'

'Well, he had an expense account. He had to lunch the account executive when the new contract was falling due. And he did use it, because I used to have to make up his expenses claims. But it wasn't a hard job, by any means. The agencies knew they'd have to take space in the *Advertiser*, and that was all there was to it.

'The reps were always horsing around, but not Mr Bednall. He was a nice man, with beautiful handwriting. I went out to his house and had dinner with his family. They were lovely people, distinguished. All the children did really well. He didn't get on with your father.'

Joyce had to get up out of her seat to turn on the fan. She had been swimming and had hurried back to shower and change for my visit. The lowering sky that I brought with me had closed over the little flat like an anaesthetist's mask. I could see that she was very uncomfortable but I made no reference to it. She was a real working girl, uncomplaining, staunch and straightforward. And there was something she wanted to say to me. As yet I had no inkling what it was.

'Your father was always scared there'd be a call from Lloyd Dumas, Sir Lloyd he was later.' (I never heard Daddy refer to him as anything else.) 'Sir Lloyd didn't smile much. Your father was engaged to your mother then. Your mother used to come into the office sometimes in the late afternoon. She seemed very impressed by the office. All carried away by the glamour. It was quite swish, I suppose. I was getting thirty shillings a week, and the usual wage for that kind of work was a guinea, so it was well paid. That was the hey-day of newspaper advertising and it was quite glamorous. Your mother was always very smartly dressed, wonderful little hats, you know. A milliner, wasn't she? Very striking. Slim. Tall.'

'And a lot of lipstick.'

Joyce laughed. 'A lot of lipstick. I remember your father had to go and take instruction sometimes at the church. "I don't know why I'm doing this," he'd say.'

Joyce paused, then she said rather hurriedly, 'Your father was a sensual man.' For a second I thought she meant an *homme moyen sensuel*, then I cottoned on. She caught my expression of dawning surprise, and explained, 'He flirted a lot. Flirted with everyone.'

'Joyce, you mean he made passes.' Suddenly we were just two working women discussing an employer.

'The Bull women all have big bosoms,' she said. 'They were always making references. I just laughed it off, but your father was always brushing past me. I was just a kid. Only sixteen. Wasn't even allowed to go out at night, unless my father knew where I was going and who with. We usually went out as a family, to movies and live shows. And Dad had explained to us what men were like. We weren't sheltered or anything. We just weren't silly. He'd take us to the Tivoli, anywhere, and we'd get the risqué jokes and all that. Once or twice I came into the office too quietly and I'd hear your father and his mates talking dirty in his office, and I'd just go out again and come in making a bit more noise. They wouldn't do it in front of me.'

The vision of my father as the office masher was unappealing. Joyce was at pains to explain to me that she wasn't a prude, and I believed her. The undeniable fact was that she was young, serious and hard-working and he couldn't keep his hands off her.

And 'poor old Gerry', as Daddy called him, saw what was going on and despised him for it.

'He must have had a car, now I come to think of it,' said Joyce. 'He used to offer to drive me home to Flemington after work. I always made an excuse.'

I slumped in my chair, looking dark. Sod the bastard. Joyce was the one keeping the damned office going while he coffeed and lunched and coffeed and cocktailed, and she couldn't accept a comfortable ride home because my father, my father! would force his attentions on her. (*Daddy, Daddy, you bastard, I'm through.*)

'Surely he was engaged then?'

'I asked him about that. He said that he was impressed with my looks. He told me men could have different feelings towards women. He was very keen on female beauty. He was great on those art books, you know, all these arty studies of nudes.' Doubtless showing these to his staff was Reg Greer's way of inviting them up to see his etchings.

At least he didn't tell her that he loved her, I thought sourly. I suppose he couldn't really without breaking his engagement.

'When I moved to another job upstairs in Newspaper House, he told me that his new girl was much more co-operative. "I've made the office much more comfortable," he said. "I've brought in a blanket. We have wonderful lunchtime sessions." '

So much for my claim that my father was one of nature's gentlemen. A cold fist of contempt began to tighten in my chest.

'Did you believe him?'

'Well. . . . He used to fantasise a lot, I think.'

I remembered an unsavoury little story that my father told my brother, of taking some girl-friend to the train at Spencer Street and giving her a quick one in the carriage before the train moved off. He even supplied the woman's name in the account he gave my brother. The evidence was not adding up to reveal my father as officer material.

'By that time he must have been married.'

'I think so,' said Joyce.

'Do you think he was in love with my mother? Why do you think he got married?'

'I think he wanted to propagate,' said Joyce drily.

'Did you believe what he said about his new secretary?'

'Well, he was attractive. Not that good-looking, but he was always beautifully dressed and he had a great line, great charm. He gave the impression of being quite well-educated, with that posh voice.'

'But you didn't think he was English?'

'All I ever heard about was Adelaide. I thought he was born in Adelaide.'

'He never mentioned Tasmania? Launceston?'

'Never. He gave the impression of being quite a well-educated man. But now I come to think of it, he really was mysterious. I've worked in all kinds of jobs all over the world, and I've never worked for anybody I knew so little about. Something murky about it.'

Everything murky about it. I was wrestling with the unfamiliar experience of feeling sorry for my mother. She was not much older than Joyce when Reg Greer stood beside her at St Columba's Church. She married him in the forms of the Catholic Church, linked herself indissolubly to a philanderer. He had a flash job, flash clothes and a flash voice. He was a lounge lizard, a line-shooter, a larrikin, a jerk. When he and his mates were bored, they would put false death announcements in the paper and have wreaths and condolences sent to the widow of someone who was still alive. Rib-tickling stuff.

'There was an executive from the radio station, a woman, who used to come across every few months from Adelaide, and she'd have me working flat out setting up her appointments and all that. Sometimes she'd ask me out to lunch, three-course lunch, with linen tablecloth, all very nice, and I was happy to go.' (Catch Reg Greer asking Joyce out to lunch! You can't grope people at lunch.) 'Then one time she asked me out to dinner at the Hotel Alexander, which was a new hotel then and really elegant. When I told your father I was going he created. He was quite upset. "What do you want to go to dinner with her for?" Anyway I went, and dinner was beautifully served and I enjoyed myself. And while we were taking coffee, a demi-tasse in the lounge, you know, she said that there was a beautiful view from her room upstairs and why didn't we go up? I thought try anything once. I was curious to see the room but, just as we were about to go upstairs, a well-dressed gentleman came up and said good evening to her. She wasn't the least little bit pleased to see him. "I'm going to insist on buying you a liqueur. I won't take a refusal," he said. So of course I said yes. I was dying to taste a liqueur. And then he asked what time it was and it was a quarter to eleven. I jumped up and said I had to rush, because I was late already but he stopped me. "I'm going to order a car, for you," he said, and he did. And I had a wonderful ride all the way home in a chauffeured car. When your father came into the office next morning, he put a book on my desk. "I think you ought to read this," he said. It was *The Well of Loneliness*. Do you know it? By Radclyffe Hall?'

I was thunderstruck. The man who never read a book and certainly never suggested any book for his daughter to read had somehow got his hands on to a book and given it to a young woman who might genuinely profit by reading it. Perhaps he never suggested that I read any particular book because he seldom saw me doing anything else. Or he was afraid of my flashing answers. Maybe he was afraid that I would snap that I had read it and it wasn't any good. There was a fuss when I turned up at home with a copy of *The Well of Loneliness*, but that was when I was in love with Jennifer and everyone was worried that I might be unnatural.

'Did you read it?' I asked Joyce.

'I couldn't put it down,' said Joyce. 'I realised that the lady from Adelaide wore tailored suits and flat-heeled shoes, and was not like other women.'

Another victory for heterosex.

The office masher abuses his authority in trying to flip you on your back on the office carpet, but his casual lust is preferable to the careful courtship of the lady in the grey flannel suit. This is morality.

'I saw your father in the street one day, after he went into the Air Force. He was all dressed up in his uniform and loving it. Poor man, he must have hated losing his teeth. He was very vain about his teeth.'

'The *Advertiser* never promoted him, you know. He had to plead to be given the title of manager a few years before he retired.'

236

'Well, they wouldn't,' said Joyce. 'Not without any background they wouldn't.'

We stood together on her balcony, looking at a sulphur-crested cockatoo that had perched on a television aerial and was shrieking dementedly for its mate. The storm was almost upon us. Through the traffic noise I thought I could hear the roar of the curtain of rain as it tramped towards us from the northern shore of the harbour. The female cockatoo joined her mate and they flew off across the tin roofs of Paddington to their roost in Centennial Park.

The next day I bought yet another air-ticket. I knew how to find him. It was only a matter of running him to earth. I packed up all my things, sent sacks of mail back to England. I would not be passing this way again.

Eureka

He kissed Briar Rose
And she woke up crying,
Daddy! Daddy!
ANNE SEXTON, 'BRIAR ROSE'

IT WAS hot. Horribly hot. Sheep drifted across the dry pastures
eating the yellow fluff that was all there was left of the grass.
In the gaps between the ragged clouds the sky showed blue as a
gas flame. A few of the farmers were ploughing, raising a smoke
of brown dust that blew for miles. Since my last visit, Tasmania
had somehow missed out on half her annual rainfall. Now that
the rainclouds were bumping across from the west the more
industrious – or more desperate – farmers were ploughing up the
crusted ground to make the best of whatever rain was due.

I was running away, driving fast, up into the rain forest, I
hoped, away from the emblems of colonisation, away from the
banks of gorse and brambles that disfigured the roadside, and
disfigured it most hideously where they had been browned by
poison. 'BRUSH OFF did this,' a sign said proudly. The inevitable
cypresses alternated with Scots pines swollen to mastodontic
proportions, and great stands of poplars coppiced like dragon's
teeth, and sallows spreading along the moister ground until they
burst through the very tarmac of the road. It was a landscape
that made no sense, full of false starts and miscalculations, trees
that grew too big, planted too close together and straggling
hedges of quickset and hawthorn marching up and over the
naked slopes, against the grain. The hawthorns didn't look like
English hawthorns, for they were all wood and small wrinkled
leaves, reddened with berries as small and hard as peashot.
Everything panted, the faded grass, dotted with bulrushes, and
the hot sheep ugly in their brown and greasy fleece and the cattle

238

that trod the dry pasture to dust.

Some of the most beautiful landscape in the word is man-made, the hill farms of Tuscany, the paddies of Nepal, the stone-walled fields of the British uplands. Australian farming was ugly, is ugly, and, like all the farming in the world, it is getting uglier. I turned my eyes to the hills.

I was running away because I knew that the chase was coming to an end. We were closing on our quarry. Surrounded by gifted and hard-working women the lazy man didn't have a chance. Between my new friends, Mrs Nichols and Mrs Eldershaw at the Archives Office, and Mrs Rosemann at the Local History Room and Miss Record of Launceston College, and his doggedest of daughters, Reg Greer was about to be flushed from his cover. His bluff was about to be called.

It was not as if I had not given him the benefit of the doubt. For two years I had persisted in believing his own vague intimations about his background. I had investigated Greers living in England, in Ireland, in South Africa, in Tasmania, Victoria, New South Wales, South Australia, and Queensland, Quaker Greers, Methodist Greers, Presbyterian Greers. I had written more than fifteen hundred letters to all the Greers in Northern Ireland, in Australia and in Africa, and to all the family historians researching Greers. I knew Greer history from the plantation of Ulster to yesterday. And I loved them, found family resemblances among them, supplied other puzzled Greers with information for their family trees, visited the graves of dead Greers. I was a Greerologist, a Greerographer, a Greeromane. But the result of all my searching bore inexorably towards one conclusion; though I might be all of the above, I was not a Greer.

For more than a year I had known of the existence of a series of strange coincidences involving the family of Greeney. My father said his mother's name was Emma Rachel Wise; Emma Greeney's maiden name was Wise. He said his father's name was Robert; Emma's husband was called Robert. He said he grew up in Launceston; Emma and Robert lived all their lives in Launceston. The date of their marriage at the Manse of the Baptist Church was too early, I thought, for my father was not born until 1904, fifteen years later, but an Ernest Henry Greeney 'clerk' appeared on the electoral rolls with them in 1925. This was a mite surprising for they were old to have a first child born in 1903 or so. No other son appeared on the rolls, only two girls, Hazel Margaret Sylvia and Gwendoline. Robert Greeney was no journalist; at his wedding he signed the register with an 'X'. In the electoral rolls Robert's calling was given as 'labourer'.

While I scanned the newspapers and university calendars for indications of Reg Greer's having passed any public examinations, I had noticed that in 1918 Ernest Henry Greeney of Launceston State High School had passed in all the usual subjects and got a credit in book-keeping and business practice. Mrs Nicholls at the State Archives Office knew of the Greeneys but, under my influence perhaps, she had discounted a relationship. Still she thought it would be a good idea if I searched the Launceston school files, which had not been forwarded to Hobart.

Before I left Hobart I made one last gesture of faith in my father. I went to the Registrar General's Office and asked for searches for the death in Tasmania of any of three individuals, Emma Rachel Wise, Emma Rachel Greer and Robert Greer, from 1904 to 1949. And I paid for them, $180, cold cash. 'You won't find anything,' I said to the counter-clerk and went my way.

The primal elder's guffaws still ringing in my ears I took the high road up to Launceston. As I crossed the highest point on the Midland Highway the road became a slalom through the bodies of Forester kangaroos killed by motorists dashing down to the Hobart Cup. I began to wonder if I was losing my mind. Certainly I had lost my sense of proportion. Why else did I risk my life by corkscrewing around on one pair of wheels and then another, just so I wouldn't have to hit the dead kangaroos again? Why else did the sight of a dead 'possum bounced off the road into a bush make my heart hurt and my tired eyes prick and burn? All life seemed cruel and unbearable, senseless and empty. I felt sorry for everyone, sorry for the pretty little towns that had started off so bravely, building their little churches out of stone, walling their small graveyards against marauding creatures whose excrement would foul the tombs, planting avenues of pines and cypresses that were now choked bulwarks of rushing darkness that tore up their walls and engulfed their houses. I felt even sorrier for the shabby weatherboard houses that offered 'O'nite' or 'Colonial' (i.e. uncomfortable) accommodation and the fruitgrowers selling off their decaying produce from battered utility trucks by the side of the road. 'Spuds', 'Toms', their hand-lettered signs said, or 'Apricots'. The prices they were selling their fruit at would have hardly repaid the labour of picking it.

Though I felt sad as hell, I did not feel merciful. I felt like hell, implacable, hard and bitter. My heart was wrung out, shrunken to a stone. I was exhausted without being sleepy, famished without appetite.

Launceston Grammar had early dismissed my enquiries about Reg Greer. The history of the school has been written after a fashion and published, with details of the yearly intake but, as the book has the names of two of my Greers wrong, I was not convinced. Besides a memory popped into my head, which seemed to my indulgent fancy to associate my father indissolubly with Grammar. He told a story at least once of a visit to a factory by his school. According to this, the boys were dressed in boaters and Eton collars, and 'bumfreezer jackets,' in colours of black, blue and white. The factory hands gave them a terrific shi-acking on account of their effete appearance. End of story. Inconsequential enough, but like every detail I could learn about my father I hoarded it. In fact the Launceston Grammar boys did hate their 'dorkers' and their Eton collars, and in 1924 succeeded in getting rid of them once for all, for the same reasons that the factory hands found to laugh at them.

The school archivist, himself from one of Tasmania's oldest and most distinguished families, kindly rang me to answer my insistent questions, but the answer was still, no Reg Greer. And no choral scholarships as far as he could tell. He suggested I ring St John's Church who might have financed such scholarships at one time, but I knew that I was just tying off loose ends. I don't know whether my father told me or I imagined that he went to his 'secondary senior public' school as a choir scholar. I had been tossed in this blanket of lies and fantasies for the last time.

The loose end of Scotch College, the other private school my father might have gone to, was not so easily tied up. For an establishment of rather grand pretensions, the school displays a peculiarly uncouth attitude to correspondence. My first letter waited months for a reply, which then simply told me that it had arrived at the beginning of term, and nothing had been done by way of investigating my query. The connection between the two facts was inconspicuous. Presumably, if the letter had arrived out of term time, I would have been told that everyone was on holiday and I would have to wait until they returned.

The only possible course was to visit the school myself. One secretary turned me over to another woman whose function was never explained to me. She found the correspondence in her file, and there was my second letter unanswered since July. 'It's not my fault,' she said. The head had passed the letter on to the archivist and the archivist had ignored it. No, she couldn't ring the archivist; he was not due at school until the next day and she wouldn't dream of disturbing him for such as me. Compared to the sanctity of Mr Skirving's privacy, the fact that I had come all the way from England to follow up my unanswered letter was a mere bagatelle.

'And tomorrow he will be at meetings all day, and have a perfect excuse not to speak to me,' I said.

'That's right,' she said.

There was a good deal more in the same vein. For the life of me I couldn't understand why a competent woman would go so far to cover for her better-paid male 'superior', but it is a phenomenon often to be observed in the lucky country.

She offered to ring me with the answer to my July letter and so she did. 'Records before 1920 are non-existent' the message said, in typical Australese. Eighteen months before they could simply have written to say, 'We have no records before 1920,' which, as it happens, is not quite true.

Having exposed myself to such embarrassments (for the call from Grammar was even more embarrassing in its courteous way) I figured I had done my best for the Reg Greer legend. I turned to the state schools; one had been founded in 1923, and the other led me to Miss Record. In as long as it took to tell she had ingested all the salient details of my request. I had played my last card. And I shot through. Went bush. But I knew that I would not get far.

When I first encountered the Greeneys I felt a cold fear that they would indeed be the end of the trail. As I burned up the narrow road to the coast, sweltering behind huge lorries, I went over what I knew about them. Robert Greeney the elder was a convict; he married an Elizabeth and begat another Robert, born 1866. If Robert Greeney was my grandfather, I was the great-granddaughter of a genuine transportee! Yippee! I thought. Then I thought that Daddy must have been ashamed of him, ashamed of them, god-fearing, hard-working, united family that they seemed to be, for I knew that when Ernest married, Gwendoline and Hazel had appeared on the rolls. When Robert disappeared, Emma lived with Ernest until death claimed her too, a year or two later. The worm of dislike for my father that had been nibbling off and on ever since I talked to Joyce gave me a proper nip. Lying bastard, I thought, and got out of the car to inspect some gum-blossom by way of psychotherapy.

The blossom was so satisfyingly gorgeous that I forgot my self-scarifications for an hour or two under its benefic influence. The tree was stout and mahogany-green, with dark matt leaves, against which the great umbels of burning red blossom and the clusters of magenta-tipped buds on the point of bursting shone with astonishing clarity. Despite the heat and the wind, the blossoms were velvety and fresh. Their fringes of vermilion stamens were like those of some sea-creature gleaming under water, while the leaves and twigs were as solid as rock. On the end of each stamen shone a tiny grain of pale gold pollen. Inside, the calyces were a luminous pale jadey-yellowy green except where they were packed full of bee. In the phantasmagoria of wilting petunias and yellow marguerites fried brown by the salt wind, the gums were unruffled, triumphant in their bee-loud glory.

When the road reached the sea, I looked for a place to stop and dally until the time should arrive when I could call Miss Record. The waters of Bass Strait were grey and fidgety that day; there are no ocean rollers in this narrow channel, but a kind of nervous seethe of water. Snappy little waves broke against the long ridges of burnt-looking crumbly rock with loud plops. Along the fore-shore runs a railway-line, right on the edge of the sea. And the road runs alongside it, and then the ugly houses gaze across both to the uneasy horizon, in all a pretty good example of scenic vandalism. The place I stopped at was called Goat Island.

It was the kind of place I loved to escape to when I was a child. In the basins and crannies in the wrinkled rock were dozens

243

of rock pools, some shallow and weed-filled, others deep and mysterious, others quivering with energy as the tide water slopped in. I ground the heel of my slipper onto a sea-snail, and dropped the smashed thing into the water. As the juices spread the sea creatures got the message. First came the transparent sea-fleas with their crimson punching gloves at the end of very long arms. Their pecking order was causing them some difficulty, for the largest fed first and most, and the others were obliged to make do with what fell from his table. Then a hairy little crab appeared, sidling along the rock wall of the pool. He boxed with the fleas and eventually, after a good deal of weaving and bobbing and feinting, made his run and tucked the booty under himself with all his legs. He was being watched by a crab three times his size, as smooth as he was hairy, with huge pincers that seemed made of pink china. Hairy had almost got back to his lair when Pink China made his run. I expected a furious fight. To my disappointment the little crab clean dropped his bundle into the waiting pink china claws.

I try not to believe in omens, but I knew that the episode of the little crab meant that there is a time when it is wise to give way, give up. Even a banquet is not worth getting injured for. I remembered Jeffrey, 'Don't be too hard on yourself. Tell yourself a few little lies.' Turn back, give up, go home. I drove on frantically into the mountains, longing for the moss and the cancellation of the horizon, longing for the drift of the leatherwood petals. But the black ant cannot give up. For two years I had dragged my burden backwards up one side of the grassblade and down the other. I had staggered miles out of my way pulling with my great jaws, for I could detour, but I could not give up. I stopped the car at a place called Yolla and went to ring Miss Record.

'There's no Greer,' she said. 'You said there might be a name change. Ernest Henry Greeney came to the Launceston State High School from Charles Street School on 30 January, 1917. He left on 19 December, 1918 and became a clerk at the *Examiner*. He was born on 19 May, 1903.' I said nothing, thinking that she had researched the wrong name. 'His brother, Eric Greeney, born 1 September, 1904–'

'We've got him! Got him! That's my father's birthday!'

Miss Record went on, imperturbable, as if it was the most

natural thing in the world. 'Same father, Robert Greeney, carter, of 136 Bathurst Street. He went to Wellington Square School, and was admitted to the High School on 29 January, 1918 to D class, but he only stayed two months. Left to become a book-binder. Oh, it says religion C of E but they all say that.'

I had thought the news would make me sad, but for the moment I was delighted. 'Gotcha!' I kept saying to Daddy. 'Gotcha! Didn't lie quite enough, did you? You left just enough truth in amongst the lies for me to get you. If you'd changed your date of birth, if you'd changed your first name, if you'd made a clean break with your parents' names, if you'd denied Launceston, you'd have got away with it. I'd never have found you, you liar. Just didn't lie quite enough.' And I laughed aloud. 'Liar! Liar! Liar!' I kept yelling as I tore back along the narrow highway to Launceston.

'You love truth better then your father,' said a voice over the whine of my Japanese engine. 'Damn right,' I said and cackled again.

I dashed into the library and checked all the Greeney addresses. Then I dashed out to buy a camera so I could photograph my father's birthplace. Again, the primal elder had his laugh. Of the dozen or so houses the Greeneys lived in, all in the same congested area of west Launceston, not one is still standing. Three of the houses they lived in are now a huge supermarket, another is the back of a small factory, another is a parking lot. Another was swept away by a new road. I began to wonder if Robert Greeney hadn't been feckless, a drunk perhaps, unable to provide a stable home for his children, seeing as they moved every couple of years, a few doors up, a few doors down, never outside a half-mile area of terraced workmen's houses.

In the hot dark night other thoughts rose up and gibbered around my hot bed and seething plastic foam pillow. Through the fly-screen on my open window burst fusillades of Friday night revelry, a scream of tyres, a blast of distorted rock music, a confused noise of yelling and cursing, spiked by an occasional crash of breaking glass or a woman's shriek. Then the small-town silence would resume. I went into the bathroom to wash my sweaty face and neck, and caught sight of my reflection.

I hardly knew myself. My face was set, my eyes staring, the pupils fixed as if suddenly grown insensitive to light. My brows had collapsed over them like a No mask of unutterable severity. My top lip was drawn down in a rictus with harsh wrinkles like hooks at the corners.

I tried to laugh at myself but what happened was merely a ghastly simper, a short convulsion of my rigid features, before the face returned as hard as ever. My eyes looked like eyes that had never wept.

'You're mad,' I said to myself.

The face answered, 'This is what you wanted, isn't it?'

'No, no, it isn't. It can't be,' I answered myself.

'Did you really think you'd find out that your father was a brilliant refined young man with a great future and distinguished connections who just happened to lose touch with his family? You never really believed in him.'

'I did,' I wailed, trying to soften the cruel face staring at me, which didn't resemble Daddy's beloved face at all. 'I thought he was a prince in disguise.'

'That was just your own vanity. You knew he was illiterate. Jesus, you've been a teacher all your life. How could you not know the man could barely read and write? Why do you think he read his tabloid newspaper from cover to cover, because he'd rather have been reading the Tractatus? You knew he was a fraud. Dammit, you treated him as a fraud.'

'Did I?'

'Of course you did. Whenever he tried to give you advice, you snorted at him and turned your back.'

'Well, he was always wrong. He never knew the circumstances. He pontificated without ever bothering to find out what the circumstances were.'

'Don't you think he knew that if he ever got into a real conversation with you, his cover would have been blown? Of course he always spoke to you from a lofty distance. He didn't do that with Barry because Barry accepted him as he was and didn't want him to be any better or any different.'

'He still didn't level with him though.'

'How do you know?'

I didn't. I left the face, and went to lie on my bed in the dark to think about it. Despite the heat I would have liked the red cat's purr to reassure me that I was not congenitally unlovable. I buried my face in the plastic foam pillow instead and tried to suffocate myself to sleep. A pair of drunken lovers were slugging it out in the street below. An hour later I went to take a cool shower. The face was still looking at me.

'So you think Barry and Jane knew that Reg Greer was actually Eric Greeney?'

'Not really,' said the face. 'He couldn't really level with them, after all that time, could he?'

'You don't reckon that it's my fault he got stuck with the lie? The lie was made up before I was born!'

'Yes, but you and your pretensions locked him into it. Your questions forced him to embroider it. He didn't do that for anybody else.'

'Mum wasn't interested. She didn't care who the fuck he was.'

'You're so worried that he didn't love you. Have you ever considered whether you loved him?'

'I did. I do.'

'You never loved him. You've never loved anyone.'

'Don't *say* that!'

'Love is no detective.'

'Don't quote Tsvetayeva at me.'

'You know it's true. You didn't hunt him down because you loved him, but because you hated him. He rejected you and you hated him.'

'No, no. If I hated him why did it all hurt so much? Nothing has ever hurt me so hard and for so long as his dying did.'

'You think you're so warm-hearted, so noble. You never gave the poor bugger a second thought. After you left home, you never wrote. You never called.'

'Oh, bullshit. All he had to do if he wanted to know where I was was call the University. He never bothered.'

'You sound like him.'

'There's a limit surely. I did my best at school. I did my best to be good. And there was never a word of encouragement. He never noticed anything I did. Perhaps I should have got polio or started sniffing petrol or something. Perhaps I would have been rewarded for being a fuck-up.'

'Oh, poor little genius you. Why don't you burst into tears or something?

'You sound like my mother.'

'Who did you think I was?'

I turned off the light and lay across my bed again. How he must have hated the child who constantly pecked away at his flimsy cover. It was my fault he stayed so far out of my reach. I was a harpy chick. But no, it wasn't my snobbery. It was his. His snobbery was inbred. Sir Lloyd this and Sir Lloyd that. I began to wonder if I was ever really convinced by his toff act, and if he knew that I wasn't and feared that I would bring his house of cards tumbling down. And I bethought me of the cold-blood-edness of a man who could marry a young and virginal woman under an alias, knowing that she was estranged from the father who would have sussed him in an instant. Then there was the dreadful possibility that he had been married before. Perhaps he learned the art of lying in a prison, seeing as he had been unable to cope with school. How the hell did he change from a semi-literate book-binder to Reg Greer the toff? I knew I would have to confront the Greeneys still living in Launceston and my heart misgave me. The bed was heating up again. The sheets were strangling me. I got up once more.

As I stood gasping at the window, the first drops clanged against the pane. The patter became a roar. Water poured from the sky in a solid curtain. The drought had broken. If it would only keep raining. 'Send her down, Huey!' I yelled and realised that I was quoting Daddy. But my tears did not fall. In half an hour the rain had gone. The morning sky ached overhead as blind and blue as ever.

Strange things happened in those days. The piles carrying the mains water supply across the Tamar to Launceston subsided because of the drought. The three great pipes sagged and their joints split open, so that the reservoir began emptying its last tons of water into the river. For four days the water board struggled to restore the supply. In the unnatural late February heat the gardens of Launceston withered and died. Brides who came into the public gardens to be photographed stood astonished among the frizzled blossoms. The Tamar valley had never looked less Cornish.

One of the hydro-electric stations suffered a seizure that sent a massive surge of current through toasters and irons and computers and dialysis machines. I was not yet so mad as to think all such catastrophes were my fault. But I did think that I was part of them. I was definitely bad news.

My father, I am told, was brilliant on the telephone. Perhaps he liked to talk to people who weren't able to look him in the eyes. I hate it. Even with people I know well, I hate to rabbit away without being able to see if they are reading some paper on the desk or making signs to someone else. I don't know how to capture wandering attention on the phone.

'Mrs Greeney,' I began, 'this will seem rather an odd request. Are you related to Ernest Henry Greeney?'

'Yes,' said a crisp voice. 'He's my husband's father.'

'I'm the daughter of his brother, Eric. I didn't know this until yesterday, so I'm still rather fluttered.'

Mrs Greeney thought it best to call her husband. 'Why would you be writing a book about your father?' he wanted to know.

'My name is, or rather it was, Germaine Greer, until yesterday. I'm quite a well-known writer. . . .' I trailed off miserably, but Mr Greeney bore me up. 'My father never spoke about his background. He became quite a toff–' I stopped again, embarrassed, not wanting to make it seem as if I thought the Greeneys were low-life.

Mr Greeney made no odds about my floundering. 'Would you like to come and see us?' he asked. 'At two-thirty this afternoon? I'll see what I can find out from the other foster brothers and sisters.'

'I beg your pardon? Did you say foster–?'

'Oh yes. They were all adopted. Didn't you know?'

Here was I thinking I had reached the end of the trail and it was just the beginning.

While unbeknownst to me Mr Greeney rang around the family and went to his aunt's house and looked for pictures, and Mrs Greeney baked a fruit-cake, I fidgeted in my hotel room and stared out of the window at the hideous bulk of the Myers building with its bi-centennial flaggery straining in the sharp wind that shoved the rain-clouds out of the sky. The irregular tiers of houses with roofs pitched this way and that, all different and chaotic and yet all the same, stared depressingly back. The town seemed as open as a fishbowl. If Reg Greer, sorry, Eric Greeney, was a ward of the state adopted by the Greeneys there was no question of fecklessness or brutality, I thought. There was no justification for jettisoning this family except snobbery and selfishness. Certainly Reg Greer had found no other to replace it, for the only parents he could produce were the Greeneys thinly disguised as Greer. The poor man probably never knew who his real parents were.

I was early to the Greeneys' house and sat in the car listening to boy sopranos grieving for the death of God. I saw a pretty woman and a girl in pink arrive after me and walk into the house before me. At two twenty-nine I took a deep breath and walked up the hill and rang the bell. Mr Greeney opened it, and took me inside. For the second time I blessed Australian directness and simplicity. There was great kindness but no ceremony, nothing to make me feel more awkward than I already did. They welcomed me, even though they must have known that their privacy was seriously breached.

They showed me a photograph of Mrs Greeney, an old lady in a high-necked dress with a cameo at her neck. Her face was strong and kindly, with a handsome nose and a determined chin and real merriment in her smile. Her glee was occasioned by the rather grumpy-looking infant she held in her arms, my adoptive cousin John in whose house I was sitting and eating fruit-cake. 'She died not long after the picture was taken.' The pretty lady, who is another of my adoptive cousins called Geraldine, chimed in: 'She loved it when the new babies arrived in the house, and she'd stay up all night with them, feeding them, holding them. She got them all as tiny babies, and they all kept their given names. The Greeneys did their job really well; all of the children went on to make something of themselves in the world. They weren't really so poor, were they? There was a lot of silver-polishing went on.'

'How many of them were there?'

'There was Ernest Henry, Eric, Eli, Hazel, Gwendoline, Dulcie, Kathleen and Bessie. We talked to Hazel, and she said that Eric was tall, with a fair complexion and curly hair. And he had very good teeth. But she couldn't remember much about him at all. She said he worked at F. and W. Stewart's the jewellers for a while and then at Mackinlay Proprietary Limited, selling menswear. Then he got mixed up with theatrical people at the

Lyceum Theatre and went away with the Black and Whites.'

'Went away with the Black and Whites? As what?'

'He was in the show, wasn't he?'

Everyone seemed to think he was. I was astonished.

Geraldine went on: 'They all had good teeth. Mrs Greeney must have nourished them properly. According to her obituary in the *Examiner*, Mrs Greeney worked hard for St John's Church. All the children sang in the choir.'

Poor Daddy, I thought. How he must have hated it. He did despise bible-bangers so. He went on hating organised religion with the last spark of his sentient life. Perhaps he did not believe that Emma Greeney loved him, but bred him up for the maintenance money, the golden opinions and the heavenly reward. He was wrong of course. According to the way of women the world over, Emma probably loved her lazy, curly-headed boy the best. She may have found it hard to say so, or to show it, for she treated all her children equally, but his disappearance with never a letter – or rather one letter – must have cut her to the heart.

'Mrs Greeney was a great homebody. She did everything herself.'

'She even soused her own eels. You had to eat up before you could have your sweet or leave the table. The children really hated the soused eel nights. Dulcie used to hide them in her stockings.'

'The old man was very strict; all the children had jobs to do around the house and they really got into trouble if they didn't do them.' (Nevertheless Reg Greer never so much as made his own bed or rinsed a cup. His children would all have sworn that he had never washed a sock or ironed a shirt in his life.)

We all laughed about the no speaking at the table rule, which had survived the Greeney era and afflicted all the next generation.

'You know the children weren't all poor. Some of them came from very rich families.'

'But that was the way of it then. If you were expecting an illegitimate child you went to the Salvation Army Home to have it. Didn't matter who you were. And it became a ward of court. And was given away.'

'My mother, Dulcie, found out who her mother was,' said Geraldine. 'Her mother was seduced by a lay preacher at her church when she was only sixteen. She got married later and had eight or nine legitimate children.'

There was a lot more talk, as is proper among families. I was glad I had them, proud of them, and flattered by their kindness to me. I was jealous of the Greeneys, who turned their lonely house into a noisy place, with young ones racing in and out to school, to the Tamar Rowing Club, to choir practice, playing cards on their evenings off. The Greeneys never had a house of their own. They invested their time and ambition, their love and their money in people. I'd have liked nothing better than such a well-organised houseful of busy children at Mill Farm. Funny, isn't it, that I should take after my fostermother, as if Eric Greeney aka Reg Greer had passed on her genes by spiritual osmosis? I suppose it was evidence of the success of Emma Greeney's child-rearing strategies that, when the time came, he could walk away. The Greeney family didn't suit him, obviously. But then it's doubtful whether the Greer family suited him either. He certainly spent very little time in it.

I went back to Hobart by an extremely circuitous route, because it was Sunday, and there was nothing else to do. I whizzed up into the rainforest, to be appalled once more by miles of Monterey pine, inexcusable even after I had seen the apologetic notice: 'Highly productive SOFTWOOD on this selected area is replacing low quality vegetation to supplement HARDWOOD supplies from permanent better quality Eucalypt forests.' How confidently they dismiss the mountain vegetation as low quality, I fumed, just because they haven't found a way to make money out of it. Further from the metalled highway, reachable only by the Australian Paper Mills' private roads, were more tracts of devastation. After the 'No Dams' riots it would be foolhardy to clear the land right up to the road, but from the air the gross distortion of many square miles of landscape is easily visible.

A pocket of real rainforest had been left as a public amenity by the paper mills. I walked there on sphagnum moss as thick and springy as a mattress, and marvelled how the blackberries could grow even here, anywhere a bird's shit can fall. The leatherwood petals drifted on to my face but they brought no blessing. I stood watching the laden bees dropping like stones from the treetops to the tall white beehives that stood in every glade and saw only

252

pointless insect lives fraught with struggle, toil and self-sacrifice. The thought of the honey inside the white-washed wooden ziggurats made me feel sick. My hair was full of tiny waterdrops, but my skin was dry, harsh and sore. I went restlessly on to Zeehan, where once they found gold, and grieved for the wild graveyard there, bedraggled head-stones on an unvisited hill where the charred pines leaned like drunken mutes. There were fire-scars all round Zeehan, where some inhabitant crazed by the incessant wind blowing from Africa had decided to blot himself and Zeehan, ruined for a hatful of gold, out of human memory forever. Over the bald hills to Strahan I went and watched the ocean rollers battering the dunes as I ate my pie and sauce and drank a stubby. I did not notice that the stuff I was putting in my mouth was tasteless, ersatz, chemical. The world itself had lost its savour. Months after the shock of unmasking my father, I still could not taste what I ate or what I cooked.

The Heroine
of This Story

Yet I would lead my grandmother by the hand
Through much of what she would not understand;
And so I stumble. And the rain continues on the roof
With such a sound of gently pitying laughter.
           HART CRANE, 'MY GRANDMOTHER'S LOVE LETTERS'

EMMA WISE, my grandmother Greeney, was born on 10 August, 1867, on the family dairy farm at Norfolk Plains East, nowadays Pateena, a hamlet three or four miles due north of Longford, between the meandering South Esk River and Mount Arnon. She was the twelfth of the fourteen children of Robert Wise and Mary Ann Lucas. Her father was the second son of Richard Wise, who was sentenced to transportation for life at Middlesex in 1812. His wife and children joined him in Port Jackson in 1815. In 1821 after Richard was freed the family travelled to Tasmania and took up a hundred acres of prime land in New Norfolk. Later generations of Wises believed that the first of the Longford Wises had been a free settler; the children may never have been told of their family's ordeal. Richard's sons Robert and Richard acquired more land in the same district. Emma's mother was the granddaughter of Nathaniel Lucas, who was transported to Port Jackson on the First Fleet.

Besides his own land Robert farmed a hundred acres of rented land. He and his brother, who inherited the original property at Arundale, were substantial members of the Longford community and devout members of the Church of England. In 1877 Mary Ann Wise died, worn out by hard work and continual child-bearing. As one of the youngest children of such a large family, Emma seems to have been allowed to run wild; she had no education, and probably very little supervision of any kind even after her father found another wife. Her age is never given correctly, possibly because she was not sure of it herself. She was twenty-one when she married in 1889, but her age was given approximately as twenty-three. When Emma married, on 26 March, 1889, the ceremony was not carried out in the Church of England but in the Manse of the Baptist Church in York Street, Launceston, probably because Robert Greeney refused to give even lip service to the Church of England. Emma must have known something of the bitter suffering that Robert Greeney and his parents had endured, and prayed that her husband would be given the consolation of her kind of faith.

Robert was the only son of another Robert Greeney who was tried for robbery with violence at Chelsea Crown Court on 26 October, 1846, and sentenced to fifteen years. He admitted to highway robbery and stealing nine pounds and three shillings from a Mr Clements at Whitechapel. Although he was only nineteen years old he had already served three months for stealing a handkerchief and three months for attempting to steal. He was sent to Gibraltar and imprisoned on a hulk. Eight unimaginable years later, on 26 May, 1853, he arrived in Tasmania aboard the *Saint Vincent*. The physical description of convicts is unusually precise, for it may be needed to identify absconders; Robert was five feet two inches in height, dark complexioned, with a small head, black hair, no whiskers, an oval face, a high forehead, black eyebrows and blue eyes and a small nose, mouth and chin. He was put to three years' bonded service, which he served without mishap, and was granted his conditional pardon on 16 September, 1856. In July 1858 he was in trouble again, and tried for assault, but this time he was acquitted. A month later he was tried at Hobart General Sessions for stealing a box worth a shilling together with seventy pounds from one Joseph Rogers, and for this he drew the dreadful sentence of six years at Port Arthur. Twice he was placed in solitary confinement, once for neglect of duty, and once for 'misconduct'. He was released on 28 July, 1863, and must soon after have encountered Elizabeth Smith, who became Robert's mother on 8 September, 1864. Despite the best efforts of Mary Nicholls and Shirley Eldershaw at the Tasmanian Archives Office, no trace of a marriage has been found for Robert and Elizabeth, but they lived together and she used his name for the rest of her life.

Try as he might have to keep out of trouble for the sake of his wife and son, Robert Greeney was sentenced again to three months' hard labour on 4 April, 1870, for larceny. He survived this ordeal and returned to his family in the small house in Launceston that he rented from David Dell. For seven years he kept out of trouble but greater anguish than any he had known in a life full of pain and trouble came to him and his family notwithstanding.

Four days before the Christmas of 1877 Robert Greeney was working in the bark-grinding mill belonging to Mr Sidebottom. What happened is probably best told in the dispassionate words of the *Examiner*: 'On Friday last at about 2 o'clock, [Greeney] was occupied at the mill; the belt of the wheel fell off and [Greeney] leaned over to put it on, his feet being still on the truck. As he was going to start the wheel, being in danger, [Walter Leslie] who was employed as the feeder, caught hold and pulled him back, when he fell sideways, and his trousers were caught by the cog-wheels which were working close to the truck, and the leg being drawn in the thigh was lacerated and crushed between the wheels; the belt then flew off and the wheel stopped.' By the time the wheel had stopped, Greeney was grievously wounded. When he arrived at the hospital he was found to be 'suffering from an enormous wound in the left buttock, and upper part of the back part of the thigh. The muscles were completely torn away, the hip joint exposed. . . .' Unfortunately for Robert the femoral artery had not been ruptured, and death was many hours away. 'The man was quite sensible, but was suffering from the shock and was very weak.' They drew the edges of the terrible wound together and bound them close. Tough as he was, Robert Greeney had come almost to the end of his endurance. For two days and three nights he suffered, until death released him on Monday morning. It was Christmas Eve. His son, my adoptive grandfather, was thirteen years old.

The coroner did not want to cast blame on Mr Sidebottom, but he did suggest that investing a few pence in a board to protect workers from the cogwheels might be a good idea. The verdict of the inquest was that 'accidentally, casually, and by misfortune, the trousers of the said Robert Greeney became entangled in the cog wheels of the machine, whereof the thigh and buttocks of the said Robert Greeney were seriously torn and lacerated of which said injury the said Robert Greeney languished, and languishing lived until the twenty-fourth day of December ... when the said Robert Greeney did die'.

Though the coroner might not have blamed Mr Sidebottom, the verdict of history is different. Sidebottom committed a worse crime against Robert Greeney than ever he had inflicted upon society. Sidebottom did not simply kill Robert Greeney; rather, by lack of imagination and foresight, he tortured him to death. In a world so unjust, how bitterly must Robert Greeney have reviled himself for struggling so desperately to obey other men's rules? Better by far to be a desperate criminal and renegade than a drudge in a filthy industry that enriched only those who did not dirty their own hands, an expendable drudge whose life was not worth protecting.

Perhaps Elizabeth Greeney sat in the court with her boy and heard the coroner's verdict. Perhaps that unforgettable Christmas taught Robert how unforgiving life is and how tough he would have to be to survive. It would be nice to think that Mr Sidebottom made some gesture towards Mrs Greeney and her son, but so much more interesting are the affairs of the gentry than those of the poor that we would probably have heard of it if he did. The next year David Dell's house was rented to someone else. The widow Greeney and her son vanished from the record, probably because she went into service.

All his life the convict's son was clean-living and hard-working. He was also withdrawn and taciturn. He was illiterate and had only a vague idea of his age when he married Emma, who was then a domestic servant. They were both determined to survive by hard work and rigorous self-discipline in a merciless world.

Robert earned a small but steady living driving a dray for the Launceston City Council, moving earth away from the new building sites and roadways. For thirteen years he and Emma lived together without the arrival of any child, which for Emma, who had grown up in a big country household, must have been very difficult to bear.

Under the provisions of the Destitute and Neglected Children's Act, the cities of Hobart and Launceston ran a boarding-out system for children whose parents could not take care of them.

Married ladies of good character could earn twenty-one shillings and sixpence a month for each child they took in. Out of that they were expected to feed, clothe and bring the children up to be useful members of society. The law required that the children go only to households of the same religion, that they go to church regularly, and that they go to school until they turned thirteen. Then they were to be apprenticed to learn a useful trade. In the first year of their apprenticeship they were to be paid five shillings a week, two shillings to be given to them as pocket money and the rest placed in a trust fund kept by the Department of Neglected Children, which retained jurisdiction over the children until they were twenty-one. Children who were uncontrollable or got into trouble with the police were sent to reformatory schools where a combination of hard rations and harsh discipline effectively suppressed their anti-social behaviour.

In September 1903, Emma took her courage in both hands and approached the Neglected Children's Department. One of her neighbours was giving up a four-month-old baby boy whom she had taken for fostering, because she had been ill and felt unequal to the work. On the application, shakily written in her own hand, Emma called herself 'Emma Amelia Greeney' by way of gentrifying her name, for much the same reasons that her boy Eric was later to call her Emma Rachel Wise. It was an affectation of which she soon had no need. Robert had jibbed at being described as Church of England, and so she put him down as Presbyterian, to explain why he was not seen to attend church with her. Her application was endorsed by the Rector of her local church, St John's.

Her application was successful. Henry Ernest Millhouse was 'handed to' Emma as the department jargon has it. She brought him home and sat up all night holding him in her arms, as she did with all the children who came to her as babies. Emma was tall and sturdy and buxom; she knew instinctively about babies and bonding and the anguish of children. She worked hard to build real relationships with her children, giving them physical closeness, real affection, support and unfailing loyalty. Her first little boy never left her, never asked what his 'real' name was, and closed her eyes when she died. He was my father's brother, 'Ernie'.

Emma's first year of motherhood was an anguished and uncertain time. Ernie's genetic mother, Florence Millhouse, was never very far away. Florence was a lucky girl, for although she had been foolish and easy and had got herself into the family way, kind Mrs Groves had offered to take her into her service, without her bastard, needless to say. With heaven knows what anguish, Florence handed her baby over to the state and went off to 'better herself in the world'. Out of her tiny wages, she was expected to pay two shillings and sixpence a week towards the child's keep, which she conspicuously failed to do, mainly because she did not often succeed in getting paid at all. She lost her position at Mrs Groves's because of her 'bad temper and want of self-control'. There were no allowances made for her distress or disorientation. Florence was known to be a bad girl, insensible of her guilt and ungrateful for the kindnesses she received. She found other positions, but something always seemed to go wrong. The Neglected Children's Department adopted a stern tone and demanded its two and six a week. A position was found for her (possibly through Emma Greeney's intervention) with a Mrs Simmonds at 'The Oaks' in Longford, and she was sent there to escape the blandishments of the boom town of Launceston.

She was told however that at the end of June 1904 she would have to take her baby back and rear it herself. Poor Florence, deprived of her baby at the very time she was supposed to have been bonding with it, now found herself about to be lumbered with a toddler. She came to Launceston one day and failed to return to Longford, claiming that, as she sat in the park, her pocket was picked of the money she had been advanced by Mrs Simmonds. Then she refused to go back to Longford, and refused to take her baby back with her to her mother's house. Instead, she did what every persecuted Launcestonian did, she ran away to Melbourne.

At last Emma Greeney had Ernie all to herself, but it had been a worrying and uncertain time for her. She was to realise again and again that a foster mother had no rights in the child, and was merely a public amenity to be used whenever convenient by the welfare bureaucracy.

Florence Millhouse was not a cold or unnatural person, although she showed no sign of interest in her baby boy. She was

259

cornered and fighting for survival. She was a servant in the house of a Mrs Burgess when she was seduced or raped by Jack Burgess, who gave her three pounds to cover the expenses of her lying-in and considered that he had discharged his responsibility to her. Florence kept to her part of the bargain and did not name Jack Burgess as her baby's father. If she had given his name to the Neglected Children's Department they might have made a claim on him for the child's support. If he had been a working man, they certainly would have. The Department files bulge with demands for payment of child support by labouring men and instructions to the police to collect such payments or arrest the putative fathers. In the case of a working man, a mother's word was two-thirds proof of paternity. A working man had only to fail to deny the charge to be considered to have admitted it. Gentlemen were not usually named at all and if they were the matter was not taken up.

If she had named her child's father Florence would have been considered a brazen hussy, and because she did not she was considered worse. In any event she was unfit to raise a gentleman's child; if she had kept the baby with her, both would have lived in penury and hence moral danger. So poor Florence gave him up, as she was told, only to be constantly threatened with having to take him back. Her mother offered to take Florence and her baby to live with her but Florence saw no escape that way. The only way to make a fresh start was to disappear.

In December 1904, another ward of state was confided to Emma's care, but Emma was very busy with a new little boy whose name does not figure on the files of state wards; he was my father, Eric. The new little girl, her mother's third illegitimate child, was placed with Emma when she was only ten weeks old. Six months later the Neglected Children's Department placed her with another foster-mother, to see if she might not thrive better. Eight months later she was claimed by her mother who was getting married.

Emma had always lived in a house full of children. As she began to realise that she had a way with children she made herself available to take in more. She had the example of another neighbour, who employed a handyman to knock up extra rooms that were added to her rambling house whenever a new waif appeared on her doorstep, for she could never bring herself to refuse a destitute child. The Greeneys were too poor to own a house, and the growth of Emma's family was relatively slow. In March 1907, she was given Eli, whose father had disappeared, and whose mother was considered 'loose'. He had been declared a neglected child when he was eighteen months old; his mother had conceived her first child by her father and in 1911 this boy too, Eli's half-brother Edgar, came under Mrs Greeney's wing. About this time she had a girl, Vida Turner, but Vida was moved on to another foster-mother.

Emma built up the relationship with each child gently and gradually. All the state wards kept their given names, for no one knew when they might be claimed by a parent, but at school they were all Greeneys. Emma made no distinction between the state wards for whom she was paid and her own informally adopted children, or between the dolts and the dazzlers, the industrious and the lazy. She did her best to imbue the children with confidence and optimism, despite their poor beginnings. Her chief help in that was the Church of St John's, where they all worshipped and sang in the choir and even the dullest won prizes in the Sunday School.

The Neglected Children's Department had not only a responsibility to the children, but also to the public. The children could not continue indefinitely being coddled by a doting foster-mother at the state's expense. No matter whether the child had its growth or not, or if it was seriously emotionally disturbed, at thirteen it had to go to work. Applications for 'a lad for service' or 'a girl for service' came into the Department every day. Each had to be supported by a referee, a Justice of the Peace or a clergyman. The employer had to promise to send the child to church and Sunday School; this was one way that the situation could be unobtrusively monitored, but many country clergy did not understand the significance of a child's absence or truculence. The monitoring simply did not work, and many a child was kept to long hours and hard rations, reviled and struck when it did not understand what it was supposed to do or how. More letters came into the Department; the children were 'too small' for the work they had to do, or 'useless', lazy, untruthful, disrespectful.

Most who wrote in search of cheap labour were farmers, needy and otherwise. Most of the letters in the Department files are ill-spelt, ungrammatical scrawls, with a perfunctory endorsement from a local dignitary, usually a parson of one denomination or another. The youngsters were packed off from jolly households full of children to bleak hill farms where no one spoke to them except to give them orders from dawn to dusk. Bereft and grieving, they became confused. Their blunders were punished, sometimes brutally. The Neglected Children's Department found itself wedged in a dilemma; the lives of farmers' children were necessarily hard and the state wards could hardly be seen to be having a better time of it. The state wards were poor children and would have to be self-supporting eventually. It was never too soon to learn just how hard life is. Generally the Inspector tended to ignore complaints and simply exhorted the children to knuckle under and learn how to work. The foster-mothers watched and waited anxiously for news of their children, understanding how alone, bewildered and betrayed they must have felt. The children, tossed by the tempests of adolescence, stumbled through their grim round of daily chores, hungry, tired and heart-broken. Occasionally total strangers wrote to the department protesting that the system was little better than slavery. Sometimes the children were employed in lieu of an adult worker who pocketed the full wage and gave the child the departmental allowance. Some children worked more than sixteen hours in a day, and were given no shoes or clothing. When the letters that described ill-treatment showed in their style and orthography the evidence of a first-class education, the Department took the hint and removed the child before further opprobrium should attach, but the children's furtive scrawls on filthy paper with a pencil stub usually led to more and severer punishment.

The children were not permitted to write letters without their employers' knowledge; if any such letter was smuggled out and found its way to the Inspector's office it was sent back to the employer, who was asked to explain it. Occasionally the Department moved swiftly, if a child was thrashed or debauched; in one case a boy managed to get word back to the Inspector that he was obliged to share his employer's only bed, which was verminous, and his rail warrant back to Launceston was issued the next day. Mostly the children were utterly alone, menials in the house of strangers. They developed strange habits born of stifled mourning; one little girl stole small things from her mistress and buried them in the garden. Many refused to wash, became catatonic, and were declared weak-minded or psychopathic by ludicrous professionals who examined them at the receiving home.

'Let me only have him back and he will be well,' the foster-mothers chorused, but the Department told them curtly to desist from interfering, and blamed them for spoiling the children. Emma could not be said to have spoilt her children. Behind her stood the dark figure of Robert Greeney, of whom the children were afraid. Better to meet a policeman than Robert Greeney if you were up to no good. All the boys sang in the St John's Church choir, regardless of how they were ragged; they all attended church and Sunday School, and they were always neat and clean. They attended school regularly and played sports. None of them ran wild with the barefoot street kids. But they did have fun and they did have each other until the dreadful thirteenth birthday when they were suddenly thrust into a hostile world.

The first of Emma's boys to turn thirteen was Edgar. In 1914 he was sent into service with Mrs Frances E. Cockerill at 'Killarney' near Nicholls Rivulet, to learn the trade of orchardist. The local Inspector checked up on him in February 1916 and declared that he was 'a very good boy indeed: he has gained two prizes at his Sunday School, one for regular attendance and another for helping at the lessons and kindness to the younger children. He has a very good home and is very deserving of it.'

Suddenly Mrs Cockerill wrote to Mrs Greeney explaining that Edgar had not written because he was 'a very bad boy very lazy disobedient and untruthful' and to punish him she had told him that he would not be allowed to write to Emma. 'He does not seem to mind,' she added maliciously. He had chummed up with a boy from the Boys' Training School, who he said was a cousin, a thoroughly bad egg. Emma, alarmed, showed Mrs Cockerill's letter to the Inspecting Nurse, Sister Heathorn, explaining anxiously that Edgar was 'not altogether responsible for his actions'. In fact Edgar suffered a degree of mental defect; he was fast turning into a gentle giant, easily led and slow to anger, but potentially dangerous. Emma begged to be allowed to sign the

263

service conditions and take him on herself; Nurse Heathorn added her approval. 'If Mrs Greeney fails to make a decent citizen of him it will not be any fault of hers.'

Mrs Cockerill was furious that Mrs Greeney had gone to the authorities. Edgar was not so dreadful a boy that she was prepared to do without his labour. 'Of course he was no trouble to Mrs Greeney,' she wrote. 'She never made him do any work except in the house.' Her reason for writing to Mrs Greeney was simply to get her to write to Edgar and encourage him to behave better. The letter was so venomous that Nurse Heathorn wrote again to the Inspector. 'Mrs Greeney has always seemed able to bring out the best qualities of this lad,' she argued, but Edgar's stumbling letter to Emma was sent back to Mrs Cockerill and the poor fellow stayed where he was, even though his employer had found another little boy, only eleven years old, who made himself more useful than Edgar ever had.

When she realised that she had no further need of Edgar, Mrs Cockerill decided to send him back, giving as her reason that Mrs Greeney was 'always interfering with him', and that he was only able to do the simplest tasks such as hoeing around the trees. Edgar then played his trump card; instead of hoeing he went fishing and Mrs Cockerill threw him out. A new job was found for him with a Mr Richardson and for a time all seemed well.

When Ernie's thirteenth birthday came round, Emma moved to prevent another debacle. She signed the conditions of service herself, undertaking to pay him a salary which she could ill afford, which was waived because she intended to keep Ernie at school. On the application she had to list the male members of her household; she had living with her besides her husband her brother (Robert Wise) aged seventy-one, an adopted boy of thirteen, my father, and two state boys aged fifteen and nine. The Inspector added a comment, 'Mrs Greeney is an excellent foster-mother.'

Edgar Greeney's half-brother Eli came to Emma when he was about twenty months old. From the beginning he had special problems; at nearly two years old he was not able to walk. He was less intelligent than her other children and poorly co-ordinated. The other children played tricks on him. Awkwardly enough, his age was within a month of my father's. A teacher at

Wellington Square school noticed one day from the roll that the two Greeney boys in the class were born within a month of each other and stupidly remarked on the fact, whereupon the whole class hooted with laughter, for everyone except the teacher knew that the Greeney boys were foster-children. It was the sort of embarrassment that Reg Greer did not forget easily, although he had no difficulty in forgetting almost everything else.

In 1915 Emma acquired a peck of trouble in the form of two of the three Radford boys, whose father had been killed by a falling tree. The eldest boy, who had been rejected by an earlier foster-mother who complained that he beat his little brothers and was very dirty in his habits, was sent to the Boys' Training School. This foster-mother allowed the boys to sell confectionery at one of the Launceston theatres and, because she continued to do so after she had been warned by the Department of Neglected Children, they were taken away from her and given to Mrs Greeney, who had moved to a larger house so that she could take in more children. Percy went into service on Flinders Island, where he was made to work such long hours in the fish-processing factory that an anonymous observer wrote accusing the Department of Neglected Children of condoning white slavery, because he was being paid the apprentice rate while working at a job which was usually paid at the rate of a shilling an hour. The Department wrote to the employer at once asking for the boy to be sent back to Launceston, where, because he was then too old to be fostered, he was sent to the Boys' Training School.

Fostering the Radford boys was a painful experience for Emma; they were big boys when they came to her and already declared uncontrollable. Her gentle ways made little impression on them, especially as their mother kept writing extraordinary letters to them, urging them to come and work in Burnie where they would be able to have lots of fun and plenty of girls. As the boys remained under the jurisdiction of the Department until they were twenty-one, their mother's demands to have the boys back were invariably refused.

Another newcomer to the bigger house in 1915 was Thurza, whom Reg Greer did remember. He had told my mother that he had been brought up more by the maid, Thurza, than by his mother, who was delicate. Thurza was no maid, but his foster-sister. Thurza was four years older than Eric Greeney, a handsome, strong and energetic girl, with a distinct and unforgettable personality. She came to Mrs Greeney with her small brother, Clifton. Their mother had married and her illegitimate children could not adapt to the new situation. 'They have on several occasions run away and slept in hollow logs for a week at a time before they were found,' said a note on the file. On 20 October, 1915, Thurza opened a mailbag and stole the two pennies left inside it to pay postage, which she spent on sweets. That night she and her brother did not come home. To feed her little brother and herself Thurza lifted cans of food from the store. A logger saw them sitting on a fallen tree, sharing out a can of fish, but when he came closer they dropped the can and ran away. Neither the post-mistress nor the store-keeper wanted to press charges, saying that they were afraid the children's stepfather would burn their outhouses down.

The Department knew desperate children when it encountered them. Ragged and dirty, the exhausted children were immediately brought to Mrs Greeney, who applied for their clothing allowance the very next day. Nurse Heathorn was confident that Emma would know how to deflect Thurza from her self-destructive course and reassure her that Clifton would be safe.

Thurza was with Mrs Greeney for less than a year, but Eric Greeney was at an impressionable age and he did not forget the adolescent girl who was later described as a 'splendid little worker, when she is in the mood'. As soon as she was of age, Thurza went into service, but she was not separated from Clifton, for she went to Nurse Heathorn's sister-in-law in Launceston. Mrs Heathorn was not as adroit in handling disturbed children as Mrs Greeney, and fifteen months later Thurza was sent to work at New Town Infirmary in the south of the island. This changed the quality of her life completely. Thurza became taciturn and unpredictable. A request from her mother in 1919 to have Thurza home to help with her other children because she expected soon to be lying-in was not passed on by the department. Instead Thurza went to work for a Mrs Patterson, but she was having great difficulty humbling her proud heart. A passionate mis-spelt letter suddenly arrived at the Department of Neglected Children, in which Thurza said that she could not stay with Mrs Patterson another moment. 'Miss Patterson through it up at me tonight about my mother and Father not being married which has upset me very much.... I cannot bear anyone to say anythink about my mother ...,' wrote the servant-maid sitting on her bed in the privacy of her own room. Her indignation casts an interesting light on Emma Greeney's ways with her children, for clearly Thurza had never been subjected to this kind of humiliation before. She did leave her menial employment and ran as far away as she could, all the way to Sydney, where she married under an assumed name and never told her husband that she had been a ward of the state, let alone that she was a bastard child who had hidden from her mother's husband in a hollow log.

Thurza's little brother came of age to go into service in 1919; the offer of work was not made until 1920 but Emma asked that Clifton might be allowed to stay in Launceston for the celebration of the visit of the Prince of Wales, and her request was granted. Clifton had just a little more childhood left, and Emma must have been one of the few people who was glad when the Prince's visit was delayed. Clifton's apprenticeship on a farm at Spring Banks was unusually short; in October his employer caught the four-teen-year-old 'in the act of sodomy' with his nephew aged nine. Clifton was immediately recalled to Launceston and sent to the Boys' Training School. When Emma heard she went at once to the Children of the State Department and begged to have him back. She would find him a job in Launceston, as she had for all her boys. The reply was a cold note from the Secretary who did not consider the child's release advisable. Emma kept trying, and in December 1921 Clifton was finally released to her care.

If Clifton knew about her efforts on his behalf, he did not thank her for them. Instead he wrote a letter to another sister who was living in Victoria. 'Mrs Greeney is not a very good lady. I had a bit of a row with her and I asked Mr Henery [Inspector Henry of the Children of the State Department], if he could get me a place but he could not.... I am working for Standage' (he was doing a milk round) 'for 10/- a week and out of that I have to give Mr Greeney 8/- and I am not having a pleasant time.' The first thing Emma knew of this libel was when the Department, now called the Children of the State Department, requested an explanation of the distraint of most of Clifton's money. Emma produced a savings book in his name; she was trying to build up a clothing fund so that he could appear better dressed and get a better job. This was not the first or the last time that Emma had to face disloyal accusations from her children; her charges, irked by her strictness and vigilance, nursed the usual adolescent quantum of grievance, but Emma was more vulnerable to their accusations than their natural parents would have been.

As soon as the new clothes were bought Clifton disappeared and Emma never heard of him again. When he would have turned twenty-one, his mother wrote to the CSD: she was 'drooping a few lines' to ask for the money held in trust for him from the short time of his apprenticeship. The Department replied in freezing tones; the money belonged to her son, not to her. Clifton never claimed it and it was eventually paid into the Treasury.

By 1918 Mrs Greeney had acquired some little girls; she had taken the tiny five-month-old daughter of a fifteen-year-old girl seduced by a miner. She took in three older girls called Edwards, whose mother had boarded them out with an old couple in Devonport, in a two-roomed house where ten children lived. The older girl went to Hobart, where she bore an illegitimate child in 1923; one of the others who were twins bore an illegitimate child in 1929. As neither girl was twenty-one at the time of the birth, and therefore both were under state jurisdiction, these lapses reflected badly on Emma who had insisted that they were good girls and should be allowed a little liberty. Her old colleagues in the State Children's Department were retiring; the new brooms occasionally thought Emma too soft. Besides, eugenicist ideas were becoming fashionable; children of tainted stock needed to be under institutional control, to prevent them mixing with the uncontaminated. Emma clung to her own brand of tough-love. If her children were tainted then so was she and so was Robert, hard-working, honest and clean-living as they were. She knew in her bones that the doctrine of inherited moral defect was a doctrine of despair.

In 1920, when Eric was approaching his sixteenth birthday, Emma's household comprised, as well as Ernie, Eric, and Eli, five smaller children. There were two eleven-year-old schoolboys, both of whose mothers had absconded, leaving their fathers to look after them. George's father was incapacitated by miners' pthisis. Raymond's father was a shepherd, who had no way of caring for his three little boys. The Department official who collected them from Longford added a compassionate note to their file, 'They seem nice, decent little fellows.' Then there were the girls, seven-year-old Dulcie, who had been with Mrs Greeney from the age of twelve months, three-year-old Gwendoline, and another little girl called Hazel, whose name cannot be found in the files of state wards, because like Eric she was privately adopted and brought up at the Greeneys' expense.

Even with all the tumult of such a large household around her, Emma did not forget her older children. At the same time we find her writing for news of Edgar, now eighteen. 'I am writing to know when Edgar is coming home as he was 18 years of age the 3rd Sept of this year and I have written two letters to him but I have received no answer, and I feel terribly broke up through his not answering. I think as much of him now as I did when he went away.' She included a letter for Edgar, which was not forwarded but remained in the Department file. Instead Edgar was to visit the office for an interview, which he did, saying that he was very contented at his place of work. A few weeks later a telegram arrived at the Inspector's office, 'Edgar Wm Thow, barefooted, left employment of Wm Richardson, Sandford, yesterday, having decided not to stay owing to the young children of Richardson being permitted to throw things at him, and illtreat him.' Emma's concern was justified.

Edgar did not come back to Mrs Greeney; instead he found lodgings in Cascade and went to work as a milkman. He wrote to the Department and asked them to tell Mrs Greeney to send him his Sunday School prize books. It was a final breach. Others of her children were to take this step, which signified that they no longer regarded Emma's house as their home. The files of the State Children's Department do not carry any indication of Emma's reaction to this rejection.

In 1920 a comprehensive law regarding fostering and adoption was finally passed. Emma made use of it in 1923 to give her name to two of her little girls, Dulcie and Gwendoline; her application was contested on the grounds that the children were both over ten years of age, but an exception was made because Emma was the only mother they had ever known. In 1928, Dulcie's mother wrote to the Department, asking for Dulcie to be sent to her in Melbourne, 'as ther is know prosects for a girl in Tasmania. I have wrot servel letters to Mrs Green the lady that got her but got know answer.' Dulcie was then older than her mother when she bore her, and had never heard from her. The Department informed her mother that Dulcie had been adopted, and she had no further right of access to her.

Mrs Greeney did lose Dulcie eventually. In 1931 Dulcie's future mother-in-law wrote to the Department, asking for her 'real' name. 'Dulcie does not know her name, other than Dulcie Greeney. She is not friendly with Mrs Greeney and has not lived home for some months.' The answer from the Department told her in no uncertain terms that Dulcie's name was Greeney and she would be married as such. In fact Dulcie went to Mrs Greeney's house and got down the register from the top of the wardrobe and read her own name. Painstakingly recorded there was every payment that had been received and made on her account and the accounts of all Emma's children over the years. It must have been an impressive document, for altogether more than twenty-five children were brought up by Emma and Robert Greeney. The record would have showed that she never gave up on a child, never rejected any of them no matter how naughty or stupid or ugly, never did as so many other foster-mothers did, sent them back to the Department because they fancied a relief from the toil of looking after a mob of kids.

In 1931 Emma fell foul of the CSD over her last foster-child, Kathleen, who had been apprenticed to her in order to stay on at school. When she was unable to find a job for Kathleen in the deepening Depression, Emma was ordered to send her away into service. The new Inspecting Nurse was disgusted when Emma came to her, 'shed tears and said she did not want Kathleen to leave her, she was a bonser kiddie, etc.' and told her curtly that she was not entitled to Kathleen's unpaid labour. Ernest Greeney then came to his mother's aid; he explained in a letter that she would keep Kathleen in food and clothes and all necessities but she could only afford to give her two shillings a week. Kathleen was small, and suffered from eczema and a speech impediment. If her experiences in service were to be anything like those of Emma's other children she could hardly have been expected to survive it, but Emma was too poor to be able to keep her. Nurse Plummer's reaction to her low offer was scathing. Emma promised to pay the extra money into Kathleen's trust fund, and set about finding her a job at the woollen mills. Kathleen never worked more than a few weeks before being laid off, and poor Emma suddenly found herself being carpeted by Nurse Plummer and ordered to pay three weeks' arrears on Kathleen's fund. Actually Kathleen was much better off than Emma, for her mother had had the foresight to name as her father a man who went off to the Great War with the twelfth battalion of the AIF. Contributions to her support were taken out of his soldier's allotment and, when he was killed three months after her birth, a trust fund had been set up for her. When her trust fund matured in 1939, Kathleen was richer than Emma had ever been in her life. By then Robert was dead, and Emma had not long to live.

I should have been so proud to have inherited Emma Greeney's genes. She had in abundance all the human characteristics I most prize, tenderness, energy, intelligence, resource, constancy, honesty, courage, imagination, endurance, compassion.... She was true blue, dinki-di. I have made up for myself a private name, that seems to me to fit better than the ridiculous name my parents gave me, of which half is a remembrance of a character in *The Countess of Rudolstadt* and the other half my father's shonky alias. 'Germaine Greer' indeed. I call myself Frances Greeney, and realise glumly that I am simply carrying on the Reg Greer tradition of aliases. There is no bucking the genes.

It had not occurred to me to look for a reason why Emma Greeney didn't marry one of her fellow parishioners in Longford and live happily ever after on a dairy farm. I came across the entry in the parish register of Christchurch, Longford, quite by chance. On 15 May, 1887, at Christchurch, a newborn was christened George; his mother was given as 'Emma Wise, domestic servant'. That night George died of obstruction of the bowels, probably because he was born prematurely. Emma's brother Charles registered the birth and death for her, and probably took the ailing infant to the church for his christening and burial. I thought it typical of Emma that regardless of her own shame she would have wanted her tiny boy to be properly christened and buried. She never named the father of her child but bore the brunt of the scandal alone. This catastrophe deflected the course of her life, drove her out of Longford and eventually to the Manse of the Baptist Church where she agreed to share her destiny with silent Robert Greeney. She won back, by sheer deserving, the esteem and social standing she had lost; when she died, four years after Robert, on 20 October, 1940, the *Examiner* printed her obituary.

What Daddy
Never Knew

'I got thinking of the time Dad come 'ome. Walked out of the
asylum 'e did, wiv a coat over his asylum cloves. He come
'ome to the residential where Mum was stayin' wiv me and
the other kids. I was twelve. He come 'ome on the Friday, and
Saturday afternoon, when we was at the pi'tures, he cut her
throat, and then he cut his own throat afterwards. The
landlady made me go wiv a mop and a bucket and clean up
the floor. Bled to death he had, all over it. And me wringin'
out the mop wiv me own farver's blood on it. The landlady
said they was my parents and I had to do it.'

KYLIE TENNANT, THE BATTLERS

'YES!' SAID Mr Peggotty, with a hopeful smile. 'No one can't
reproach my darling in Australia. We will begin a new life
over theer!'

Why Mr Peggotty should have supposed in 1850 that Australia
was a paradise of fallen women where he should take not only
Little Emily but Martha Endell as well is a mystery. The respectable
people who paid their own passages to the other side of the world
were as anxious to demonstrate their superiority to the criminal
classes as ever respectable people were. If Charles Dickens had
travelled to Australia he would have found a more bigoted middle
class than he left behind. He might have been shocked to find Mr
Peggotty struggling to survive as a labourer, having been too
poor to acquire land of his own, and the two women married to
violent men who drank their wages and cared not at all that their
children had no shoes. Mr Peggotty, prevented by his poverty
from acquiring the wherewithal to live, might have succumbed
to gold fever and tried vainly to live cleanly in the frenetic
battlefields where most succeeded in finding only a show and
those who found more were penniless again within months. Or
they may all have gone into service in the houses of the great,
an outcome which no one associates with Australia, in which

case the women would have been more at risk than ever.

On 30 December, 1856, a few years after Mr Peggotty set out with Martha and Little Emily, David King, aged twenty-eight, a farmer from Lincolnshire, and his wife Elizabeth, aged twenty-five, arrived in Tasmania aboard the *Alice Walton*. They brought with them their four small children, John, seven, Mary Ann, five, David, three, and the baby, Elizabeth. Perhaps they expected to take up a sizeable land grant in Tasmania, in which case they were disappointed. Rather than moving out into the new districts that were being opened up, David King found work as a tenant farmer on a 150-acre subdivision of a large estate at Dairy Plains, near Deloraine.

Dairy Plains might have reminded them of Lincolnshire, for the alluvial soil is deep for Australia, and comparatively rich. Like Lincolnshire, Dairy Plains is drained by man-made canals, emptying into Leith's Brook; even in the drought of 1988, the grass on the flats was still green, or rather not quite ash-blond. On every side stand blue hills, and to the west the land is protected by the massive bulwark of the Western Tiers. King was farming at Kingsdon, one of two large estates that made up Dairy Plains. Kingsdon was subdivided into nine farms, and three smaller allotments were set aside for labourers' cottages and kitchen gardens. The owner of the whole 1,762-acre spread did not himself live in the big house, but in the pleasant township of Deloraine, enjoying the fruits of his farsighted investment in the development of the soggy plain so that it was suitable for intensive dairying. Both landlords tolerated their tenants for long periods, so that the tenancies passed from father to son, but there was never any chance of the farmers' acquiring land of their own in the district, unless they went out to the margins where the land rose steeply to the hills. The old class structure was well in place at Dairy Plains, and none of the farmers ever succeeded in bucking it. After nineteen years, although the landlord was dead and the property being managed by the public trustees, David King was still a tenant farmer on 150 acres at Kingsdon. His grown sons were existing as labourers; John had the right to farm a mere twenty acres on the edge of Dairy Plains, opposite the handsome house of Kingsdon, with its steep gables and pierced bargeboards, where his father lived. There he raised a few bushels of wheat or oats, and a few tons of potatoes, kept a couple of horses, three cows and a pig.

This is the reality behind the rather imposing statement on the wedding certificate of John King, my great-grandfather, who was married in 1873, 'in the house of Mr David King at Kingsdon'. The bride was Harriett Smith, daughter of William Smith and Ellen Donovan. Her parents were both convicts, who had been married, with special government permission because they were still serving their sentences, in Christchurch, Longford, in 1838. Thus in one generation the distinction between bond and free was wiped out; King and Smith were joined in the great fellowship of the poor, where the distinction between deserving and non-deserving has never been clear.

The two-roomed weatherboard cottage where my grand-mother was born still stands, and its tin roof still keeps out water well enough for it to be used for the occasional lambing. Against the sprung planking of the walls, sacking has been stretched. In the old days, the walls would have been papered with layer upon layer of newspaper, but even so they would have kept out precious little of the cold. In their two rooms, one for cooking and one for sleeping, the Kings would have been so huddled together that cold was probably the least of their problems.

When I visited the house the poppy seed in the long field behind it was ready for threshing. On such narrow fields as these the only sensible cultivation is a high yield crop. Tasmanians told me that the poppyseed is grown for the hot bread shops of the Australian capitals; in fact the crop is none other than *Papaver somniferum*. Tasmania is the world's third largest producer of alkaloids for the pharmaceutical industry, after India and Turkey, despite the pleas of the UN Commission on Narcotic Drugs to reduce the world stockpile of opium and the seriousness of Australia's heroin problem.

The dry seed capsules of the poppies shone pink-silver in the afternoon sun as I climbed over the rotten gate and walked through the sheep shit to the door of the tiny house, where first Selina was born, in 1874, and then Ada, in 1877, and then Albert John, in 1880. In 1880, Selina died, probably of typhus.

John's family seems to have been growing more slowly than is usual for an Australian farm labourer in the 1880s, but not all

275

the children's births were registered. Given the extreme hardships they endured the parents may have felt that there was little point in travelling to Deloraine to register children so likely to die. Though Dairy Plains is beautiful, its beauty must have become sinister for the Kings as they realised that they would never succeed to one of the bigger tenancies. They were ignorant, poor, virtual serfs on the estate. There was no chance of rising in the world unless they left the district, but without capital they had no hope of acquiring an appreciable amount of land anywhere. The bitterest irony is that they had less chance of acquiring land than the early convicts who were given a hundred acres or so upon their release.

The Kings were farm labourers who had come to the other side of the world only to continue being farm labourers. When David King arrived in Tasmania he could read and write; when his son married the daughter of convicts, neither of them, nor their witness, could sign the register. This was the reality behind the myth of the new world. The Kings joined the vast majority of Australians who called themselves 'battlers'. For some reason, David King relinquished his tenancy at Kingsdon and moved to another on the neighbouring estate of Keanefield; within ten years he had lost that too.

Although Harriett was a member of the Church of England, she was married using the forms of the Methodist Church. The ceremony was performed by John Shaw Greer and this is as near as my father ever got to being a genuine Greer. Harriett's religion soon became dominant, however, and most of her children were christened and married in the Church of England. The King family made several attempts to find a more adequate provision for its growing numbers; the Davids senior and junior took up tenancies in more than one of the new areas being opened up in the eighties, but they also clung to the twenty acres in Dairy Plains, living in the tiny cottage by turns, which was as well, because none of their new tenancies lasted.

My grandmother, Rhoda Elizabeth King, was born in the Dairy Plains cottage on 28 January, 1885.

To the north-west, the hills behind Forth were being opened up, and land was being sold for clearing and intensive planting of vegetable crops. John's brother David had tried his hand at tenant farming in near-by Sassafras and New Ground for speculative landlords without conspicuous success, for as soon as the land was cleared it was, predictably, sold out from under him at a profit. The family pooled its meagre resources and acquired ten acres at a place called Sprent. In 1895 they left old David King in the cottage at Dairy Plains and took the children with them to Sprent.

This was very different country from the idyllic river meadows of Dairy Plains. The thickly wooded hills though not high were spectacularly steep, crushed one upon another in a succession of crazy folds; in the deep gullies tree ferns showed the soil to be rich and sweet, but the clearing of the stands of eucalypts from the slopes was back-breaking work. Once the native hardwoods had been ringbarked and left to fall in their own time, for there was little point in blunting good axeheads on them, the farmers planted potatoes and kept pigs, much as they had in the old country, and for much the same return.

The Kings would have knocked up some kind of dwelling on whatever level land they could find; it was probably much like other selectors' houses: 'with four slab-sides and a top, a place to get in at and two small, square holes, one on each side of the door, to look out through. The whole was guarded by a dandy-looking dog-leg fence, that kept everything off except cattle, goannas, kangaroo-rats, snakes and death adders. Inside, tidy and natty. Curtains on the bed, a cloth on the table, the legs of which were screwed into the earth; two gin-cases that served as chairs wore crochet coverings, while the holes in the floor, in and out of which snakes used to chase mice, were covered with bags and a heavy round block was placed on them for additional safety.'

Steele Rudd's selection was a corner of a degraded cattle run in Queensland, but the newly cleared land in Sprent must have been similarly infested with nocturnal wild life. Potatoes are unlikely to be eaten by cockatoos, but wombats and bandicoots would enjoy rootling in them, and kangaroos and wallabies would have grazed them down to the soil, whether the Kings fenced their ten acres or no. There was no way the grown children could be supported on the yield of ten acres, supposing the caterpillars and borers held off and there was a yield. The Kings

277

however had more serious problems than flood, drought or infestation by plant pests. John William, Rhoda's father, was losing or had lost his mind.

William Henry King told the justices at his father's committal that his father had threatened his life and that of his mother, and had offered to cut his son-in-law's 'inside out' because he had stolen a horse from him, which he had not. John William was also claiming falsely that a Mr Louth of Ulverstone had stolen a horse from him. He believed that he was a great horse doctor and told Dr Stuart of Ulverstone that his horse had worms, which he diagnosed by putting his ear to the horse's hoof and listening for them. The justices believed that he might prove dangerous but in the five months that he remained in the New Norfolk asylum he gave no trouble. He employed himself usefully, although he was piteously confused most of the time and imagined that the other patients were people he had worked for outside the hospital.

By this time my grandmother would have been working as a domestic in Ulverstone. In September 1902 her father was in trouble again. Mr Bishop of Sprent found him in a highly excited state intent on setting fire to his barn, saying that it was infested with anthrax, and, as Bishop would not burn it himself, he would have to do it for him. When they were bringing him to Ulverstone he insisted that the willow trees, the cattle, sheep and horses that they passed all had the disease. He gave tobacco to a police constable, advising him to smoke it to fumigate the diseased vegetation around him. 'He knelt before a notice paper printed in Hindustanee and sang aloud, the words being those of the National Anthem, saying he was singing the words.' This time the justices opined not only that he was likely to become dangerous, but that the cause of his distress was 'hereditary tendency'. He was more difficult to control, constantly quarrelling and fighting with his fellows. He was allowed to go home at the end of June 1903. For four and a half years he kept his wits, but by April 1908 he was singing and dancing in the street, declaring that he had anthrax and bot-flies were coming out of his mouth. Six months later he was discharged and remained calm again until 1915 when he started threatening Harriett with an axe, and running about the streets on hands and knees like a dog; again he was discharged after six months. The diagnosis of hereditary disorder was never repeated.

John William was in the asylum on 10 June, 1903, when William Henry got married at Holy Trinity Church in Ulverstone, to Jane Agnes Rodman, sister of the man his sister Ada King married in 1896. Rhoda witnessed the marriage, signing her name in a wobbly fashion which missed out half of one letter altogether. At Christmastime, the same year, she conceived a child. She was not yet twenty.

De occultis non scrutantur. Let us assume merely that what happened so often to poor girls happened to my grandmother. Far from home, struggling to learn how to adopt the manners pleasing to the Australian gentry, to keep herself clean and tidy, low-voiced and inconspicuous, my grandmother probably had also to repel the advances of one of the men of the household. To make a fuss about this harassment would have been to lose her place. She was lonely and defenceless. The gentleman's casual caresses were probably the only human warmth she felt from one month's end to the next. Perhaps she even deluded herself that he loved her.

She can hardly have foreseen the appalling consequences of her lapse. The man's affection, such as it was, would have vanished as soon as her trouble became apparent. The lady of the house would have blamed only her servant, for men will be men. She would have directed the seducer to give the girl money to pay for her lying-in and get rid of her. And so my grandmother, in dread and misery, made her way to the big city, to Launceston.

On 1 September, 1904, in a mean house in Middle Street, Launceston, my grandmother gave birth to a boy. She gave him the name Robert Hamilton, and because she was unmarried he bore her own surname, King. The name Robert Hamilton was probably the name of the child's father, for neither name ran in her own family. Mrs Helena Beston, usually called Lena, the tenant of the house, registered the child for her. Robert Hamilton King was my father.

In saying so, I say more than my poor father knew. He was never a ward of the state and his name did not show in the register of her charges that Emma kept on top of her wardrobe. There was no government department keeping a file on him in his own name. After Mrs Beston had the baby entered as Robert

Hamilton King in the register, the name was never heard by mortal ear until the Registrar read it out to me in Hobart. It is entirely owing to his kindness that I have any name for my father at all; he agreed to read the register for me, looking for any male child born in Tasmania on my father's birthday. He had other names in other places, but I did not even ask what they were.

'Do you think that's the one?' he asked, not convinced.

'It has to be,' I answered. 'How many illegitimate boys were born on the first of September in Launceston that year? How many illegitimate boys were born in Launceston that year? There were only 23,000 people in Launceston, for heaven's sake! It could be a coincidence, but I don't think so.'

Some days later Mary Nicholls found the christening entry in the register of St John's, Launceston, Emma's parish church. On 9 November the tiny boy was given the names Robert Henry Eric Ernest. The curate had some difficulty reading what was painfully written on the piece of paper Emma Greeney brought. He entered the child's father's name as 'Robert Hambett', or something like it, when it was in fact Robert Hamilton, and the column where his occupation should have been entered remained vacant. Perhaps the curate actually meant to shield a good middle-class family from a servant-girl's accusations and simply refused to believe what was written.

For there was a Robert, or rather a Richard Robert Ernest Hamilton, who would have been known to the vicar at St John's Church, if not to his curate, for he had been a member of the Rev. Beresford's congregation when he was Vicar of Holy Trinity Church, Ulverstone. The Rev. Beresford had married him, come to that. Robert Hamilton was born at Colenso, near Ladysmith, north-west of Durban in 1865, and educated in England. He emigrated to Tasmania in 1887 and set up as a house, estate and general commission agent in 1888; he married a Tasmanian girl in 1895. A daughter was born in 1897, another in 1902, and another in 1908. In 1905 he extended his operations to include customs, shipping and forwarding, representing Holyman's White Star line of steamers, and Commercial Union Assurance. He was also a district valuer. When Robert Hamilton King was born, R. R. E. was secretary to the Leven Road Trust which eventually became the Ulverstone Council, with R. R. E. still lending his services as secretary until a town clerk could be appointed. He was also secretary of the Leven Harbour Trust.

But R. R. E. was not the kind of man to get a servant girl pregnant and turn her out. For one thing he was married and his wife had had a baby the year before Rhoda became pregnant. Respectable middle-class men do not seduce the help when their wives are pregnant or pre-occupied with new babies. There was no way a bad ignorant girl like Rhoda King was going to compromise Mr Hamilton's reputation by putting his name in the St John's Church register as father of her child for all the world to see. Everything I have told you about the man is irrelevant; it is also irrelevant that he was tall, narrow-chested, had a moustache, a long face, a narrow nose, deep-set eyes, very fair skin and rode a bicycle around Ulverstone. He lived to the great age of ninety-one and died of athero-sclerosis of the brain. All utterly irrelevant.

Rhoda was not there when her five-week-old son was christened; she had already given him up and gone her way sorrowing. None of the people standing round the font knew what to answer when the curate asked what the child's father's occupation was. The curate opted for discretion. If Robert did eventually become a charge upon the state legal proceedings to secure a contribution from the father for the child's support had to be instituted, and the curate was not prepared to furnish material for a scandal.

If my grandmother dreamed of her baby each night, and woke calling his name, she did no more than relinquishing mothers usually do. If when she went to Launceston she stared at little boys his age, looking for her own features, she did no more than relinquishing mothers usually do. A year after her ordeal she married. She had found another position, as a domestic servant in Sassafras, and there she found a husband, the son of a fellmonger from Perth, thirty-two years old, a labourer. They went to live at Deddington, a tiny place on the upper waters of the Nile River, between Gelignite Hill and Lowes Mount. They had ten children, seven girls and three boys, which is why I shall not tell you her married name, for I have not been able to tell all of them or my eighteen half-cousins, about their half-brother. Rhoda died in 1968, fifteen years after her husband.

My father's names, 'Robert Henry Eric Ernest', were probably chosen partly by his mother and partly by Emma. Perhaps Emma was preparing her new little boy as a replacement for Henry Ernest, whom she still seemed likely to lose. So Robert Hamilton King became Eric Greeney, and later, Eric R. Greeney, as the name appears in the register of results from Wellington Square school. From the beginning my father hardly had a name to call his own.

His mother was the first of several women left to grieve for my father and helplessly wonder what had become of him. For his part, he never knew her name. It seems unlikely that he would not have known of the existence of Emma Greeney's register and its place on the top of the wardrobe. He probably knew that his name was not to be found in it. He was too smart not to realise that he did not have the same encounters with officialdom that so harassed his foster-brothers and -sisters. Yet Emma never concealed from him or from any of her children that they were adopted. The state wards all knew what their entitlements were, although they often misunderstood the nature of their trust funds and the limitations on their access to them. Until Emma Greeney legally adopted them the state wards were entitled to their own names if they wished to assume them, and their files were kept in their own names. No legal form of adoption existed when Emma took Robert/Eric away from Middle Street, but this was one child that Emma had to call her own, after the uncertainty and anguish of expecting month by month that Ernie would be returned to his mother. Robert and Emma's only hope of keeping Eric was to hide him from his mother, for they had no legal claim to him. For several years after they got Eric, Robert Greeney's name did not appear in the post office directory.

If Rhoda wandered the streets of Launceston, looking for her little boy, she never found him. He may have thought that he had been abandoned and forgotten but he was almost certainly wrong. Middle-class women might try to pretend that the birth had never happened, but working-class women usually confessed their lapse to their husbands and took their children back from the state when they married. The mothers of state wards wrote letters to the Neglected Children's Department, many years after their children had been given up, mostly without success. Robert Hamilton King's mother, persuaded or duped into countenancing private adoption, had no way of knowing if her son was alive or dead, well or ill, happy or unhappy.

Actually he was happy, although he may not have realised the fact.

Eric

A bachelor and a bohemian, [the female impersonator Perce Lodge of the Smart Set Diggers] always upheld noticeable dignity, which gave him a certain air of distinction. This was an acquired art which proved very successful, enabling him to gatecrash any of the high society functions he wished to attend. He was tall, extremely good-looking, had charming manners and was an exquisite dancer ... it was never apparent to anyone that he was any other than an invited guest.

HECTOR GRAY, *MEMOIRS OF A VARIETY ARTISTE*

V ERY PROBABLY Eric, like his own son, Barry, my brother, was an adorable little boy. He had the kind of aquiline features that are dainty in childhood, very fair English skin, and large grey eyes. He also had a very soft heart and extremely cuddly ways. Emma Greeney would have been forgiven for spoiling him, but as far as his foster-sisters recall he was treated the same as any other of the children who slept two to a room in Emma's house in Bathurst Street.

The town children of Launceston roved the streets in barefoot gangs getting up to all kinds of devilry and considered themselves pretty hard cases. When school was out the boys at Wellington Square school used to 'duck home, whip off their boots, chuck them over the back fence and race off to be in it', according to Dave Chandler who went to school with Ernie, Eli and Eric. The Greeney boys had to be more circumspect; Robert Greeney was out and about all day with his horse and dray and might turn up in the middle of a good stoush (street-fight) or just as you jumped over a wall with your pockets and your shirt front stuffed with stolen fruit. The boys well knew how to outwit the bobby on the beat, but Robert Greeney was another matter.

Emma had no intention of letting her boys run wild; if they got into trouble the consequences were far more serious than they were for boys who lived with their natural parents. Emma's lads would not be fined or bound over to keep the peace; they would be on the way to the Boys' Training School within hours. Eric was not a ward of the state and could not have been sent away unless Emma herself declared him uncontrollable, something she only ever did when discontented older boys threatened to disrupt the household. When one of her boys threw a stone at a street boy who was tormenting him, missed and broke a shop-window, Emma stepped in at once; within hours he had penned and delivered a laborious explanation and apology, with an offer to pay for re-glazing the window.

The shopkeeper was only too happy to leave the matter there, and Emma breathed easy again, although they could ill afford the seven and sixpence that the window cost. She knew that the matter was on the boy's file at the Neglected Children's Department and would not be forgotten if he got himself into trouble again. This was the genesis of my father's constant refrain, that if we children were not good we would be sent to Father Gilhooley at the Reformatory School, but no Father Gilhooley ever was employed by the Tasmanian correctional services. This detail is probably an anti-Catholic embroidery.

Eric was not a fighter, but he was a great egger-on and manipulator of fights. He was a 'hard doer' says his foster-sister, Dulcie, by which she means I think that he was always up to something, constantly teasing and acting the fool. Dulcie, though still a small girl, used to like to eat raw onions. Eric would sniff her breath as he passed and, if it smelt of onions, he would flip at her with his bath-towel so that it stung. When Emma got on her high horse he would smack her on the bottom or make her laugh.

Though Emma was sincerely religious, and dependent upon her church for support and guidance in bringing up her crew of damaged children, she was not a wowser. The children played cards uproariously around the kitchen table after their chores and their homework were finished, and it was probably there that Eric first took on the role of official interpreter of the rules. The boys played for sixpence in the pool at the local snooker tables and became fairly proficient. They could buy cigarettes for a penny each and a penny ha'penny for two at Ginny Hazelwood's shop on the corner by Wellington Square school. The pennies they got by returning beer-bottles to the pub, or by offering 'dinks' on their bicycles at a penny a time.

The boys' greatest pleasure was also their greatest ordeal. St John's Church prided itself on its all-male choir. The choir-master was none other than Mr George Hopkins whose grandfather had been choirmaster to George III. Every Thursday night the trebles were paraded through the town in their surplices and cassocks to sing on Cleaver's corner by way of attracting custom for the church. The street urchins with whom they fought on other days used to gather round and insult them with impunity, as they chirped their way through the boy soprano repertoire. That was how Reg Greer came to warble 'Oh for the weengs, for the weengs of a derv' in the shower, many years later in a nicotine-laden baritone.

Dave Chandler sang in the choir with Eric and Eli and Ernie, and he loves to tell a story of Eric Greeney's derring-do. Mr Hopkins habitually wore 'apple-catchers', i.e. plus-fours, with the curious addition of a bowler hat. When he conducted the choir he would remove the hat and leave it at the head of the choir loft staircase. As the boys filed out one night, Eric Greeney said, 'I hate to see a hat without a dent in it.'

'Bowler hats don't have dents,' said Dave.

'There's a bowler hat gunna have a dent now,' said Eric and gave the crown of the bowler a sharp downward chop with the side of his hand. The boys hid in a side chapel to enjoy the spectacle of poor Mr Hopkins confronted with his ruined hat, first trying to punch out the dented crown and then marching down the church steps with an extremely misshapen object on his head. It is remembered by the surviving choristers as a rattling good laugh.

In December of each year the Wellington Square school students who were considered bright enough were presented for the qualifying examination for entrance to the Launceston State High School. In 1916 Ernie gained a very creditable pass, 452 marks out of a possible 700 and went on to graduate from the high school two years later with credits in book-keeping and business practice, as well as passes in English, History, Geography, French, Arithmetic, Algebra and Geometry. In 1917, thirteen-year-old Eric took the qualifying examination for the high school. Mary

Nicholls found the record of his results for me. Here at last was the answer to my question of how intelligent my father actually was. His colleagues all thought him very sharp. Dictation (dictation!) 48 out of a hundred. Writing 28 – out of fifty, we thought. Composition 52 out of a hundred. Grammar 43 out of a hundred. Maths 124 out of two hundred, geography 12, out of fifty we hoped, and history 32 out of a hundred. He tied for second bottom of the class with a girl called Esther Begent. Both of them had their marks adjusted to a bare pass of 350 so that they could after all enter the high school. The only child with lower marks failed outright. Joint twenty-ninth out of thirty-one. I had my answer.

'Bad teaching,' said Mary, smiling at my consternation.

'They all had the same bad teaching. It still makes him the worst of a bad lot. Besides, it's not down to the teaching really.'

'Perhaps he didn't work?'

'I can't see Emma not making them work. What else did they have to do? He wasn't serving in a shop after school or milking cows or anything. The state wards weren't allowed to do part-time work and Emma wouldn't have made a distinction for Eric. He was obviously an air-head.'

If I said that I worked very hard at school I would be lying. The fact is I couldn't have got marks as low as my father's no matter what I did or didn't do. When I was thirteen I was learning three languages and physics and chemistry as well as the subjects my father had taken. The standard he reached was much lower than his age would nowadays indicate. My poor father was barely literate. And yet he affected a lordly disdain of my convent education, which was light-years ahead of his own. The only time I remembered him commenting on my examination results was when amid high marks for all my other subjects he spied a mere fifty per cent for maths.

'What is the meaning of that?' he asked.

'I don't like maths,' I said unhappily. 'I suppose I wasn't trying. It's only half term. I'll have it sorted out by finals.'

'I hope so,' he said coldly. 'That mark is a disgrace.' Not a word about the other marks. If I could get such high marks in those subjects they must all have been easy.

I applied myself to the dreary maths and got a hundred per

cent at the end of the year. 'Hm,' said my father. 'That's more like it.'

And now I find that the bloody man was never better than a fifty per center in anything. 'Don't be so hard on him. He might have been a bad examinee,' said my conscience. 'They thought he was good enough to go to high school. They must have, to have put up his marks.'

The Eumenides answered back at once. 'I should think so too. Good enough to go to high school? You won scholarships to go to high school, and he pretended it was all in a day's march, the old fraud.'

'Well, he did give me a watch.'

'Don't remind me!' shrieked the fury. 'The bloody song and dance about that watch, you'd have thought it was a Rolex instead of the cheapest of the cheap. Price of winning all your secondary education gratis, a two-bob watch. And it was supposed to be your Christmas present and your birthday present as well. He probably got the damn thing free from a client anyway.'

'More to the point,' said I to my worse self sternly, 'is that I completely mistook the way to his heart. I only threatened him by being so clever. I should have tried to be lovable.'

'Flirted with your father? Been cute? With that face? Spare me,' screamed the Fury.

'Nobody likes a clever child,' I said miserably. 'Well, only teachers like clever children.'

'Crap!' said the Fury. 'No Australian likes a clever child. Italians, even the most illiterate Italians, burst with pride and delight when their children do well at school. Nothing is too good for them.'

'And Jews,' I said to myself as my halves drew back together again. 'Perhaps that's why I wanted so much for Daddy to be a Jew.'

The next academic year Eric Greeney entered the Launceston State High School, as we have seen. He lasted two months before Emma withdrew him. She had got him a job with a book-binder, perhaps because, as she was not receiving any money for his support, she could not afford to keep him at school. Perhaps she realised that he did not have academic ability, but she ought also to have realised that he had little manual dexterity or mechanical aptitude. He didn't last long at the bindery. He was soon, I don't know how soon, doing what he was really good at, using his gift of the gab, selling.

The jeweller's shop where he worked for a year or so still functions in Launceston. The ornate scrolling and gold leaf painted on its glass windows is as fresh and bright as it was when handsome Eric Greeney waited on its customers. For the bicentennial they had placed some of their old ledgers in the window as evidence of the venerable antiquity of the firm. The shop had very little merchandise displayed, and very few customers as far as I could see, but when I called hoping they had searched their ledgers for Eric Greeney's name, they explained that they had been much too busy. After three visits of an excruciating nature one of the women behind the counter said that they had after all cleared out all their ledgers before 1940. 'Yairs,' said the lady behind the counter, nodding her head slowly up and down as if to agree with herself, a habit Australians seem to have acquired by dint of watching thousands of hours of American television. I regret to say that I was not convinced. It seemed to me most odd that after searching upstairs in the shop she had discovered something that she should have known before she started. As the woman's vowels were bringing tears to my eyes, for she was talking to me as if I was on the opposite side of a busy street and a moron to boot, I abandoned the quest as hopeless.

'What could it possibly matter if a man called Eric Greeney worked here in 1919?' I could see her thinking, as she and her off-sider exchanged glances and their one client wandered disconsolately along the half-empty showcases. Because he was supposed to be bloody jackerooing, that's why, I thought, but I had no intention of explaining who I was or who he was or of buying the silver frame I meant to give to Cousin John for Emma's picture. He did know jewellery, after all; the diamond he bought for my mother's engagement ring is one of the best I have ever seen.

The mystery of Eric Greeney's dressing so well was quickly solved. He was employed for about a year by McKinlay Proprietary Limited in Brisbane Street as a salesman, probably but not certainly, of menswear. He may have had to measure out the 'smart and exclusive frockings' from the bolts that McKinlays opened in preparation for Race Week, the taffetas, grenadines, foulards, pongee tussores and fujiettes, in fashion shades of mole, mastic, putty, nigger and bottle, but he would not have been allowed to counsel ladies on the correct choice of bloomers or madapolam camisoles or long-cloth combinations, or wedding robes of ivory charmeuse. I wondered if he wrote the copy for the advertisements that the *Examiner* carried on the front page of every edition, advising ladies that 'Nautilus corsets – the secret of a commanding figure' were to be had at 'Launceston's busiest store'. The newspaper relied on the half-dozen drapers' stores in Launceston, who placed large advertisements every day, in a veritable trade war. At sale times they took half pages with lists of slashed prices. Eric Greeney may not have learnt anything at school, but once out of school he quickly mastered the business of selling clothes and the role that newspaper advertising plays in it.

When Eric Greeney turned fourteen he had to train as a cadet in the working boys' battalion. One night a week they had to drill, and they had to spend a week a year under canvas. They were supplied with weapons and with uniforms and had to turn out in good order. Their employers were required to give them time off for parades. The working boys did not succumb to this regimentation with a good grace. On at least two occasions the entire corps was put on a charge for rowdiness and insubordination. They chiefly resented the interminable time that this pointless discipline was intended to continue; after seven years of compulsory drilling, they were required to serve five years' compulsory membership of the militia. After much agitation the last requirement was waived. None of the boys wanted to be commissioned; they despised the ranks and usually refused to volunteer for officer training. But I suspect that Eric Greeney liked the idea of stripes and became some sort of officer in the cadet corps. He used to say that he had been a cadet major, but this seems unlikely.

(It was the Fury who wrote that last bit.

My better self demurs. 'Just because a man lied about one thing does not mean that he lied about everything. Besides he doesn't lie much. If he lied more, if he enjoyed lying, you'd never have pierced his alias. He'd have got away with it.'

'The bloody man is driving me crazy,' said the Fury.

'No he's not. You're driving yourself crazy.')

In 1920 came the biggest parade of all. In an attempt to damp down the furious anti-imperialist sentiment that swept Australia after the grim debacle of 1914-18, the Prince of Wales was to undertake a gruelling tour of the colony. His job was to convince Australians that their contribution to the war effort had been noticed and appreciated. (This expedient never fails; after the visit of their Royal Highnesses in 1988, republican sentiment in Australia became most unfashionable.)

The Launceston cadets were told that they would 'march from the forming up position in Cornwall Square, via the Esplanade to Victoria Bridge, thence along the route of the procession until they reach their allotted positions'. The military cadets, under the command of Captain A. L. Weston, accompanied by the band of the Twelfth Military Regiment, were to form up at the Railway Station at 10.45 a. m. to receive his Royal Highness.

Reg Greer used to tell a story that he was part of the cadet guard of honour for the Prince, and, although it was not a hot day and the wait was not long, he fainted. He came to on a wool-bale in a shed by the station. 'Feeling better now?' asked the Prince.

'Yes, sir,' answered my father, stood up and snapped a salute. There is no verification of this fable in any contemporary source.

Eric Greeney really liked to sing. He would pretend that his life was a musical comedy and seize any pretext for a song. If Emma touched something of his, he would do his rendition of 'Take your hands off, that's mine.' If you asked him how he was, chances were he would give you 'Too many parties, too many pals....' If Emma asked him if he had missed her when she came back from her periodic visits to Longford, he would carol, 'You never miss the water till the well runs dry.'

The imminent arrival of Ted Russell's Black and White Costume Comedy at the Academy Theatre was announced in the Laun-ceston papers in the fourth week of January 1921. Ted Russell was occasionally described as 'Australia's premier yodeller'. This was no mean claim, for every country show featured one or two yodellers; singing jackeroos and warbling drovers were as much a part of the Aussie scene as the double-handed sawing match, the tossing a sheaf contest, stockwhip cracking and guessing the weight of a sheep. 'Ted's act is one of the cleanest, cleverest, smartest, most novel and unique ever seen in Australia.' He had 'the goods, which are always put over with a well-balanced brain,' according to *Hawklet*, a Melbourne magazine which dealt with racing, boxing and variety theatre.

In return for the advertisements Ted Russell took every day, the Launceston papers obligingly puffed the show, making it sound for all the world as if the Black and White Costume Comedy Company was world-famous. 'By the 'Kooringa' on Wednesday night,' twittered the *Daily Telegraph*, 'there arrived a band of well-known and talented mainland artists ... a big combination of vaudeville stars. ...' It was to be the first appearance in Tasmania of the Falvey Sisters, variously described as 'personality girls' and 'Hawaiian harmonists', Roy Kent, the 'eccentric comedian', Rosa Darcy, lyric soprano, 'the girl with the golden voice', Mark Ericsen, the improbably named 'genial Irishman', Edna Taylor, the 'dainty soubrette', George Blythe, 'monologist', and the husband and wife team, Ted Russell, 'everybody's favourite' and Peggy Dean, 'soubrette'. 'Dancing is a specialty turn ...'; 'mirth and song' would be the lot of anyone who went,' the papers burbled. 'Book or be sorry,' they warned. The seats were priced at three shillings, two shillings and a shilling, plus tax, showing the performance to be a cut above those that advertised a hundred or so seats at sixpence. Every Friday there was to be a talent contest for local performers. It seems very likely that Eric Greeney took his silvery tenor up on to the stage in one of the weekly talent contests and won himself a 'gold' medal. He may have even danced a bit, for in those days all the boys could dance. While Ernie and Dave were rowing on the Tamar, Eric was moving in on the girls, haunting the blood houses (as the Launceston hard nuts called the dance halls) and the Bathurst Street band-room perfecting his dance-steps as well as his line.

Though his fellow Launcestonians may have thought of this as his big break, it was an opening that led nowhere. Very few of the members of the Black and White Costume Comedy Company had ever played the major variety circuits, Fuller's or J. C. Williamson, and none had ever been at the top of the bill. The company was put together specifically for the Launceston season and never existed before or since. Ted Russell was not a distinguished actor-manager but a battler from Melbourne who usually played a one-man act or a duo on the suburban and country circuits. He seldom worked more than one day a week, because the country towns could not provide audiences for a full week's run, and was more often to be found propping up the bar at Fuller's Hotel.

The Falvey sisters, Violet and Eva, were front-line performers, who often appeared with Stiffy and Mo, fast becoming the most famous vaudeville act in Australia. The girls worked every week and had occasionally played for J. C. Williamson, 'the Firm', and the Fuller circuit; Russell got them for only three weeks on condition that they got top billing. Sweet-voiced girls like Phyllis Clay and Rosa Darcy were tuppence a dozen. Rosa's specialty was the Jewel Song from Gounod's *Faust*, in which she displayed 'brilliant technique and splendid memory' according to the *Daily Telegraph* critic. Mark Erickson, the spelling of whose name was corrected later in the season, came fresh from playing the Baron in the pantomime at the Princess Theatre in Melbourne. Edna Taylor had last appeared with the Blue Bird Costume Company at Cohuna and Leitchville.

The papers obligingly reported that hundreds had been turned away from the opening performance on Saturday night and that an 'ovation' had been 'tendered'. The Falvey Sisters left; in February 'big-voiced' Lal Logie arrived and was 'taken into the hearts of lovers of rollicking humour'. The cub reporter from the *Daily Telegraph* tried out his variety press jargon, telling us that Logie promised 'to go big from this out'. Edna Taylor left to play soubrette parts for Dora Mostyn's Dramatic Company on tour in Gippsland. Russell picked up Gladys Shaw and Fred Webber, a speciality dancing act that had played fourteen weeks in Hobart. The 'pot pourri of music and nonsense' was considered, by the tame press, to be 'entertaining to a degree almost inconceivable'.

However the show did run into difficulties. It was rumoured that it was indecent, so the advertisements announced that it was 'clean and free from vulgarity'. The weather was very hot and the advertisements promised, 'No more hot nights. Electric fans in this theatre!' Some of the audience found that they had taken home some of the less entertaining members of the theatre world, and Russell had to put a new line into their announcements, 'This theatre is disinfected and fumigated twice weekly.'

The show ran and ran. More performers left, and others arrived, Carlyon and Phillips, 'Singing, Dancing and Harmony' duo, Neil McInnes, 'Harry Lauder's rival ... direct from Scotland'. On 31 March, *Hawklet* revealed that Lal Logie had had a fit while taking an encore at the Academy: 'he suddenly stopped, grasped his throat, and fell across the footlights, striking his head on the corner of the piano, and became unconscious.'

In fact Logie had something of an alcohol problem, which almost finished his career in 1921. He stayed on in Tasmania after the rest of the company left, spending a good deal of time in hospital. He took a job as a stage manager for one of the companies that played the Academy later that year, and was sacked. For a few weeks he worked as a barman in Launceston. Then he went on the wagon and reappeared on the Melbourne suburban circuit in the spring of 1922. 'Lal has talent,' said *Hawklet*, 'and the water materially helps to purvey it.'

On April Fool's Day the run was obliged to close, for the Academy had booked another company, the Scarlet Gaieties, which played for only three weeks before moving to the Mechanics' Hall, having been adversely affected by an accident which befell one of their leading acts, Harry Webster by name. In Melbourne Ted Russell announced that he would be taking a new show back to Launceston, and invited artistes to contact him at Fuller's Hotel.

When the Black and Whites reopened in Launceston, Rosa Sinclair and Dorothy Dane, 'two sure winners with the Adelaide boys', who had recently been playing the Ozone Pavilion at Semaphore with the 'Red Gaieties', supplied the glamour. Lal Logie was back in the line-up with his Melbourne mates, Frank Crossley, Eddie Bush, 'comedy merchant, tumbler and acrobat', and Max Desmond. Eddie Bush had a 'tumbling table' routine which was considered very unusual. Frank Crossley, singing comedian, was principally famous for having been part of The Smart Set Diggers who were invited to perform at Buckingham Palace. The comics were assisted by the Fletcher Girls, Nellie Steward, and Harry Penn, 'light and pleasing tenor'. In May, they were joined, 'by special and expensive engagement', by the operatic tenor Darvell, Darville, Darval or even Daniel Thomas, 'direct from Fuller's' and 'late of Quinlan's Grand Opera Coy', who was in fact best remembered for playing King Spider in the Christmas panto at the Princess using 'two electric green bulbs in place of his own eyes'.

The new show was deemed to be 'a scream and a yell'. From 14 May the show billed Rhodesbury and Ralph, 'Australia's premier patter comedians', and Thelma Doward, 'late of the English Pierrots', that is to say, out of work since the summer season ended and Pierrot-land, at St Kilda, Victoria's answer to Blackpool, closed down for the winter.

On 19 May, the Academy Theatre management was arraigned for over-crowding, and found guilty of a criminal offence. Nothing of the sort had happened in Launceston in ten years and the daily advertisements immediately boasted of the fact. The company was joined a week later by Reg, Red or Ted Anderson. On 28 May, Ted Russell undertook a publicity stunt the like of which had never been seen in Launceston. Between noon and one o'clock he flew over Launceston in an aircraft piloted by Captain Huxley and dropped playbills and two hundred free passes to the show.

On 2 June the following 'notes' appeared in *Hawklet*: 'Ted Russell's Black and White Co is doing well, crowded houses about six times a week being the rule. Ted Anderson is very popular and witty. Dorothy Dane is a very good soprano and harmoniser. Rosa Sinclair is a fine little actress, a good ballad singer, and does some clever footwork. She is a great favourite among the male section of the audience. Ted Russell's parody singing is good, and his yodelling a specialty. Darvell Thomas is, undoubtedly, a very good tenor, and knows how to act. He is leaving Launceston this week with Miss Dorothy Dane who will be his partner from now on for a fair time. The Fletcher Sisters are a very good hit, and Lily's strong voice gets a lot of applause, and "Chick's" voice seems to harmonise well.' (At this point the style of the notes collapses into bathetic uncertainty.) 'Darvel Thomas is second to none, so far, who have visited Launceston in revue work. Rhodesbury and Ralph are clever artists, and very good at jokes, some of them being very witty. Rhodesbury possesses a very good voice, and I think will hold it for a few years yet.' The 'notes' are signed S. E. Greeney.

There was no S. E. Greeney in Launceston in June 1921. *Hawklet* always had difficulty in rendering names, even the names of the performers it was supposed to puff. The likeliest candidate for authorship of the 'notes', which are badly enough written in truth, is Eric Greeney. A letter like this from a member of the audience is both a puff and a timely reminder to those booking new shows. Eric was probably prompted by a member of the company, aware by now that the Tasmanian career of the Black and White Costume Comedy Company was about to come to an end. The prompter, one would think, given her prominence in the account given of the performances, was probably Rosa Sinclair.

In writing to *Hawklet*, Eric Greeney was acting as a 'gee-man' or 'Mickey Finn', whose job is to stir up the sluggish crowd. Or perhaps he had the less demanding job of a hampster, who has merely to stand in front of the crowd registering enthusiasm for the spruiker's suggestions and lead the way to the ticket office. It was a good induction for a street-smart young man who was to rise to the top in the new industry of advertising.

The day after S. E. Greeney's contribution appeared in *Hawklet*, the Black and Whites moved out of the Academy Theatre. The names of Ted Russell and Rhodesbury and Ralph appear amongst the passengers in the first saloon on the SS *Nairana* when she left for Melbourne on 13 June but it seems that they fitted in a short tour of the industrial towns on the west coast of Tasmania and actually left on 20 June. Part of the company went on to perform at Bendigo and Ballarat, then Ted Russell and his wife went to Wonthaggi with a company called 'Dinkum Diggers' run by Val Lee, that had played successfully in the north-eastern district of Victoria, before leaving to take up an engagement to tour in South Africa.

If Eric Greeney left Tasmania 'with the Black and Whites' he must have crossed Bass Strait in the third week of June, more than two months before his seventeenth birthday. If he stayed with Rosa Sinclair he would have been in the vicinity of the Kensington Town Hall in September, where she was appearing for impresario Frank Irons, and Sandringham Town Hall in December, for Will Hill, then at the Temperance Hall. On Tuesday,

20 December, she was married to the 'well-known' ventriloquist Eric Valentine, who was not the man who later married my mother as 'Eric Reginald Greer'.

Emma must have protested when Eric announced his intention of leaving, but she never forced a restless child to remain with her against its will. As Eric's adoption was never official she had no way of preventing what must have seemed to her a catastrophe. She had no legal right of control over him at all. Her only recourse would have been to have turned him over to the police as uncontrollable, an outcome which would have been disastrous for her and the rest of her large family. Emma never saw Eric again. He wrote once or twice and then – nothing. He put Emma, and Robert, and Ernie and Eli and Thurza and Clifford and Geraldine and Dulcie out of his mind forever.

Emma knew, none better, what a harsh and unforgiving world it is, and she probably had a shrewd idea that Eric's talent was not great. She never knew what became of him, and she was not a woman to forget. Try as I might I cannot forgive my father this cruelty, banal and commonplace as it is, compounded of indifference and lack of imagination. Whatever confidence, charm, elegance or plausibility he had, she had made possible for him. Perhaps he realised it, and could not bring himself to write and tell her that he was not a great star of stage and screen, but a well-dressed battler living by his wits.

The Gauntlet

'I mean every once in a while I'm just amazed when I catch a
glimpse of who I really am. Just a little flash like the gesture
of my hand in a conversation and WHAM there's my old man.
Right there, living inside me like a worm in the wood. And I
ask myself, "Where have I been all this time? Why was I blind?
Sleeping. Just the same as being asleep. We're all asleep. Being
awake is too hard."'

SAM SHEPARD, 'SLEEPING AT THE WHEEL'

THE YELLOW-BOUND proof copy of a new book on the media
superstars of the seventies' feminist movement cracked open
at a chapter called 'Sitting on a Fortune'. I read the slip-slop slap-
dash synopsis of my parents' life with deepening horror. I had
nobody but myself to blame for the farrago of errors that skipped
about the page. Germaine's father 'was already housed in army
barracks' when she was born. No, he wasn't. He was sitting in a
flat in St Kilda with Wally Worboys.

'In the years to come – "for the duration" as it was called –
Peggy, like so many wives of young servicemen, would wait. She
would not go back to her work as a model. Instead she would
play the role of a war wife, entertaining the American soldiers
who stopped off in the charmed middle class oasis of Melbourne
en route to the battlefields of the Pacific.'

'Can I have talked such rubbish to this woman?' I asked myself
miserably. I would have told her that my mother was tall, red-
haired, scarlet-mouthed and very striking, but surely I couldn't
have made her sound like Mamie Stover. Poor Mother, her modelling career was one photograph. She never worked after she
married her dream man, with the elegant office in the city that
Joyce Bull ran for him while he played man about town. There
was never any question of her going back to work. Wartime
austerity and millinery hardly went together. She did what she
has always done, made do with the tiny allowance she got as an

officer's wife, and went to the beach. And in any case Reg Greer didn't go for his board until December 1941. Mother used to tell a story about how Daddy rang to say he was embarking, and she fainted by the telephone. When she came to, there was I, looking down at her anxiously. 'I have something to live for,' she told herself and bravely soldiered on, a woman without a man, etc., etc.

If I imagine that scene I see myself as a tall, sallow three-year-old, with a censorious look. 'What are you doing on the floor, Mother?' I don't remember seeing my mother drop the telephone and fall as one dead, or screaming with terror until she came to. The war and fatherlessness are the first things I can remember.

The parody of my own inaccurate memories and the scenario I erected upon them continued; my own account of meeting Daddy when he was demobbed appeared in a new and fanciful garb.

'After a while they stepped back from the crowd to make a more careful study....' Oh no, we didn't. The station platform was emptying, as wives and mothers scooped up their trembling men and took them home. We wandered up and down until there were only a few men left, and one of them, grey-faced, drawn and old, was Reg Greer.

'In fact Reg Greer, his teeth lost to starvation, was returning home after a two-year stay in a hospital. He was suffering, Germaine would learn much later, from severe anxiety neurosis, the aftermath of battle shock and wartime deprivations in Egypt and Malta.'

No wonder my mother used to click her tongue and brush off my jeremiads about my father. I read on in torment, battle shock indeed. Two years in hospital. God, how could I ever have invented such stuff? Even the teeth detail was wrong.

The real cause of my father's losing his teeth was nothing to do with the war. On the report of his first medical examination in 1941 I found the initials PUD: Prosthetic upper denture. He lost his upper teeth before he went before the interview board, probably before the war. Nevertheless I'm sure we were told, as part of the endless nagging to brush our teeth, that Daddy's teeth had fallen out when his gums receded because of poor diet in Malta. Joyce Bull had said in her letter: 'He must have been very distressed about the loss of his teeth. He was very proud of his teeth.' The foster-sisters said to me in Tasmania, 'He had beautiful teeth.' I never met those beautiful teeth, but I found a photograph of them in *Newspaper News* dated 1936, which showed the gums already receding.

'Oh yes,' said Mother. 'That was because of smoking a pipe. In Western Australia, he smoked a pipe and it ruined his teeth, pulled them all out of alignment. Champing on a pipe.'

'I never saw him with a pipe.'

'Well, no. He gave it up then. Just smoked cigarettes.'

The more I think about it, the more I think Eric Greeney began to smoke a pipe in order to make himself seem older. The tale of the teeth is doubtless trivial, but it provides a very good example of the way myths grow in families. The photograph of my father that used to stand on the overmantel, that was all I knew of him until the day we met him at Spencer Street, has disappeared, but now that I think of it, I'm fairly sure that it showed him with false teeth. Nevertheless we all believed the tale of his losing his teeth in the war. He looked toothless that day on the station platform because his gums would have shrunk badly as a consequence of his anorexia. His denture probably did not fit any more and had to be built up, and out of that we made a legend of the teeth as war casualties.

'Do you know, Ann,' I said, sitting on the stool at Ann's kitchen counter in Fitzroy, 'I reckon my father dyed his hair. Not just when his hair faded, when he was old, but all his life. All his life as Reg Greer, I mean.'

'You mustn't start doubting everything about the poor man,' said Ann, laughing.

But I know, rather, I believe, that Eric Greeney's hair was the same mid-mousy-brown that mine is. Daddy had fair eyebrows and a fair nicotine-stained moustache. He darkened his top hair to age himself, and to give his head a sleeker profile. My hairline is identical to his, and I know his top hair would have been curly and fly-away, but his barber darkened it and straightened it, to strengthen the Basil Rathbone likeness. It was well and subtly done, but it was done. If Reg Greer had met Eli Greeney in the street, Eli might not have known him with his dark hair and his new teeth for his brother, Eric.

The book splashed on through a mire of errors about me. About those I could feel amused, but the inflation of my own mistakes about Reg Greer, the 'high-ranking' intelligence officer, had the effect of pushing him still further away. All I had was a heap of props, smart clothes, dyed hair, false teeth, and a script full of lying clichés, most of them embellishments of my own fantasies.

'Your father fantasised a lot,' Joyce said. Here was the evidence that I fantasised just as much. I made a myth about my father and I published it. How the poor man must have shuddered whenever, if ever, he read accounts of my childhood based on interviews with me. He of course never spoke a word, never said, 'She doesn't know what she is talking about.' He was gagged and bound by his own lies. But try as I might I cannot feel sorry for him.

What would I have done if he called me in one day and began, 'There are some things I think you ought to know about your background....'

'Fire away, Papa.'

'Well to begin with my name's not Greer, and I don't know what it should be....'

If my father had told me as much of the truth as he knew, and enjoined me to silence, I would have kept my word. Yet he was probably right in not burdening me this way; I'm sure I should have lacked all confidence and conviction if I had learned the truth in adolescence. Now that knowing the truth cannot hurt anyone, I had to impart it to my family.

First I went to my sister, because I feel closest to her. We didn't begin the story until we had loaded the picnic hamper and the thermos into her 'cuda boat and chugged around the corner of the red cliff into a sparkling bay. Feeding porpoises tumbled by us, which I thought a good omen, for the dolphin is a figure of love. Cormorants watched sleepily from the fringed piles. Jane taught me how to tell the sex of the commonest gulls. The water was like black opal and the sky trailed far off a fine scarf of cloud, signifying the first currents of high cold air, and summer's end.

Jane has married into a big Catholic dynasty. The early years of adjustment were hard for her, but she won through and became a central pivot of the family. She brought no money and no connections with her, except for the one, rather onerous, with me, but she did bring a warm heart, loyalty, perseverance, capability and creativity. She has my father's genius for making and keeping friends, which is more to be envied than her beautiful houses, her BMW and her boat.

'Is it bad?' she asked me as we pushed the boat off the jetty.

'Pretty bad. But it could be worse.'

'What do you mean?' she asked quickly.

'I don't think he was a bigamist. Or a jailbird.'

When the hamper was opened and the gulls were busy stealing everything out of it, I told her the whole story. At first her face stiffened with embarrassment. She looked past me to the shore on the other side of the heads, her dark eyes reflecting the ocean rollers' blue-grey. If she had turned to me and told me coldly that I had no call to be disturbing our father's repose, I should not have known what to answer. I need not have worried; she took Emma Greeney to her heart at once. As I described Eric Greeney to her, she said more than once, 'Just like Peter Marcus', her elder son. In the end she was glad to have her heredity, rather than the implausible façade we had always lived with.

'You always knew, you know,' she said. 'I can't remember if he told me or you told me, but someone told me that there'd been a name change. It's a good story, isn't it? I think it's really interesting. Poor Daddy. Mum'll be dark. She was sure you were way off-beam.'

That night she told her two boys and her husband, and they liked the story too.

If my sister liked the story, my brother Barry adored it. He had such physical intimacy with our father that he had felt no need to idealise him. He knew all his foibles and had forgiven him for them long ago. He put a tape-recorder on the table as I began my story. 'I want to make sure that I get it right,' he said.

All his working life, my brother, who is a primary school teacher, has been involved with poor children. He was actually pleased to discover that our father was one of the poorest of poor children. He understood Emma's noisy household and its small inhabitants immediately. It was easy to demonstrate to him how extraordinary Emma's understanding of adolescent children was for her time, and what kind of rough and tumble logic she used to build the children's self-esteem.

'She made it possible for them to escape,' he said. 'That was her greatest achievement.'

To Barry, who is a committed socialist and gut democrat, the proof that children are not limited by their heredity was manifest at every stage of the story. He brushed aside my strictures about Reg Greer's treatment of Emma.

'He did what he had to do,' he said. 'He knew what he could handle, and what he couldn't.'

'D'you reckon he loved her?'

'I reckon. But it was like it was with all of us. He couldn't show it. Or he'd have gone to pieces.'

'You think he felt too much, rather than too little.'

'I think so. After all that he made a stable family; he brought us all up well. Three out of three's not bad going.'

'But, if he knew about poverty and the struggles of the poor for any kind of a decent life, why was he so stupidly right-wing? It's funny really; none of his kids would ever vote Liberal and poor Daddy never voted anything else. Perhaps that's it. Perhaps he felt that socialism institutionalises poverty so that you can't escape from it. He wanted to live in a world where he didn't have to think about poverty any more, didn't have to acknowledge that it existed. But that'd mean that he was living in a dream.'

'Well, he was. Maybe he couldn't confront reality himself, because the early struggle knocked him about too much. But he gave us the security and confidence to get involved.'

'I don't think so, Barry. I think his version is typical of the lie of *history* that concentrates on élites; the truth about Reg Greer is a classic example of herstory, puncturing the ideology.'

Hugh and Alice, my nephew and niece, had listened to the whole story and wisely refrained from intervening. There would be time tomorrow and afterwards to go over the tape and explain the hard bits, about fostering and adoption, about illegitimacy and the seduction of servant-girls. Alice climbed onto Barry's knee for a cuddle before she went to bed. My brother looked quite beautiful, sitting with his daughter's arms garlanded around his neck, accepting her closeness without a hint of our father's self-consciousness. She fitted herself into the side of his body like a limpet, and would have gone to sleep right where she was, if her brother had not summoned her to bed.

I had to tell our mother next.

'Where've you been?' she asked over the telephone.

'In Tasmania, Mother.'

'What were you doing in Tasmania?'

'Researching Daddy's life, Mother.'

'What for?' asked Mother.

I side-stepped. 'Can I come down tomorrow and tell you what I've found out?'

'I suppose so.'

As I piloted my car down the vast chaos of the Nepean Highway, my 'touchy tummy' screamed with nerves. I knew that it was pointless to plan the conversation, because by no stretch of the imagination could I foresee my mother's contribution. Taking a leaf from my sister's book, I decided to take her out to somewhere she felt comfortable.

'I like Half Moon Bay,' she said. 'I always usually go to Half Moon Bay.'

She was whipping cream in a small enamel basin which did not sit on the mixer base, so she was steadying it with her hand. A dangerous proceeding, I thought. Another bowl, with what looked like a quart of cream in it, stood on the worktop. 'What are you doing, Mother?' I asked rashly.

'I'm making a dip,' said Mother. None the wiser, for I could see no ingredients for the dip other than cream, I reverted to the job in hand.

'OK. Let's go to Half Moon Bay.'

'Like this?' asked Mother. 'Sit on the beach in our clothes?'

She was wearing a skin-tight synthetic knit dress, striped green, yellow and white. 'It's nice, isn't it?' she had said. 'I found it on a fence. Yes. Somebody must have got wet, and it's awful to sit in a car in a sopping dress, so they took it off and left it on the fence. I found it when I was out on my bike. I find all sorts of things when I'm out on my bike.' She smoothed the dress over her hips, evidently quite satisfied with her own improbable theory about its provenance. 'Yes, no, yes, I'm a scavenger, a beach-comber. That's how I live.'

I reflected that to a woman who treated the whole world as a series of beaches, it was perfectly consistent to treat everything in it as flotsam and jetsam.

'I trust the fence is not actually nearby, Mother. The dress is rather distinctive.'

'Oh yes,' said Mother, 'I wouldn't take anything from round here.' I realised that one part of her echoing brain knew perfectly well that the dress had blown off a clothesline. On the fourth finger of the left hand of this rag-picker blazed her own fine solitaire diamond reset in a sort of steel lozenge with my grandmother's five large rose diamonds. The setting was guaranteed not to allow any of the diamonds to fall out, but as it made them look cheap as paste, the object of the re-setting seemed to me completely defeated.

'You can change, Mother, if you want.'

'What about you?' asked Mother, looking at my skirt and T-shirt as if they were white tie and tails.

'Perhaps I could borrow some shorts.'

Mother squeezed herself into a pair of pale-blue stubbies, out of which her tanned seventy-year-old legs oozed like Brown Windsor Soup sliding down a ladle. Me she kitted out in a vast pair of black Bombay bloomers.

As we walked down the concrete stairs to the beach I wondered how to introduce the subject of my father, which had not so far been mentioned. I wished Mother would say, 'Now what's all this about your father?' Instead she said in a special voice that she reserved for rhapsody, 'Oh, yes, it's been such a wonderful summer, this year. No, yes, no, last year we had hardly any real beach weather, but this, oh, this year has just been so marvellous. Day after day of beach weather. Just gorgeous. Yes, no, you wouldn't find anything like it anywhere else in the world.'

'What about Kenya?'

'What about Kenya?'

'Nothing, Mother.' I scrambled back to conversational high ground, mentally upbraiding myself for falling for one of Mother's gambits. Nothing would have been sillier at this point than to have played a game of 'beaches I have known' with a woman who has done nothing but lie on beaches for the best part of seventy years. We crunched along the coarse wet pinky-brown sand, which gave beneath my sandshoes, towards the northern end of the bay. If I had been less preoccupied I would have noticed that almost all the people sunning themselves on the sand were male and unusually scantily clad, in that their trunks were the kind I used to call handkerchiefs full of apples. Seen from behind their buttocks mooned quite bare and strangely pale.

I decided to plunge straight in. 'I found Daddy. It was a struggle but I've got him.'

'Hah,' shrilled Mother. 'You don't even know if he's your father! How do you know he's your father? You don't even know that!' She shrieked with theatrical laughter. The men on their beach-towels lifted their heads to see us, and rolled their eyes at each other.

'Mother, that is what is called an own goal. You may not know if he's my father, but I do. I only have to look at him.' Two boys in very, very tight jeans that had been torn off just above the knee minced past us, one on each side, rolling their hips. They turned their heads without turning their shoulders and stared at us insolently. 'That's about the only thing I am sure of; the man who called himself Reg Greer was my father.'

We had reached the end of the bay, where a rough tongue of rock crisped like boiling toffee dropped into cold water stuck out of the cliff and curled through the sand. We sat down side by side on a smooth patch. The two boys stared at us fixedly, looked at each other, shrugged their shoulders and sauntered away.

'What do you mean called himself?'

I began to tell her, but she interrupted. 'They've got no birth certificate for him in Durban, you know,' she said, triumphantly.

Satisfied that Daddy had never levelled with her, seeing as she sent to Durban for a birth certificate after he died, I said carefully, 'That's because he wasn't born in Durban.'

'So where was he born?'

'In Launceston, Mother. But he's not called Greer.'

'So what's his name?'

'The only name he knew was his foster-mother's name. He was boarded out.'

Mother took over. 'Oh, they only did that for the money. Yes, no, yes, they were paid to take in poor little children. They did it for money. Poor little kiddies, they just piled them in, beat them and starved them—'

'Mother!' I yelled so loud that a particularly Grecian-looking youth who was standing in the sea dabbling his fingertips in the water and turning slowly from side to side started and looked round at us. I couldn't bear to hear her slandering Emma Greeney. 'Emma Greeney was only paid 21/6 for each child. She didn't–'

'That was a lot of money in those days, but then you wouldn't know about that. No, yes–'

'Mother, I'm talking about 1904, thirteen years before you were born.'

'I know that.'

'So both you and I have exactly the same chance of knowing what 21/6 was worth when Reg Greer was born. Emma used all the money to feed and clothe and house her children adequately, and in any case she got nothing for Eric, because she adopted him privately.'

'Who's Eric?' asked Mother. The logical sequence of the story was to hell and gone. I was obliged to blurt out the facts of Rhoda King's travail out of sequence, muddling Mother with a plethora of names. Worst of all I could feel her getting agitated, and struggling for escape.

'You're not going to write all this? About the man I married? You wouldn't. The poor old man. What a cheap journalistic trick. . . . I'll stop you. You can't. You won't write this stuff.' A man in overalls suddenly appeared on the rock behind us. He seemed hurried and excited in some way but, when he saw us, he stopped in his tracks and seemed to be signalling with his eyes to one of the men on the beach.

'Mother, it's not my fault that my father was a fraud. When I took the commission for the book, I did so in good faith. I've spent two years trying to verify my father's phony biography, two years and God knows how many thousands of pounds–'

'That's it, isn't it? You've spent it and you can't give it back. You've spent it!' she jeered. 'Hah! hah! You've spent it!' Suddenly she stuck her face into mine. 'What've you been eating? Eh? You've been eating onions. God, it's awful when you put your face near anyone. God, what a stink.'

'I didn't put my face near anyone, Mother.'

Mother banged me sideways with her shoulder, to push her face closer. 'No, garlic, that's it. What did you eat?'

I stumbled into her trap. 'It must have been the Ethiopian food last night.'

'How revolting,' said Mother, having proved to her satisfaction that I was mad.

'N'jera wat. It was delicious, actually,' I said softly. 'Do you want to know about Reg Greer or not? If it doesn't interest you I shan't tell you. You can wait to read it in the book. This might be the one book of mine that you do read.'

'The poor old man. How could you bring yourself to write all that about anyone?'

'He's not a poor old man,' I said, exasperated. 'He's dead. Much you cared about the poor old man, anyway. Talk about starving and beating.'

'Oh,' she said, 'all he wanted to do was eat. I was always cooking. It was terrible. But I miss him, yes, no ...,' her voice was modulating to the rhapsodic mode.

I tried to get on with my story. 'Eric was Emma's second child. The first was Henry Ernest; Emma called him Ernest Henry—'

'Oh, your father's brother, Ernie!' Mother stopped, annoyed with herself for exhibiting a normal human reaction.

'What did Daddy tell you about Ernie?' I asked.

Mother's face went blank. 'You know the best book I ever read about you?' she said. 'It was that *Difficult Women* by whatsisname.'

'David Plante, Mother dear.'

It was the perfect wind-up. She must have known how I hated that book. I sat on the rock in the sunlight, suddenly chilled to the bone. I used to say to David, 'Isn't it time you got an honest job?' Here I was hoisted off my feet by my own petard. In her random onslaught, mother had hit home, slammed me in the solar plexus.

I stared at the human statuary that posed on the beach. A man I had seen gather up his towel and leave, minutes before, reappeared and lay down again, rolling over to show two pale globes of buttock. Several boys were watching something at the top of the cliff. I followed their eyeline and saw a man beckoning from the bushes. One of the boys laid his manicured hand on his sternum, and the man nodded. The boy gave his rivals a skittish look and ran lightly up the stairs.

'So this is your favourite beach, Mother. No wonder you like David Plante. You're a fag-hag. You've sat us here right in the

308

middle of the meat rack. Or fish rack, maybe, seeing it's the beach.'

'Yes,' said Mother, and added, 'I suppose they suck each other these days because of AIDS.' Her light carrying voice lashed round the beach like a whip. The boys stiffened and turned and stared.

'I'll get you some binoculars and a notebook, Ma, and you can do a behavioural study.' It seemed a good moment to go.

'They're not all queer, you know,' said Mother, looking hard at a very tanned, flat-bellied older man who lay by himself on a huge expensive towel with a tiny expensive radio plugged into his ear. Then I understood. Having found most of her life's necessities on a beach, Mother was now beachcombing for another husband. The older man rolled over, revealing the same moon-pale buttocks that we had noticed on the others. He began carefully to anoint them with sun-block.

Mother's steps were flagging when we tramped back along the sand, and we had to stop twice on the concrete stairs. For all her strength and her demonic energy, she needed her fantasies and I had torn them away. Occasionally I would surprise a look of panic in her eyes. She had been conditioned all her life to be a satellite and now she was spinning out of orbit, a moon looking for an earth. Reg Greer had convinced her that she was making an advantageous marriage. He cast her in the role of a raw suburban girl marrying a man about town, and though she had sneered at his pretensions she had never doubted them. Reg Greer had applauded her for being ultra-feminine and spectacular, and had done so well that even now she believed that she had only to look straight at a man and he would follow her anywhere.

I was afraid that she would suffer delayed shock when she actually considered the truths that I had told her on the beach. I asked her to call me if she felt confused. Instead she telephoned her elder brother. He could make no sense of what she was telling him, and waited until I came to lunch next day to get the facts straight. He told her that he was reading *The Madwoman's Underclothes*.

'You didn't spend good money on that rubbish, did you?' said Mother. She announced that she wouldn't come to my farewell dinner at Jane's, but would run away. When I called for her next day she had not run away, but was waiting, ready dressed and made up.

'Jane made me come,' she said. 'She's a terrible bully. She said she'd been cooking all day and I had to come. She didn't need to do that.' All the way down in the car she kept up a running diatribe against her whole family, accusing us of the most appalling crimes, wild promiscuity, drug addiction, grand larceny. Our successes were ascribed to Machiavellian machinations and luck. She, Mother, was the only intelligent, beautiful and virtuous member of the family. Things were back to normal.

At dinner on the deck of Jane's beautiful house, looking over the sloping lawn and the art nouveau shapes of the melaleucas, as we went over details of the story again, the magnitude of Reg Greer's achievement was made manifest.

'When I went to Kilbreda, I used to think of myself as a real toff,' said Jane laughing. 'I reckon the old boy knew what he was doing.'

Some of the constriction round my heart eased. They had forgiven me for digging up the dead with my nails, but I had not forgiven myself.

'Oh, look,' breathed Mother, 'no, no, just look at the moon. Isn't that gorgeous!' We had all been looking at the moon all evening as it rose silvery pale behind the solid clouds of melaleuca and sailed up through the thin cloud streamers of the eastern sky, but Mother wished to tutor our earth-bound senses in the apprehension of beauty. 'No, yes, look at it,' she said. 'Now where would you see a moon like that?'

'In the sky?' said somebody.

Mother swept on. 'It's, oh, how would you describe it?'

'Round?' said somebody. Mother made several more attempts in the course of the evening to get us to appreciate the moon, but we remained cold and matter-of-fact, to her high requiem a bunch of sods.

The job was done. My quest was over. There were huge gaps in the story but I had the answers to my most insistent questions. I seem to remember being given once a pottery figure of a lady spinning. Her arms moved back and forth and her wheel really went round. I recall the strange porous texture of the low-fired biscuit ware of which she was made. She seemed the more wondrous and intricate to me because as a result of the war I had had no toys except the kangaroo and the rabbit that my mother made of felt and stuffed with such vim that they were hard as rocks, and a pink cotton doll with white nylon hair. I picked up the spinning lady, turned her upside down and shook her to see what made her spin and lo! a quantity of sand ran out of her and she spun no more. Perhaps if my parents had told me what I needed to know I would have my spinning lady still. Instead I was beaten and told I was a destructive child. I didn't need the beating, for I was crushed already. I had owned my first mechanical toy for only half an hour.

I am at home now. The jade feathers are appearing on the acacia. The peonies are busting open in the warm border. My parrot has decided that he trusts me, and even lets me stroke his head and throat when I have Christopher the red cat purring loudly on my shoulder and dribbling down my back. There have been storms of apple blossom, and fritillaries along the drive. There is a fog of lilac along the roadside fence and frogs are dwelling in the pool in my wood which this year will cast shade for the first time. I am unmoved. For this, for every thing, I am out of tune.

There is a change – and I am poor. I cannot speak to Daddy any more because I know he lied to me. It was not the war that destroyed his love for me, but his charade and my censorious, scrutinising nature. He is no longer beside me with his face turned away, but lying in my desk drawer in tatters, a heap of cheap props. I think I know that the people who genuinely loved him were aware that his gentlemanly carry-on was an act and loved him for the way he did it, but I, like the RAF officers he met 'overseas', am not beguiled. 'He was a character,' his old friends say when they tell stories of the amazing effrontery that reduced policemen and publicans to apologetic wrecks. He was good company, but not for me. I was never his boon companion, but a full-on pain in his neck.

In finding him I lost him. Sleepless nights are long.

Acknowledgments for Quoted Material

The author and publishers would like to thank those who have given permission to reproduce the material quoted in the chapter openers and elsewhere, the sources of which are given below.

Extracts from 'Full Fathom Five' and 'Daddy' (p. 7) from *Collected Poems* by Sylvia Plath, Faber & Faber Ltd, copyright © Ted Hughes 1965 and 1981, reprinted by permission of Miss Olwyn Hughes. Extracts from poems by Marina Tsvetayeva (pp. 7, 13 & 200) from *Selected Poems of Marina Tsvetayeva*, trans. Elaine Feinstein, Century Hutchinson Publishing Group Ltd, reprinted by permission of Miss Olwyn Hughes. Extract from 'The Grey-Eyed King' from *Selected Poems* by Anna Akhmatova, trans. Richard McKane, Bloodaxe Books 1989. *Bye Bye Blackbird* (words by Mort Dixon and music by Ray Henderson) © 1926 Remick Music Corp, USA; reproduced by permission of Francis Day & Hunter Ltd, London WC2H 0EA and Warner Bros Inc. *Sometimes I'm Happy* (p. 16) (by Vincent Youmans and Irving Caesar) © 1925 Warner Bros Inc (Renewed). All rights reserved. Reproduced by permission of Warner Bros Inc/Harms Inc/Chappell Music Ltd. Sophocles, *Oedipus the King* (quote on p. 17), trans. Grene, from *Complete Greek Tragedies*, edited by David Grene and Richmond Lattimore, © 1942, 1954 by the University of Chicago. All rights reserved. Sophocles, *Oedipus at Colonus* (quotes on pp. 25–6), trans. Fitzgerald, from *Complete Greek Tragedies*, edited by David Grene and Richmond P. Lattimore, © 1941 by Harcourt, Brace and Company, © 1954 by the University of Chicago. All rights reserved. (Chicago 1954 edition is revised translation.) Extract from 'Marina' from *Collected Poems 1909–1962* by T. S. Eliot, reprinted by permission of Faber & Faber Ltd. Extract from 'Disguises' from *Collected Poems* by Elizabeth Jennings, Carcanet. *The Ramayana of Valmiki*, trans. Makhan Lal Sen, is reprinted by permission of Munshiram Manoharlal Publishers Pvt Ltd, New Delhi. 'And One for My Dame' from *Live or Die* by Anne Sexton, copyright © 1981 by Linda Gray Sexton & Loring Conant Jr., executors of the will of Anne Sexton; reprinted by permission of Sterling Lord Literistic, Inc, and Houghton Mifflin Co. Extract from 'Examination of the Hero in a Time of War' from *Collected Poems of Wallace Stevens* reprinted by permission of Faber & Faber Ltd, and Alfred A. Knopf, Inc. Extract from *Mussolini: His Part in My Downfall* by Spike Milligan reprinted by permission of Michael Joseph Ltd. 'Briar Rose' from *Transformations* by Anne Sexton, copyright © 1981 by Linda Gray Sexton & Loring Conant Jr, executors of the will of Anne Sexton; reprinted by permission of Sterling Lord Literistic, Inc, and Houghton Mifflin Co. The lines from 'My Grandmother's Love Letters' from *The Complete Poems and Selected Letters and Prose of Hart Crane* edited by Brom Weber, are reprinted with the permission of Liveright Publishing Corporation. Copyright © 1933, 1958, 1966 by Liveright Publishing Corporation. Extract from *The Battlers* by Kylie Tennant is reproduced by permission of Angus & Robertson (UK). Extract from *Memoirs of a Variety Artiste* by Hector Gray, Hawthorn Press (Australia) 1975. 'Sleeping at the Wheel' comes from *Hawk Moon*, 1981 copyright © by Sam Shepard, reprinted by permission of Faber & Faber Ltd (published in one volume with *Motel Chronicles* in the UK) and PAJ Publications (US and Canada).